BRAIN SEX

BRAIN SEX

The Real Difference Between Men and Women

ANNE MOIR AND DAVID JESSEL

A LYLE STUART BOOK
Published by Carol Publishing Group

First Carol Publishing Group Edition 1991

Copyright © 1989, 1991 by Anne Moir and David Jessel

A Lyle Stuart Book
Published by Carol Publishing Group
Lyle Stuart is a registered trademark of
Carol Communications, Inc.

Editorial Offices   Sales & Distribution Offices
600 Madison Avenue   120 Enterprise Avenue
New York, NY 10022   Secaucus, NJ 07094

In Canada: Musson Book Company
A division of General Publishing Co. Limited
Don Mills, Ontario

Published by arrangement with Michael Joseph Ltd

Queries regarding rights and permissions
should be addressed to: Carol Publishing Group,
600 Madison Avenue, New York, NY 10022

Manufactured in the United States of America

10 9 8 7 6 5 4 3 2 1

Library of Congress Cataloging-in-Publication Data

Moir, Anne.
    Brain sex : the real difference between men and women / Anne Moir
and David Jessel.
        p.   cm.
    "A Lyle Stuart book."
    Includes bibliographical references and index.
    ISBN 0-8184-0543-0
    1. Sex differences. 2. Sex differences (Psychology). 3. Brain--
Sex differences. I. Jessel, David. II. Title.
QP81.5.M65   1991
155.3'3--dc20
                                                    91-7569
                                                      CIP

CONTENTS

ACKNOWLEDGEMENTS

THIS BOOK IS based on the research of many scientists around the world and without their curiosity and search for truth it would not have been written. It is to them that we owe the most thanks. We would especially like to thank those scientists who patiently answered my questions and/or sent their latest research: Dr Camilla Benbow, Dr Anke Ehrhart, Dr Helen Fisher, Dr Robert Goy, Dr Roger Gorski, Professor Lauren Julius Harris, Dr Melissa Hines, Professor Doreen Kimura, Dr Jane Lancaster, Dr Jerre Levy, Dr Seymour Levine, Dr Catherine Mateer, Dr Bruce McEwen, Dr Dianne McGuinness, Dr Jeanette McGlone, Dr Heino Meyer-Bahlburg, Professor Julian Stanley, Dr June Reinisch, Dr Richard Restak, Dr Alice Rossi, Professor Walter Stumpf, Professor Lionel Tiger, Professor David Taylor, Dr Sandra Witleson, Dr Glen Wilson. The pioneer of sex differences, Dr Corinne Hutt, now dead, was instrumental in the past in encouraging me to pursue the subject.

There are detailed references at the back of the book for those who might be interested in investigating the subject themselves. There is a list of general reading and specific references for each chapter.

The case studies described in the book are not individuals, but profiles of the general characteristics and abilities found in a large number of case studies.

The brain sex test at the end of Chapter Three is based on scientific studies into the differences between men and women. A statistically significant sample of people have completed the test and it works. Among others we have the regulars of The Blue Boar in Aldbourne, the staff of the Canadian Broadcasting Corporation and Jenni Turner's staff at Financial Planning Services to thank for filling in the first drafts of the test and making pertinent comments which improved the final version.

We would also like to thank Bernard Cornwell and Serina Dilmot for their astute and helpful comments on the final draft, and the person who made crucial contributions but wishes to remain anonymous.

To Susan Watt, Publishing Director of Michael Joseph, we would like to give special thanks. She has given us enthusiastic support for the project from day one. She has gone through each draft of the book with painstaking care and sent us reams of excellent suggestions which have improved the book enormously.

In the end, however, the book is ours, and only we can be held responsible for any flaws it may have.

Anne Moir and David Jessel

BRAIN SEX

FOREWORD

It was some twenty years ago as a postgraduate student working for her doctorate that Anne Moir acquired her interest in the research into sex differences.

It seemed very important in the radical feminist atmosphere of the 70's to understand the truth about the differences between men and women. If there were proven differences in ability between men and women, then it was intellectually dishonest for anyone to deny those differences. It was, of course, important to get the initial premise straight – that there were scientifically and clinically demonstrable differences between the brains of men and women.

So there began, part hobby, part curiosity, the accumulation of scientific data from around the world.

I

Ten years ago, Anne Moir was a current affairs producer at BBC Television. David Jessel was a reporter. Kicking ideas around one stagnant afternoon, Moir mentioned that it would be interesting to make a programme about the differences between men and women.

Jessel said it was news to him that – anatomy and procreative functions apart – there was any difference. And surely, if differences had been discovered, that *would* be news.

The research was coming out piecemeal, Moir explained. Some of the scientists seemed almost afraid of what they had discovered. They played down the significance of what they had found, because they were worried about what it meant. Especially because what it seemed to mean was that the minds of men and women were different. And that would never do. Some pioneering authors had drawn some of the strands together, but the work was still progressing, the picture gradually emerging . . .

Jessel was intrigued, but, having a journalist's typical attention span, soon forgot about the conversation.

Ten years later, casting around on another stagnant afternoon for an idea for a television programme, he remembered Moir. She had gone off to work in transatlantic television. Pumping the BBC's telephones with all the confidence that comes from not having to pay the phone bill, Jessel traced Moir from London . . . to Toronto . . . to London, where she was now European Editor for the Canadian Broadcasting Corporation. In fact, she and her husband lived 150 yards away from Jessel's London flat.

They met over a lunchtime curry. Moir had kept up her interest with brain-research developments. In the intervening years, there had been an explosion of academic effort. The findings were dramatic and conclusive. Scientists could now incontrovertibly prove that there was a difference between the male and the female brain.

Only a few scientists and a few specialist authors knew about this, but the information was there for anyone with the wit and inclination to gather. Her own attic was bulging with Xeroxes of monographs, sometimes impenetrably learned, by eminent people.

Would you be able to explain it to a layman? asked Jessel, whose interest in, and knowledge of, biology evaporated on the day that he was asked to dissect a pickled cockroach.

Moir said she thought so. What worried her, with her scientist's training, was what it all meant, and how these new findings explained our behaviour as men and women.

They reached an agreement. Moir would explain the science to Jessel. They would both then argue about how the science could explain one aspect or another of human behaviour. Moir would then go back to the scientific papers and see if the suggestions were valid.

Every month for a year, Moir would hand Jessel a stack of box files full of academic articles, and notes about what she considered the most important and significant findings. Jessel would hand back thirty pages of what he understood it all to mean.

They both became intrigued by what they were learning. It had all the ingredients of a fascinating television programme. Meanwhile, Moir and Jessel found that they had written a book.

INTRODUCTION

MEN ARE DIFFERENT from women. They are equal only in their common membership of the same species, humankind. To maintain that they are the same in aptitude, skill or behaviour is to build a society based on a biological and scientific lie.

The sexes are different because their brains are different. The brain, the chief administrative and emotional organ of life, is differently constructed in men and in women; it processes information in a different way, which results in different perceptions, priorities and behaviour.

In the past ten years there has been an explosion of scientific research into what makes the sexes different. Doctors, scientists, psychologists and sociologists, working apart, have produced a body of findings which, taken together, paints a remarkably consistent picture. And the picture is one of startling sexual asymmetry.

At last there is an answer to the exasperated lament 'Why *can't* a woman be more like a man?'; it is time to explode the social myth that men and women are virtually interchangeable, all things being equal. All things are not equal.

Until recently, behavioural differences between the sexes have been explained away by social conditioning – the expectations of parents, whose own attitudes, in turn, reflect the expectations of society; little boys are told that they shouldn't cry, and that the way to the top depends on masculine assertion and aggression. Scant attention was paid to the biological view that we may be what we are because of the way we are made. Today, there is too much new biological evidence for the sociological argument to prevail. The argument of biology at last provides a comprehensive, and scientifically provable framework within which we can begin to understand why we are who we are.

If the social explanation is inadequate, the biochemical argument seems more plausible – that it is our hormones which make us behave in specific, stereotypical ways. But, as we will discover, hormones alone do not provide the whole answer; what makes the difference is the interplay between those hormones and the male or female brains, pre-wired specifically to react with them.

What you will read in this book about the differences between men and women may make both sexes angry or smug. Both reactions are wrong. If women have reason to rage, it is not because science has set at naught their hard-won struggle towards equality; their wrath should rather be directed at those who have sought to misdirect and deny them their very essence. Many women in the last thirty or forty years have been brought up to believe that they are, or should be, 'as good as the next man', and in the process they have endured acute and unnecessary pain, frustration and disappointment. They were led to believe that once they had shaken off the shackles of male prejudice and oppression – the supposed source of their second-class status – the gates of the promised land of equal achievement would be thrown open; women would be free at last to scale and conquer the commanding heights of the professions.

Instead, in spite of greater emancipation in terms of education, opportunity, and social attitudes, women are not noticeably 'doing better' than they were thirty years ago. Mrs Thatcher is still the exception which proves the rule. There were more women in the British Cabinet in the 1930s than there are at present. There has been no significant increase in the number of female MPs over the past three decades. Some women, seeing how far their sex has fallen short of the supposed ideal of power-sharing, feel that they have failed. But they have only failed to be like men.

Men, on the other hand, should find no cause for complacent celebration, although some will inevitably find ammunition for their bar-room prejudices: it is, for instance, true that most women cannot read a map as well as a man. But women can read a character better. And people are more important than maps. (The male mind, at this point, will immediately think of exceptions to this.)

Some researchers have been frankly dismayed at what they have discovered. Some of their findings have been, if not suppressed, at least quietly shelved because of their potential social impact. But it is usually better to act on the basis of what is true, rather than to maintain, with the best will in the world, that what is true has no right to be so.

Better, too, to welcome and exploit the complementary differences between men and women. Women should contribute their specific female gifts rather than waste their energies in the pursuit of a sort of surrogate masculinity. A woman's greater imagination can solve intractable problems – be they professional or domestic – at one apparently intuitive stroke.

The best argument for the acknowledgement of differences is that doing so would probably make us happier. The appreciation, for instance, that sex has different origins, motives, and significance in the context of the male and female brains, that marriage is profoundly unnatural to the biology of the male, might make us better and more considerate husbands and wives. The understanding that the roles of father and mother are not interchangeable might make us better parents.

The biggest behavioural difference between men and women is the natural, innate aggression of men, which explains to a large degree their historical dominance of the species. Men didn't learn aggression as one of the tactics of the sex war. We do not teach our boy children to be aggressive – indeed, we try vainly to unteach it. Even researchers most hostile to the acknowledgement of sex differences agree that this is a male feature, and one which cannot be explained by social conditioning.

The writer H. H. Monro, 'Saki', wrote an instructive little story about a liberal household where the parents sought to suppress their son's natural male aggression by refusing him a set of tin soldiers; instead, they supplied a set of tin civil servants and teachers. All, they felt, was going well, until they sneaked into the playroom and saw that he had set out a battle royal between the regiments of the toy teachers and the model bureaucrats. The child was lucky, in that his parents in the end saw the futility of trying to make him something he wasn't, nor could ever be.

We are an arrogant species. Our superiority to other animals, in terms of our capacity to reason and discriminate, has been said to put us closer to the angels than to the chimpanzees. Perhaps that makes us, thinking of ourselves as masters of our destinies, ignore the notion that we are still subject to the biological imperatives of our bodies. We forget that, ultimately, like other animals, what we are and how we live is largely dictated by the messages that mould and inform our brains.

Men and women could live more happily, understand and love each other better, organise the world to better effect, if we acknowledged our differences. We could then build our lives on the twin pillars of our distinct sexual identities. It is time to cease the vain contention that men and women are created the same. They were not, and no amount of idealism or Utopian fantasy can alter the fact. It can only strain the relationship between the sexes.

Understanding that men are strong and weak in areas where women are weak and strong could be, in the boardroom and the bedroom, the beginning of wisdom and the start of a happier relationship between the sexes.

It's an old joke that the book 'All that Men Understand about Women' is a thin volume, and that the pages are perfectly blank.

It is time to write on those pages.

CHAPTER ONE

The differences

A HUNDRED YEARS ago, the observation that men were different from women, in a whole range of aptitudes, skills, and abilities, would have been a leaden truism, a statement of the yawningly obvious.

Such a remark, uttered today, would evoke very different reactions. Said by a man, it would suggest a certain social ineptitude, a *naïveté* in matters of sexual politics, a sad deficiency in conventional wisdom, or a clumsy attempt to be provocative. A woman venturing such an opinion would be scorned as a traitor to her sex, betraying the hard-fought 'victories' of recent decades as women have sought equality of status, opportunity and respect.

Yet the truth is that virtually every professional scientist and researcher into the subject has concluded that the brains of men and women are different. There has seldom been a greater divide between what intelligent, enlightened opinion presumes – that men and women have the same brain – and what science knows – that they do not.

When a Canadian psychologist entitled an academic paper 'Are men's and women's brains really different?' she acknowledged that the answer to the question was self-evident:

> Yes, of course. It would be amazing if men's and
> women's brains were not different, given the gross
> morphological [structural] and often striking
> behavioural differences between men and women.

9

Most of us intuitively sense that the sexes are different. But this has become a universal, unshared, guilty secret. We have ceased to trust our common sense.

The truth is that for virtually our entire tenancy of the planet, we have been a sexist species. Our biology assigned separate functions to the male and female of *Homo sapiens*. Our evolution strengthened and refined those differences. Our civilisation reflected them. Our religion and our education reinforced them.

Yet we both fear, and defy, history; we fear it, because we are afraid of seeming to be in complicity with the centuries-old crimes of sexual prejudice. We defy it, because we want to believe that mankind has at last achieved escape velocity, released from the muddy gravity of our animal past and neanderthal assumptions.

In the last thirty years a small but influential collection of well-intentioned souls have tried to persuade us to adopt this new defiant appreciation. They have discovered that the religions and the education were a male plot to maintain the subordinate status of women. The discovery is probably correct. They have found that our so-called civilisations are founded on male aggression and dominance. That's probably true as well. So far so good.

The problem comes when you look for an explanation of why this happened. If men and women are identical, and always have been, in the degree and manner in which they use their identical brains, how did the male sex manage so successfully, in virtually every culture and society in the world, to contrive a situation where the female was subordinate? Was it just men's greater musculature and body-weight that have made the realm of womanhood an occupied country for the past scores of thousands of years? Was it the fact that until recent centuries women were pregnant most of the time? Or is it more likely – as the facts suggest – that the differences between the male and the female brain are at the root of the society we have and the people we are? There are some biological facts of life that, with the best, and most sexually liberated will in the world, we just cannot buck; would it not be better, rather than rage impotently against the differences between the sexes, to acknowledge, understand, exploit, and even enjoy them?

For the last hundred years, scientists have tried to explain those differences – although it has to be said that the first science of brain sex differences began with a methodology as crude as its assumptions. Simple measurement of the brain apparently proved that women lacked the necessary cerebral endowment to claim an equality of intellect. The Germans were particularly obsessed with this tape-measure scholarship. Bayerthal (1911) found it a minimum requirement for a professor of surgery that he have a head circumference of 52–53 centimetres: 'Under 52 cms you cannot expect an intellectual performance of any significance, while under 50.5 cms no normal intelligence can be expected.' In this connection he also observed, 'We do not have to ask for the head circumference of women of genius – they do not exist.'

The French scientist, Gustave Le Bon, noting that many Parisian women had brains closer in size to those of gorillas than of men, concluded that female inferiority was 'so obvious that no one can contest it for a moment'. And he warned, forebodingly, of

> the day when, misunderstanding the inferior
> occupations which nature has given her, women leave
> the home and take part in our battles; on that day a
> social revolution will begin and everything that
> maintains the sacred ties of the family will disappear
> . . .

That social revolution has been with us for some time; there has also been a revolution in the science of brain differences. Many – perhaps most – of the mysteries of how the brain works have yet to be unravelled, but the differences between the brains of males and females – and the processes by which they become different – are now clear. There is more to be known, more detail and qualification perhaps to add – but the nature and cause of brain differences are now known beyond speculation, beyond prejudice, and beyond reasonable doubt.

But now, just at the very moment when science can tell us what the differences are, and where they spring from, we are asked to banish the assumption of difference as if it were a guilty thought.

Recent decades have witnessed two contradictory process-es: the development of scientific research into the differences between the sexes, and the political denial that such differ-ences exist. These two intellectual currents are, under-standably, not on speaking terms. Science knows it dabbles in matters of sexual differences at its risk: at least one researcher into the field of gender differences was refused a grant on the grounds that 'this work ought not to be done'. Another told us that he had given up his work because 'the political pressure – the pressure on the truth' had become too much. On the other hand, some of those working in the field of sex differences seem to evince an almost wanton disregard for scientific findings, blinkering themselves against findings whose implications they might find too uncomfortable to recognise.

The first systematic tests to explore sex differences were conducted in 1882 by Francis Gatton at the South Kensington Museum in London. He purported to have identified signifi-cant sex differences favouring men in strength of grip, sen-sitivity to shrill whistle sounds, and ability to work under pressure. Women were observed to be more sensitive to pain.

Ten years later, in the United States, studies discovered that women could hear better than men, had a more conven-tional vocabulary, and preferred blue to red. Men preferred red to blue, used a more adventurous vocabulary, and had a preference for abstract and general thought, while women preferred practical problems, and individual tasks.

Havelock Ellis's *Man and Woman*, published in 1894, aroused immediate interest and ran into eight editions. Among the differences he chronicled were women's superior-ity over men in memory, cunning, dissimulation, compassion, patience, and tidiness. The work of female scientists was found to be more precise than that of men, but 'perhaps a little lacking in breadth and initiative, though admirable within a limited range'. A woman genius seemed to need the close support of a man; Ellis gave the example of Madame Curie, who was the wife of an already distinguished scientist, and pointed out that Mrs Browning's finest poems were all written after she had the good fortune to meet Mr Browning. Ellis found that women disliked the essentially intellectual process of analysis – 'They have the instinctive feeling that analysis may possibly destroy the emotional complexes by which they are largely moved and which appeal to them.'

These observations would have remained mere curiosities of scholarship, were it not for the development, beginning in the 1960s, of new scientific research into the brain. Paradoxically, the finding of gender differences corresponded with the period when the political denial that any differences existed was at its most vocal.

Paradoxically, too, interest in these differences grew out of an original scientific motive to suppress them. The problem arose from IQ tests. Researchers noticed consistent differences favouring one sex over the other in some of the abilities tested. This did not result in a chorus of eureka from the scientific community. In fact, it was regarded as something of a nuisance, muddying the waters of accurate measurement of intelligence. In the 1950s Dr D. Wechsler, an American scientist who developed the IQ test most commonly used today, found that over thirty tests 'discriminated' in favour of one or the other sex. The very use of the word suggests that the tests themselves were somehow to blame for the fact that different sexes achieved different success rates.

Wechsler, among others, sought to resolve the problem by eliminating all those tests which resulted in findings of significant sex differences. When it still proved difficult to produce 'sex-neutral' results, they deliberately introduced 'male-slanted' or 'female-slanted' items to arrive at approximately equal scores. It is an odd way of conducting a scientific study; if you don't like the result you get from an experiment, you fix the data to produce a more palatable conclusion. The sporting equivalent would be to handicap Olympic pole-vaulters with lead weights, or poles of different length, to ensure that the desired truth prevails: that all pole-vaulters, regardless of prowess or agility, are created equal.

Even so, sex differences stubbornly emerged, like recalcitrant dandelions in a chemically treated lawn. Wechsler even came to the conclusion from a series of sub-tests that it might be possible to demonstrate a measurable superiority of women over men in general intelligence. On the other hand, out of 105 tests assessing skills in solving maze-puzzles, involving the most heterogeneous populations throughout the world, ranging from the most primitive to the most highly civilised, 99 showed an incontrovertible male superiority. Perhaps the safest and least controversial synthesis of these findings would have been that girls are too intelligent to bother with anything as silly as a maze-puzzle test.

Preoccupied with finding sex-neutral IQ techniques, Wechsler regarded the evidence that the sexes *were* different as a mere nuisance. Rather as Columbus might have regarded his discovery of America as something of an irrelevance, since, after all, he was looking for the East Indies, Wechsler observed, almost parenthetically,

> Our findings do confirm what poets and novelists have
> often asserted, and the average person long believed,
> namely, that men not only behave, but 'think'
> differently from women.

What an early British pioneer of sex differences has called 'a conspiracy of silence surrounding the topic of human sex differences' was soon drowned in a babble of sociological explanations. Children, it was argued, were born psychosexually neutral; then parents, teachers, employers, politicians, and all the wicked fairies of society get to work on the innocent virginity of the mind. The main group championing the neutrality theory was led by Dr John Money, of Johns Hopkins University in the USA.

> Sexuality is undifferentiated at birth and . . . it becomes
> differentiated as masculine or feminine in the various
> experiences of growing up.

14

So, if men and women were different, it must be the result of social conditioning. Society was to blame, which, in the view of sociology, it usually is.

If there is still a dispute about how sex differences arise there is now no argument in the scientific community that such differences exist. It cannot be stressed often enough that this book concerns itself with the *average* man and the *average* woman. In the same way, we might say that men are taller than women. Look across any crowded room and this will be obvious. Of course some women will be taller than some men, and the tallest woman may possibly be taller than the tallest man. But statistically men are on average 7 per cent taller, and the tallest person in the world, rather than in the room, is certainly a man.

The statistical variations in sex differences which we will explore, in skills, aptitudes or abilities, are much greater than they are in relation to height; there will always be the exception to the average, the person with exceptional 'wrong-sex' skills, but the exception does not invalidate the general, average rule. These differences have a practical, social relevance. On measurements of various aptitude tests, the difference between the sexes in average scores on these tests can be as much as 25 per cent. A difference of as little as 5 per cent has been found to have a marked impact on the occupations or activities at which men or women will, on average, excel.

The area where the biggest differences have been found lies in what scientists call 'spatial ability'. That's being able to picture things, their shape, position, geography and proportion, accurately in the mind's eye – all skills that are crucial to the practical ability to work with three-dimensional objects or drawings. One scientist who has reviewed the extensive literature on the subject concludes, 'The fact of the male's superiority in spatial ability is not in dispute.' It is confirmed by literally hundreds of different scientific studies.

A typical test measures the skill of men and women in the assembly of a three-dimensional, mechanical apparatus. Only a quarter of the women could perform the task better than the average male. At the top end of the scale of mechanical aptitude there will be twice as many men as women.

From school age onwards, boys will generally outperform girls in areas of mathematics involving abstract concepts of space, relationships, and theory. At the very highest level of mathematical excellence, according to the biggest survey ever conducted, the very best boys totally eclipse the very best girls. Dr Julian Stanley and Dr Camilla Benbow, two American psychologists, worked with highly gifted students of both sexes. Not only did they find that the best girl never beat the best boy – they also discovered a startling sex ratio of mathematical brilliance: for every exceptional girl there were more than thirteen exceptional boys.

Scientists know that they walk on social eggshells when they venture any theory about human behaviour. But researchers into sex differences are increasingly impatient with the polite attempt to find a social explanation for these differences. As Camilla Benbow now says of her studies showing a male superiority in mathematically gifted children, 'After 15 years looking for an environmental explanation and getting zero results, I gave up.' She readily admitted to us her belief that the difference in ability has a biological basis.

Boys also have the superior hand-eye co-ordination necessary for ball sports. Those same skills mean that they can more easily imagine, alter, and rotate an object in their mind's eye. Boys find it easier than girls to construct block buildings from two-dimensional blueprints, and to assess correctly how the angle of the surface level of water in a jug would change when the jug was tilted to different angles.

This male advantage in seeing patterns and abstract relationships – what could be called general strategic rather than the detailed tactical thinking – perhaps explains the male dominance of chess, even in a country like the USSR, where the game is a national sport played by both sexes. An alternative explanation, more acceptable to those who would deny the biological basis of sex differences, is that women have become so conditioned to the fact of male chess-playing superiority that they subconsciously assign themselves lower expectations; but this is a rather wilful rejection of scientific evidence for the sake of maintaining a prejudice.

The better spatial ability of men could certainly help to explain that male superiority in map-reading we noted earlier. Here again, the prejudice of male motorists is confirmed by experiment; girls and boys were each given city street maps and, without rotating the map, asked to describe whether they would be turning left or right at particular intersections as they mentally made their way across town and back. Boys did better. More women than men like to turn the map round, physically to match the direction in which they are travelling when they are trying to find their way.

While the male brain gives men the edge in dealing with things and theorems, the female brain is organised to respond more sensitively to all sensory stimuli. Women do better than men on tests of verbal ability. Females are equipped to receive a wider range of sensory information, to connect and relate that information with greater facility, to place a primacy on personal relationships, and to communicate. Cultural influences may reinforce these strengths, but the advantages are innate.

The differences are apparent in the very first hours after birth. It has been shown that girl babies are much more interested than boys in people and faces; the boys seem just as happy with an object dangled in front of them.

Girls say their first words and learn to speak in short sentences earlier than boys, and are generally more fluent in their pre-school years. They read earlier, too, and do better in coping with the building blocks of language like grammar, punctuation and spelling. Boys outnumber girls by 4 : 1 in remedial reading classes. Later, women find it easier to master foreign languages, and are more proficient in their own, with a better command of grammar and spelling. They are also more fluent: stuttering and other speech defects occur almost exclusively among boys.

Girls and women hear better than men. When the sexes are compared, women show a greater sensitivity to sound. The dripping tap will get the woman out of bed before the man has even woken up. Six times as many girls as boys can sing in tune. They are also much more adept at noticing small changes in volume, which goes some way to explaining women's superior sensitivity to that 'tone of voice' which their male partners are so often accused of adopting.

Men and women even see some things differently. Women see better in the dark. They are more sensitive to the red end of the spectrum, seeing more red hues there than men, and have a better visual memory.

Men see better than women in bright light. Intriguing results also show that men tend to be literally blinkered; they see in a narrow field – mild tunnel vision – with greater concentration on depth. They have a better sense of perspective than women. Women, however, quite literally take in the bigger picture. They have wider peripheral vision, because they have more of the receptor rods and cones in the retina, at the back of the eyeball, to receive a wider arc of visual input.

The differences extend to the other senses. Women react faster, and more acutely, to pain, although their overall resistance to long-term discomfort is greater than men's. In a sample of young adults, females showed 'overwhelmingly' greater sensitivity to pressure on the skin on every part of the body. In childhood and maturity, women have a tactile sensitivity so superior to men's that in some tests there is no overlap between the scores of the two sexes; in these, the least sensitive woman is more sensitive than the most sensitive man.

There is strong evidence that men and women have different senses of taste – women being more sensitive to bitter flavours like quinine, and preferring higher concentrations and greater quantities of sweet things. Men score higher in discerning salty flavours. Overall, however, the evidence strongly suggests a greater female delicacy and perception in taste. Should more great chefs be women? Or do many great male chefs have more than their share of feminine sensibilities?

Women's noses, as well as their palates, are more sensitive than men's; a case in point is their perception of exaltolide, a synthetic musk-like odour associated with men, but hardly noticeable to them. Women found the smell attractive. Interestingly, this superior sensitivity increases just before ovulation; at a critical time of her menstrual cycle, the biology of woman makes her more sensitive to man.

This superiority in so many of the senses can be clinically measured – yet it is what accounts for women's almost supernatural 'intuition'. Women are simply better equipped to notice things to which men are comparatively blind and deaf. There is no witchcraft in this superior perception – it is extra-sensory only in terms of the blunter, male senses. Women are better at picking up social cues, picking up important nuances of meaning from tones of voice or intensity of expression. Men sometimes become exasperated at a woman's reaction to what they say. They do not realise that women are probably 'hearing' much more than what the man himself thinks he is 'saying'. Women tend to be better judges of character. Older females have a better memory for names and faces, and a greater sensitivity to other people's preferences.

Sex differences have been noted in the comparative memory of men and women. Women can store, for short periods at least, more irrelevant and random information than men; men can only manage the trick when the information is organised into some coherent form, or has a specific relevance to them.

So men are more self-centred – so what else is new? What's new is that the folklore of gender, which is always vulnerable to dismissive, politically motivated, fashionable opinion, is now shown to have a basis in scientific fact.

Many people resist the thorough-going biological explanations we will propose for so many of the differences between the sexes, but are prepared to believe, in a rather vague manner, that they probably have 'something to do with the hormones'.

That's half right. The hormones, as we will see, determine the distinct male or female organisation of the brain as it develops in the womb. We share the same sexual identity for only the first few weeks after conception. Thereafter, in the womb, the very structure and pattern of the brain begins to take a specifically male or female form. Throughout infant, teenage, and adult life, the way the brain was forged will have, in subtle interplay with the hormones, a fundamental effect on the attitudes, behaviour, and intellectual and emotional functioning of the individual. Most neuroscientists and researchers into the mysteries of the brain are now prepared, like the American neurologist Dr Richard Restak, to make the confident assertion

> It seems unrealistic to deny any longer the existence of
> male and female brain differences. Just as there are
> physical dissimilarities between males and females . . .
> there are equally dramatic differences in brain
> functioning.

The way our brains are made affects how we think, learn, see, smell, feel, communicate, love, make love, fight, succeed, or fail. Understanding how our brains, and those of others, are made is a matter of no little importance.

Infants are not blank slates, on whom we scrawl instructions for sexually-appropriate behaviour. They are born with male or female minds of their own. They have, quite literally, made up their minds in the womb, safe from the legions of social engineers who impatiently await them.

Recent years have brought us the means to build a new framework for understanding sex differences through two, independent and converging scientific advances. The first is the giant progress which has been made in understanding how the brain works; the second, the new discoveries about how, biologically and behaviourally, we are what we are – male or female.

CHAPTER TWO

The birth of difference

IT IS NOT until six or seven weeks after conception that the unborn baby 'makes up its mind', and the brain begins to take on a male or a female pattern. What happens, at that critical stage in the darkness of the womb, will determine the structure and organisation of the brain: and that, in turn, will decide the very nature of the mind. It is one of the most fascinating stories of life and creation; a story largely unknown, but now, at last, beginning to unfold in its entirety.

We have known some of the story for some time. We know that the genes, carrying the coded blueprint of our unique characteristics, make us either male or female. In every microscopic cell of our bodies, men and women are different from each other; because every fibre of our being has a different set of chromosomes within it, depending on whether we are male or female.

Our identity blueprints come in the form of forty-six chromosomes, half contributed by the mother, half by the father. The first forty-four team up with one another, forming pairs of chromosomes which determine certain bodily features of the eventual individual, such as the colour of the eyes, the length and shape of the nose. But the last pair are different.

The mother contributes an 'X' chromosome to the egg (the 'X' describes the rough shape of the chromosome). If the father's contribution on fertilisation of the egg is another 'X' chromosome, the outcome will – normally – be the formation

Normal genetics and sex determination

Woman

Man

Eggs:
All 22 chromosomes + X

Sperm:
22 chromosomes + X
or 22 chromosomes + Y

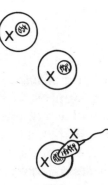

Girl

Boy

of a girl baby. If the father's sperm contains a 'Y' chromosome, normally a baby boy will be born.

But the genes alone do not guarantee the sex of a child. That depends on the intervention, or the absence, of the other factor in sex determination – the hormones. Whatever the genetic make-up of the embryo, the foetus will only develop as a male if male hormones are present, and it will only develop as a female if male hormones are absent. The proof of this has come from studying people who have inherited abnormalities. It is only by looking at where development goes wrong that the scientists have been able to build a picture of what happens during normal development. These studies have shown that male hormones are the crucial factor in determining the sex of a child. If a female foetus, genetically XX, is exposed to male hormones, the baby is born looking like a normal male. If a male foetus, genetically XY, is deprived of male hormones, the baby is born looking like a normal female.

Hormonal sex determination

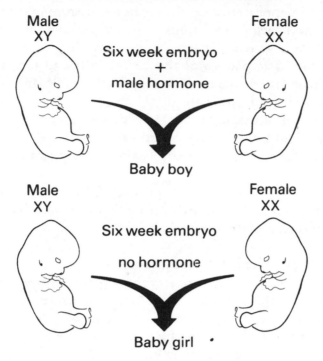

Male
XY

Female
XX

Six week embryo
+
male hormone

Baby boy

Male
XY

Female
XX

Six week embryo

no hormone

Baby girl

In the first weeks in the womb, the tiny foetus isn't noticeably a miniature girl or a miniature boy. It has all the basic equipment, such as vestigial ducts, tracts and so on, to develop as either sex. But as the weeks go by, the genes begin to put the message across. If things go normally, and everything follows the XY blueprint of a boy, the chromosomes will cue the development of the gonads into testes.

It's now, at around six weeks, that sexual identity is finally determined – when the male foetus develops the special cells which produce the male hormones or androgens, the main one being testosterone. The hormones instruct the body not to bother with developing a feminine set of sexual equipment, while stimulating the development of embryonic male genitalia.

At about the same time, if the baby is female, genetically XX, the reproductive machinery develops along female lines, produces no significant amount of male hormone, and results in a girl baby.

Just as the six-week-old foetus wasn't recognisably male or female in appearance, so the embryonic brain takes some time before it begins to acquire a specific sexual identity. If the embryo is genetically female, nothing very drastic happens to the basic pattern of the brain. In broad terms, the natural template of the brain seems to be female. In normal girls it will develop naturally along female lines.

In boys it is different. Just as male gender depended on the presence of male hormone, so a radical intervention is needed to change that naturally female brain structure into a male pattern.

This literally mind-altering process is the result of the same process that determined those other physical changes – the intervention of the hormones.

It has always seemed something of a puzzle that nature should put such a high priority on organising the sexual machinery of the unborn child. After all, its reproductive mechanism isn't going to come into its own for years to come. The answer is that the formation of the sexual equipment is not simply an end in itself. Once formed, the sexual machinery has work to do. It produces those crucially important male hormones. They, in turn, have work to do – on the unformed brain.

Embryonic boy babies are exposed to a colossal dose of male hormone at the critical time when their brains are beginning to take shape. The male hormone levels then are four times the level experienced throughout infancy and boyhood. A vast surge of male hormone occurs at each end of male development: at adolescence, when his sexuality comes on stream, and six weeks after conception, at the moment his brain is beginning to take shape.

But, as with the development of the rest of the body, things can go wrong. A male foetus may have enough male hormones to trigger the development of male sex organs, but these may not be able to produce the additional male hormones to push the brain into the male pattern. His brain will 'stay' female, so he will be born with a female brain in a male body. In the same way, a female baby may be exposed in the womb to an accidental dose of male hormone – we'll see later how this can happen – and end up with a male brain in a female body.

Ten years ago, most of this was tentative theory. Now, it's accepted, to a greater or lesser degree, by virtually every brain specialist or neuroscientist. Yet most non-scientists – that is, most people – are unaware of this fundamental fact of life. If most of us do not know that our brains are made differently, it is not surprising that we have difficulty in acknowledging, or understanding, each other's differences.

So how did the scientific detectives discover the truth of how the brain becomes sexed as male or female in the womb? The clues came from two sources – from children who for one reason or another have had an abnormal dose of hormones in the womb, and from experiments with animals.

The rat has many vices, but one redeeming virtue; it is in some respects an ideal subject for experimentation. It has genes, hormones, and a central nervous system just as we do, but it has one extra trick up its sleeve; its brain does not develop in the womb, as ours do. Its brain takes final shape only after birth. So it is easier for us to see what is going on, and find out why. We can watch the development of the brain, and manipulate its very nature.

A male rat comes into the world with its brain roughly at the same unformed stage as the seven-week-old human embryo. When scientists castrate him, he becomes to all intents and purposes (except procreation) a female rat. He certainly thinks she is. (Let's call him/her 'it'.) As the neutered rat grows up, it is much less aggressive than its intact, male companions. It is altogether a much more social creature, at least by the standards of rats. It will groom and lick other rats like a good mother.

The later the rat is castrated, the less obviously feminine its behaviour is – because the more opportunity the brain has had to be bathed in male hormone, the more it will be organised into a male pattern. Once the critical time of brain development is past, no amount of additional male hormone can make the rat regain its original masculine identity. Stripped of its sexual machinery at the crucial time of brain development, it never produced the male hormones that could kick the brain into male shape.

If you inject it, as an adult, with female hormones, its sexual behaviour becomes that of a female, curving the back in the presence of males in the typical, submissive manner of a female rodent. It is a male rat, but with a female brain.

The experiment works in reverse. If you take a new-born female rat – again, with its brain still unorganised on any specific sexual lines – and inject it with male hormones, the brain cells will be exposed to a sluice of male hormone. This female then develops into a rat which, when 'turned on' by injections of male hormone, behaves just like a male. It will be more aggressive and try to mount other female rats. Yet if you inject it with female hormones, nothing happens.

A picture is emerging of the critical interplay between the hormones and the unformed brain. The developing male brain needs the male hormones to organise it into a specific male pattern – to wire it to produce male behaviour. It only stays wired as a female brain if the male hormones are absent at the time of brain development. A normally developed female brain is immune to later doses of male hormone, and a normal male brain does not change its behaviour if soaked in female hormone. Once the brain is 'set' in its male or female structure, the intervention of wrong-sex hormones does not affect it.

Having found that there was a connection between hormones and behaviour, the next step was to see whether physical differences in the structure of the brain could be found.

The obvious place to look for a difference between the brains of the sexes was in the part of the brain controlling sexual behaviour. This area is called the hypothalamus. It took microscopic examination to detect the differences – but differences there were. The pattern of cells and structure of the hypothalamus, in male and female rats, were distinct and different.

Scientists could see differences in the structure of the nerve cell network of the male and female animal brain. They have detected specific differences in the length of some nerve cell connectors, a different pattern of branches, different pathways which the chemical messengers of the hormones take to reach different destinations in the brain. The strands of nerve cells are much denser in the male rat, for instance, and some of its brain-cell nuclei are up to eight times larger.

Their curiosity aroused, the scientists wanted to find out if they could remould the hypothalamus, this crucial area of the rodent brain. They knew that manipulating the hormones at a critical time changed behaviour from male to female, and female to male. Now they found that, by manipulating the hormones in the same way, they could alter the very structure of the brain. If they deprived a developing male rat of male hormones, his hypothalamus followed the female pattern. If a female rat was given extra male hormones, her hypothalamus was designed according to the male blueprint.

Further research revealed other differences between the sexes in the structure of the brain. The cerebral cortex is like a rind over the two hemispheres of the brain. In the cortex are located key control centres governing relatively complex behaviour. It was discovered that this rind was measurably thicker in males – but only on the right side. In females, the left side was thicker. Manipulate the hormones at a critical time, and, again, you could reverse the pattern.

Male hormone alters the way in which the brain network is laid down; when it is present, the pattern is male, and when it is absent, the pattern is female. A connection – or at least a relationship – had been discovered, and experimentally demonstrated, between behaviour, hormones and brain structure.

There is a graphic example of this process from another part of the animal kingdom. Among certain songbirds, the male sings but the female does not. The capacity to sing can be shown to depend on the presence or absence of male hormone. Female chaffinches and canaries can be induced to wax lyrical – by the injection of the male hormone, testosterone. Once again, under the microscope the differences in the brain-cell network are visible. The female brain lacks the neurones, the connections between some cells, which give the creature the capacity to sing. Exposed to male hormone, however, the female chaffinch brain acquires the relevant neurones and the gift of song.

'The brain', according to a Canadian psychologist who has made some of the most recent contributions to sex-difference research, 'is a sex organ'.

There is more precise proof of the power of the hormones in determining brain sex and behaviour in animals. Experiments have shown how specific behaviours can be influenced by manipulating the hormones at various stages of the brain's development, while the animal embryo is still in the womb.

For these experiments, rhesus monkeys make useful subjects, sharing similarities with the nervous system of humans; female rhesuses have the same twenty-eight-day menstrual cycle as women.

You don't have to be a monkey scientist to spot the males among rhesus monkeys. They're rougher and tougher, they initiate play more often than females, and have distinctive male sexual monkey tricks; they mount other monkeys of the same age (whether female or male), and they also mount their mothers more often than do female monkeys.

Scientists can now fundamentally alter, and redetermine, the behaviour of monkeys, by injecting the pregnant mother with male hormone – at a time when, like humans, the brain pattern is being set.

Their female offspring will behave in the boisterous male manner. Intriguingly, by giving the injections at different times during the pregnancy, the scientists can induce specific masculine behaviour; they can make the females mount other monkeys of the same age group, but not mount their mothers, or they can produce females who are more aggressive in play, but do not mount their peers. In other words, the imprinting of male behaviour is not a drastic, one-off business: it happens gradually, the hormone causing different behaviours by altering the wiring in discrete areas of the brain bit by bit, function by function.

Tweaking the developing brain of an animal with extra hormones changes its structure; and a change in structure corresponds with a change in behaviour.

So where does that leave us?

> The brains of male and female mammals, from rodents
> to primates, exhibiting hormonally mediated differences
> in neuro-transmitter levels, neural connections, and cell
> and nuclear volume, strongly suggest that similar sexual
> dimorphism of structure and function exists in human
> brains as well.

Scientific caution makes most people shrink from drawing
human parallels from our knowledge of other animals. But,
after all, we share quite a lot of our behaviour with the rest
of animal creation, and there are many areas where the
separate activities of boys and girls are mirrored by similar
differences in other species. It's not just young male rats who
play more aggressively, or young female monkeys who like
to spend their time looking after babies. Conversely, it's not
just men who are better than women at reading maps; male
rats are better at finding their way out of mazes.

In the early days of scientific gender curiosity the wisdom
was that biology had a comparatively minor influence on
our behaviour and attitudes. The assumption was that, in
terms of our minds, we were born sexually neutral, our minds
a blank slate on which our parents, our teachers, and the
expectations our societies had of us would chalk their determinant messages. In most of us, of course, our minds, bodies
and the way society expects us to behave, are so tightly
bound up together that it is difficult to prise them apart. But
today there are hundreds of cases which show that social
conditioning alone cannot determine our sexual mind-set.

Many of these cases concern accidents of nature which
have resulted in trapping a female brain in a male body, or a
male brain in a female one.

The Case of Jane

Jane is a happily married mother of three children. When she
was born, the doctors were disturbed. As a baby she had
underdeveloped, and somewhat ambiguous, sex organs – not

quite male, not quite female. The confusion was such that the doctors conducted a genetic test. Jane had XX chromosomes, so she was a female. After some surgical correction, she was brought up as a typical girl. Except that Jane wasn't typical. She was noticeably rougher and tougher in play. She was an intensely physical, outdoor person. She also went out of her way to seek out the company of boys as playmates. She had no time for dolls, preferring to play with her brother's trucks, cars and building blocks. At school, she was a late developer in reading and writing. She would also get into trouble for starting fights.

As a young teenager, she refused to be a bridesmaid at her cousin's wedding. Later, she displayed no interest at all in babies. Alone among her female friends, Jane always refused invitations to baby-sit. She had absolutely no interest in feminine clothes.

When she got married, she had an unromantic, down-to-earth view of marriage. She describes her husband as 'my best friend'. When she had children, she was devoted, in equal measure, to her family and to her career. Her hobby is orienteering, the strenuous cross-country sport where success depends on stamina and an accurate sense of direction.

Her younger sister is nothing like her, although the children were brought up in identical circumstances.

So what made Jane Jane? While the doctors were sorting out her problems as a baby, they discovered that she had an abnormality in the adrenal glands of her kidneys. This so-called adrenogenital syndrome resulted in the secretion of a substance much akin to male hormone while she was in her mother's womb. This condition often results in the formation of underdeveloped male external genitalia, along with a normal set of internal, female, reproductive apparatus. Surgery can correct the unnecessary boyish bits — but it cannot reverse what has already happened to the brain. While in the womb, Jane's developing brain had been exposed to the male chemical. Her brain, then, had felt itself 'instructed' to develop along male lines.

Jane had a male brain in a female body. It didn't stop her

being a woman, and having babies. But it stopped her behaving completely like a woman and, to a great extent, feeling like one.

Sometimes, the kidney abnormality results in so high a release of this male-like hormone that the genetically female (XX) baby comes into the world with the sexual equipment of a boy. Naturally, such babies are brought up as boys. It is only at puberty, when the boy fails to develop into manhood, that the doctor is consulted, and the hospital laboratories find that 'he' is genetically female.

The parents usually opt for treatment involving supplementary doses of the male hormone – and the boy becomes a man. He may marry, but will not have children; being a genetic woman, of course, he does not produce sperm and so cannot be a father.

But in his mind, whatever the genetic code is insisting, he has always been male. That same, abnormal, bathing in male hormone that turned a would-be girl into a sexually identifiable boy, didn't just affect the growth of the genitals; it also cast the embryonic brain into a male pattern.

Just like the girls, the brains of these children had already been set in the womb as male – because of their exposure to an overdose of mind-altering androgen hormones.

The evidence suggests that brain sexing is a matter of degree: the more male hormone the foetus is exposed to, the more the adult will be male in behaviour. The less the amount of male hormone, the more feminine the adult behaviour.

Further evidence for this comes from women who are missing one of the two XX female sex chromosomes. Their genetic make-up is XO and the condition is known as Turner's syndrome. These women have exaggeratedly female behaviour. The ovaries of the normal female foetus produce tiny amounts of male hormone. The Turner's syndrome foetus has no ovaries, so no male hormone at all reaches the developing brain. The brain retains a fully female organisation.

The Case of Caroline

Caroline suffers from Turner's syndrome. Like most girls with her condition her behaviour as a child was exaggeratedly feminine. She played with dolls to the exclusion of virtually everything else. As a teenager she loved to imitate her mother and do the household chores. She was always the first to volunteer as a baby-sitter. As Caroline grew up she became obsessive about pretty clothes, make-up and personal appearance. She was ultra-romantic, yearning to be married, and dreaming constantly of having babies – something, alas, which she could never do. Intellectually, she scored the average for her sex on verbal IQ tests, but in mathematics and tests for spatial ability she fell far below the level of normal girls. Her sense of direction was very poor. It took a long time for her to learn her way to and from school.

Caroline's hormonal imbalance resulted in an exaggeratedly female brain bias, which in turn accentuated her feminine behaviour and comparative mental strengths and weaknesses.

Further evidence for the power of the hormones on our behaviour has been shown by studying the after-effects of artificial hormones. Hormones, both male and female, were routinely used in the 1950s and 1960s in the treatment of difficult pregnancies. The findings of this study give us the closest human parallels with the earlier animal experiments.

Some diabetic mothers-to-be suffered frequent spontaneous abortions. Doctors knew that the problem was caused by a low level of natural female hormone, a side-effect of diabetes. They treated the mothers with a synthetic female hormone, diethylstilbestrol. The treatment solved the problem of the miscarriages, but time has revealed that it has been responsible for other complications. The additional hormones changed the brain, and the behaviour, of the male children born to these mothers.

The Case of Jim

Jim is one of a group of sixteen-year-olds surveyed after their diabetic mothers took supplementary female hormones during pregnancy.

Like most of the group, Jim is shy, unassertive and has a comparatively low level of self-esteem. He ranks himself in the bottom 25 per cent of his class when it comes to popularity, influence, sporting and physical prowess. He has had no heterosexual experience (though some homosexual). His occasional masturbatory fantasies involve a nude, faceless girl, with whom he never comes into physical contact.

In the course of the survey, Jim's mother made a spontaneous comparison between Jim, and her older son, Larry. While pregnant with Larry, she had not taken any of the hormone treatment. She commented that her younger son was an extremely poor athlete, was regarded as a 'sissy' by the other boys, would never fight back, and never developed an interest in electronic devices or chemical sets as his older brother had done. These were children of the same family, brought up in culturally identical situations.

What happened with Jim is that the extra female hormone had feminised his brain while it was developing. Scientists now believe they can explain the process. Female hormones inhibit, or counteract, the effect of male hormones. Jim had enough male hormone to develop male sexual equipment, but the additional female hormone prevented the organisation of his brain into a male pattern.

Male hormone was given to mothers-to-be who suffered from toxaemia. The treatment alleviated the discomfort caused by this condition, but is now known to have had some effect, this time on the girl babies born to these mothers. Their subsequent behaviour was very like that of Jane, the girl whose own adrenal gland malfunction had resulted in her producing abnormal amounts of male hormone. Like Jane, they had little interest in conventional feminine pursuits.

The psychologist Dr June Reinisch, now director of the Kinsey Institute in Ohio, describes the influence of the hormones on us. She says that we are all 'flavoured by our prenatal chemical development'. Depending on the nature, the dose, and the timing, Reinisch explains the nature of tomboyish girls, or of boys with an unusual preoccupation with clothes, dolls or children; of girls better than the average for their sex at maths, or of boys who were less aggressive and assertive, less athletic, perhaps, but more willing than their peers to co-operate and sacrifice their own individualism to the will of the group.

All of which has disturbing implications; if hormones are really that influential, what have we done, what may we still be doing, and what could we do to the brains of our unborn children? We are standing on the very brink of pre-natal mind-control, social engineering now made possible by the administration of hormones which can change the way we are, the way we behave, and the way we think.

If we are really unhappy about the way men and women are, and if we truly want to engineer a society in which traditional gender roles evaporate, there is clearly an easier, synthetic solution than teaching boys needlework or girls metalwork. It could be done with a syringe.

There are more immediate implications. Accepting that sexual differences are so much the product of biology is to throw a hand-grenade into the middle of the happy consensus that we are what society expects us to be; and that we can change what we are by changing society's expectations of our hitherto stereotyped roles. Women's liberationists – and that often-overlooked group of men who are restless at the role they are expected to undertake – have believed that to a large extent we can take control of our destinies and direct them, irrespective of gender, wherever we want. Free will may exist in both the male and the female brain – but is will itself enough to free us from the way we are made? We can always change our direction, but we cannot alter our biology.

There is no room for any residual suspicion that it is conditioning and culture rather than biology which determines the sexual identity of the mind. The nail in the coffin of that social theory comes with studies of boys who, due to a chemical deficiency, are born with what look like female sex organs, and are brought up as girls.

The Case of Juan, née Juanita

Juan is one of a group of cases, most of which have been discovered in New Guinea and the Dominican Republic.

At birth, his scrotum had the appearance of the female labia, his infant phallus was tucked in like a clitoris, and the testes were pouched out of sight in the abdomen. It was assumed that a baby girl had been born, and the child was brought up in accordance with the explicit, sex-specific female role of the primitive society village.

At puberty, Juanita's parents came in for something of a shock – as did their daughter. Her voice deepened, testes suddenly popped out and descended, and the penis rapidly grew.

It was clear that Juanita was no girl.

Intriguingly, in spite of having been brought up as a girl (and, according to old behavioural theories gender identity is firmly established by the age of four) Juanita/Juan and nearly all the children who turned from girls to boys said that as early as twelve years of age they began to become concerned about their sexual identity. By adolescence, the suspicion had become absolute: they simply didn't 'feel' like girls. They changed their clothes, and fell in love with girls.

There was nothing in their environment to give them a hint of what 'feeling like a boy' was, and strict social taboos kept them to their assigned gender identity – but, deep inside them, they knew they were not girls. And they were right.

We now know that there are a number of different male hormones responsible for sexing different aspects of infant masculinity in the womb. The particular hormone which prompts the male sex organs to drop down is present in these children, but in very low amounts, so that the penis and testicles remain internal until puberty. Then, there is a sufficient concentration of the relevant hormone to provoke the emergence of the sex organs. But the crucial male hormones responsible for sexing the brain in the womb had always been present, and at the right concentration, to pattern their brains along male lines. Their brains had been formed in

35

the male mould; their brains would always 'know' they belonged to a male being when once the hormonal floodgates of adolescence had been opened and those hormones had come into contact with a receptive, male mind. But they were trapped in a body which society assumed was female. Biology overcame conditioning.

What gives us a male or a female brain, then, is not a matter of our genes; for we have seen how a genetic male may have a female mind, and vice versa. It is a matter of the hormones that our developing bodies make, or which surround us in the womb. What matters is the degree to which our embryonic brains are exposed to male hormone. The less they get, the more the natural, feminine mind-set will survive. More precisely, it is a matter of the concentration, timing, and appropriateness of those hormones. The die is cast *in utero*; that's when the mind is made up, and the luggage of our bodies, and of society's expectations of us, merely supplements this basic biological fact of life.

Scientists have concluded that in man and other animals, at a critical stage of brain development, there are critical phases of nerve cell growth which are influenced by male hormone. As one of them sums up the process, 'Hormonal influence at this critical stage is important for gender differentiation, since brain cells acquire a "set" . . . highly resistant to change after birth. It is this organisational effect of the hormones on neural circuitry that has led neuroscientists to speak of a "male" or "female" brain at birth.'

If the hormones hold so much of the answer to our behaviour, mental attitudes and outlook, could they also dictate our sexual inclinations? The answer is yes – but the reasons are so fascinating that the subject deserves, and will get, a chapter to itself. Sufficient, for the moment, to mention that just as some drugs taken during pregnancy can misdirect the development of the foetal brain, so a chemical imbalance in the womb can also alter sexual inclinations in the eventual adult. We know how to make homosexual rats and monkeys. Some scientists argue that we know how to prevent homosexuality in man – before birth.

How the brain circuitry is arranged affects more than our

36

sexual inclination. It will make us, male or female, tend towards different attitudes, responses, feelings about ourselves and others, priorities . . . all the hundreds of differences noted throughout the ages by poets, writers, and ordinary men and women, in blissful scientific ignorance.

It even explains how and why we think differently.

But to understand that, we need to explore a little more deeply into the different mechanisms of male and female brains.

CHAPTER THREE

Sex in the brain

WHAT WE ARE, how we behave, how we think and feel, is governed not by the heart, but by the brain. The brain itself is influenced, in structure and operation, by the hormones. If brain structure and hormones are different in men and women, it should not surprise us that men and women behave in different ways. Understanding the exact relationship between brain structure, hormones and behaviour would take us a long way to discovering the answer to some of humanity's most exasperating riddles. We are on the threshold of that understanding.

The first step was the discovery that the hormones have a dual effect on the brain. While the brain is developing in the womb, the hormones control the way the neural networks are laid out. Later on, at puberty, those hormones will revisit the brain to switch on the network they earlier created. Their action is like the process of photography: it is as if a negative is produced in the womb, which is only developed when these chemical messengers return in adolescence. Differences in human behaviour depend on the interaction between hormones and the brain.

The next step was to discover whether the differences in behaviour between men and women were echoed by differences in structure between the male and the female brain. This would establish an incontrovertible connection between hormones, brains, and behaviour.

It was not an easy task. Even our current knowledge of the brain – the most sophisticated of our organs – is in many ways rudimentary. Our brain functions reside in a three-pound lump of tissue, helmeted by the skull, and looking dispiritingly like a monstrous pickled walnut. Female brains are a little smaller than male brains, but this seems to have no significance. The higher thought processes of the brain – those which distinguish us from other animals – exist in the cortex, a half-inch-thick grey rind which covers the two halves of the brain.

Different ages have compared the brain with different things; in the nineteenth century they compared it with one of their new-fangled mechanical looms, while today, inevitably, we think in terms of the computer. Each new model spawns a new hypothesis, to be countered by corresponding rebuttals. But slowly, proposition by proposition, argument by argument, an accepted, time-tested set of conclusions gathers from which we can begin to construct a more solid basis of understanding.

Before we look at the differences between the male and the female brain, we should understand the general structure of the human brain, and then see how precise areas of the brain are different in men and women.

The earliest clues to how the brain works came from examining the behaviour of people with brain damage. Different areas of the brain control specific functions.

It is now known that the left side of the brain deals predominantly with verbal abilities and the detailed orderly processing of information. That is, speaking, writing and reading are all largely under the control of the left-hand side of the brain. Damage to the left side of the brain causes all sorts of problems related to language. The left side controls the logical, sequential thought processes.

The right side of the brain is the headquarters for the visual information. It deals with spatial relations. A person with brain damage to the right-hand side often loses their sense of direction, unable even to find their way around their own home. The right side is responsible for taking in 'the big

General brain geography

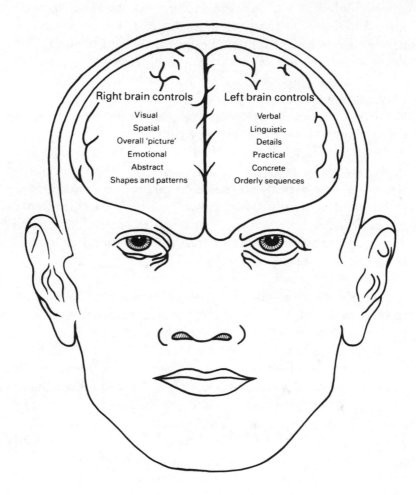

Right brain controls

Visual
Spatial
Overall 'picture'
Emotional
Abstract
Shapes and patterns

Left brain controls

Verbal
Linguistic
Details
Practical
Concrete
Orderly sequences

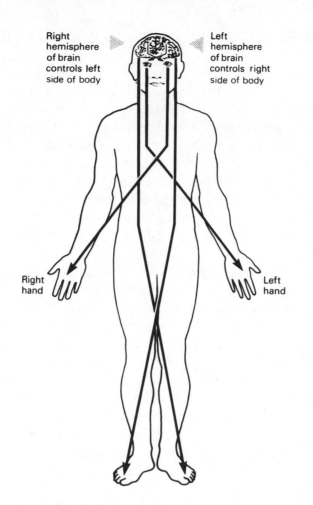

Right
hemisphere
of brain
controls left
side of body

Left
hemisphere
of brain
controls right
side of body

Right
hand

Left
hand

picture', basic shapes and patterns. It controls the abstract
thought processes and some of our emotional responses.

The right side of our brain controls the left-hand side of
our bodies, and the left side of our brain controls the right-
hand side of our bodies. Damage to the left side of the
brain can lead to the paralysis of the right side of the body.
In addition, what we see with our left eye is processed in the
right side of our brains, and the right eye in the left.

THE DISCOVERY OF BRAIN DIFFERENCE

The early knowledge of which areas controlled which functions came mostly from the laboratory of the battlefield. One disadvantage of this methodology, from a scientific point of view, is that the war game is almost exclusively a male pursuit, so there was little data on women. As in so many things, the easy assumption was made that what was true of the male brain probably held good for the female. The specific study of the female brain is comparatively recent; but it is now clear that there are major differences in the structure and organisation of the brains of men and women.

The first indications that this was the case came nearly thirty years ago. In his Bethesda, Maryland research centre, the psychologist Herbert Landsell discovered that men and women, when damaged in the same area of the brain, were differently affected. He took a group of epileptics who had had part of their brain removed – some of the right hemisphere which deals with the shape of things and the space they occupy.

The men with right-side brain damage did badly in tests relating to spatial skills. Yet the relative performance of the similarly brain-damaged women was scarcely affected. Men lost all their capacity for spatial IQ tests; women with right-sided brain damage did not.

Landsell moved on to the left hemisphere, where language skills are located. Once again, men with left-side damage lost much of their command of language; but women with damage in the same area retained most of theirs. Men were three times more likely to suffer from a language problem than women – in spite of their having been damaged in exactly the same place.

This led Landsell to the conclusion, now accepted, that in women language and spatial skills are controlled by centres in both sides of the brain; but in men such skills are much more specifically located – the right side for spatial skills, the left for verbal ones. Numerous studies have confirmed the early findings.

In women the functional division between the left and the right sides of the brain is less clearly defined. Both the left and right sides of the female brain are involved in verbal and visual abilities.

Men's brains are more specialised.

The left side of the male brain is almost exclusively set aside for the control of verbal abilities, the right side for the visual. Men, for example, tend to use the right side of their brain when working on an abstract problem, while women use both sides. Tests have measured electrical activity in the brains of boys and girls engaged in the mental task of working out what three-dimensional shapes can be made out of a flat sheet of paper. In boys, the right-side hemisphere was consistently activated. In girls the electrical activity took place in both hemispheres of the brain. Boys also did better when a problem was presented exclusively to the left eye – which feeds directly to their specialised right hemisphere. In girls, it didn't seem to matter which eye – and therefore which hemisphere – assessed the problem. Men faced with a test of artistic judgement – calling upon their visuo-spatial skills – were severely impaired when the right hemisphere was damaged. Women with identical damage coped better.

Another piece of the puzzle showed that the more feminine the brain, the more diffused the brain functions were. This evidence came to light with the study of Turner's syndrome women. These are the girls already described who have exaggeratedly female behaviour. The study showed that the brain in these women was also super-female in organisation. The visual and language functions were even more scattered between the left and the right sides of the brain than in normal females.

Men who are known to have been exposed to a below average amount of male hormone in the womb, are also found to have a female pattern in the distribution of their skill functions in the brain.

New research has added a more complex layer to the sex differences in brain organisation. It is found that men and women have a different brain organisation even in the left-hand side of the brain. Professor Doreen Kimura, a Canadian psychologist, made the discovery (since confirmed by other scientists) that the brain functions related to the mechanics of language such as grammar, spelling and speech production, are organised differently in men and women. In men these functions are located in the front and back areas of the left side of the brain. In women these functions are more focused and are concentrated in the front area of the left-hand side of the brain.

The difference in the layout of the average male or female brain is found to have a direct effect on the way men and women differ in their ways of thinking.

How the difference in the brain structure relates to the differences found in behaviour and ability between the sexes is an area of intense debate among scientists. After talking to the world's principal specialists, we have arrived at this picture of their current working hypothesis.

What makes us better at one thing or another seems to be the degree to which a particular area of the brain is specifically devoted to a particular activity – whether it is focused or diffuse. Men and women are better at the skills that are controlled by specific areas of the brain – but different areas of their brains are focused for different things. This means that the male and female pattern of brain organisation has advantages and disadvantages for both sexes. The male pattern, with more brain functions specifically organised, means that men are not so easily distracted by superfluous information.

Yet the human brain – male or female – cannot cope with too much information. There is a limit to the amount of brain capacity we can efficiently apply. A study done on concert pianists showed that they could accurately play two different tunes, one with each hand. If they tried to hum as well, the right hand accuracy declined. This is because humming and movement of the right hand are both controlled by the left-hand side of the brain. The capacity of the left-hand side of the brain has been overloaded when too many of the activities it controls are carried out simultaneously, and so the activities are not performed as efficiently. The same is true for other activities and means that the difference in brain organisation in men and women will lead to differences in the efficiency with which they perform certain tasks.

A leading Canadian brain sex researcher, Sandra Witleson, suggests that this difference may make it easier for men to perform two different activities at once. She suggests, for example, that talking and map reading can both be done at the same time much more easily by a man than a woman. In a man each activity is controlled by different sides of the brain. In a woman the same activities are controlled by areas on both sides of the brain. The two activities can interfere with each other and she will not be as good at talking and map reading at the same time.

The differences in brain organisation, according to many research workers, also provides an explanation for male superiority in spatial ability. A woman's spatial skills are controlled by both sides of the brain. There is an overlap with areas of the brain that control other activities. The female is trying to do two things at once with the same area of the brain and the spatial abilities suffer. In a man the spatial abilities are controlled by a more specific area of the brain, so there is much less chance that other activities will interfere.

There is a further difference in that women often apply verbal methods to solve abstract maths problems. This approach will not be as effective as the male who is using the right, visual side of the brain to solve that type of problem. It is far quicker and easier to solve such problems with the right-side brain skills than with the verbal left-side brain skills.

The superiority of women in verbal tests can also be explained by the difference in brain organisation. The language skills related to grammar, spelling and writing are all more specifically located in the left-hand side of the brain in a woman. In a man they are spread in the front and back of the brain, and so he will have to work harder than a woman to achieve these skills.

So far we have mostly discussed language and spatial

BRAIN ORGANISATION: THE DIFFERENCES

FUNCTION	BRAIN LOCATION		SUMMARY
Mechanics of language, e.g. speech, grammar	MEN	Left hemisphere front and back	More diffuse
	WOMEN	Left hemisphere front	More specific
Vocabulary Defining words	MEN	Left hemisphere front and back	More specific
	WOMEN	Left and right hemispheres front and back	More diffuse
Visuo-spatial perception	MEN	Right hemisphere	More specific
	WOMEN	Right and left hemispheres	More diffuse
Emotion	MEN	Right hemisphere	More specific
	WOMEN	Right and left hemispheres	More diffuse

skills; but the brain is more than a mere calculating machine. It determines our emotions, and our capacity to respond to them and express them. Sandra Witleson has studied how people respond to emotional information fed to the right hemisphere and then the left hemisphere. She made use of the fact that visual images restricted to the right-hand field of view are transmitted to the left side of the brain, and those restricted to the left-hand field are transmitted to the right side of the brain.

The visual images she used were emotionally charged. She found women recognised the emotional content whichever side of the brain the image was transmitted to. Men only recognised the emotional content when the image was transmitted to the right-hand side of the brain.

Women have their emotional responses residing in both left and right sides of the brain. In men the emotional

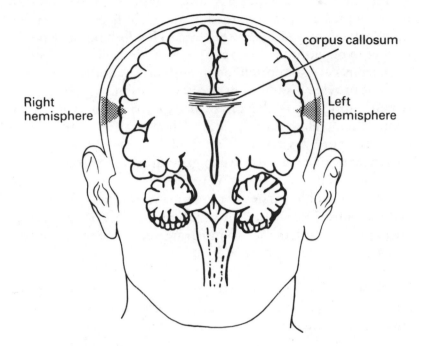

Right hemisphere

Left hemisphere

corpus callosum

functions are concentrated in the right side of the brain.

The importance of the differences in brain organisation for emotion becomes clearer in the light of the latest discovery of sex differences in the brain.

The difference relates to the corpus callosum, the bundle of fibres that link the left and right sides of the brain. These nerve fibres allow for the exchange of information between the two halves of the brain. In women the corpus callosum is different from in the male brain.

In blind tests on fourteen brains obtained after autopsy, the scientists found that in women an important area of the corpus callosum was thicker and more bulbous than in men. Overall, this key message-exchange centre was bigger, in relation to overall brain weight, in women than in men. The difference could be precisely discerned.

The two sides of the brain, connected by the corpus callosum, have a larger number of connections in women. This means that more information is being exchanged between the left and right sides of the female brain.

47

And the latest research has shown that the more connections people have between the left and right hemispheres, the more articulate and fluent they are. This finding provides a further explanation for women's verbal dexterity. But could the corpus callosum provide the answer to another mystery; could it provide a somewhat prosaic solution to the secret of female intuition? Is the physical capacity of a woman to connect and relate more pieces of information than a man explained not by witchcraft, after all, but merely by superior switchgear? Since women are in general better at recognising the emotional nuances in voice, gesture, and facial expression, a whole range of sensory information. They can deduce more from such information because they have a greater capacity than men to integrate and cross-relate verbal and visual information.

Some scientists suggest that the difference in emotional response in men and women can be explained by the differences in the structure and organisation of the brain.

Man keeps his emotions in their place; and that place is on the right side of his brain, while the power to express his feelings in speech lies over on the other side. Because the two halves of the brain are connected by a smaller number of fibres than a woman's, the flow of information between one side of the brain and the other is more restricted. It is then often more difficult for a man to express his emotions because the information is flowing less easily to the verbal, left side of his brain.

A woman may be less able to separate emotion from reason because of the way the female brain is organised. The female brain has emotional capacities on both sides of the brain, plus there is more information exchanged between the two sides of the brain. The emotional side is more integrated with the verbal side of the brain. A woman can express her emotions in words because what she feels has been transmitted more effectively to the verbal side of her brain.

The differences in brain structure, and the consequent differences in ability, bias men and women towards dealing with problems by employing their best attributes. Sandra

Witleson calls this 'the preferred cognitive strategy'. What it broadly means is playing to your mental strengths. Witleson suggests that there may be fewer female than male architects (and, for that matter, scientists and mathematicians) because, the female spatial sense being weaker, they tend to prefer a different 'cognitive strategy' — to use another, stronger, part of their brain. It could also explain the riddle of why there are so many more female musicians than composers, because they play to strengths in the female brain such as control over fine movement of the hands and voice. Composing music demands the capacity to see the pattern and involves abstract mathematical ability, primarily a function of the right side of the brain. Obviously our culture and our history has something to do with this; but, clearly, so does our biology.

A picture is emerging, and it is the image of two brains, differently organised, and differentially connected, in the male and the female of our species. The knowledge is growing, day by day, as new papers and monographs appear in the learned journals. This information is too important to be left floating in academic outer space because it is about *us*. It shows how we are different because our brains are different.

From the earliest age, the difference begins to show.

BRAINSEX TEST

Introduction

It is possible to test how male or female your own mind is.

The extent to which men and women exhibit masculine or feminine behaviour is dependent on the organisation of the brain into male or female patterns.

It is possible to be female and have some male mind attributes, and this simply depends on the presence or absence of the male hormone during certain stages of pregnancy.

1. You hear an indistinct meow. Without looking around how well can you place the cat?

   (a) If you think about it you can point to it
   (b) You can point straight to it
   (c) You don't know if you could point to it

2. How good are you at remembering a song you've just heard?

   (a) You find it easy and you can sing part of it in tune
   (b) You can only do it if it's simple and rhythmical
   (c) You find it difficult

3. A person you've met a few times telephones you. How easy is it for you to recognise that voice in the few seconds before the person tells you who they are?

   (a) You'd find it quite easy
   (b) You'd recognise the voice at least half the time
   (c) You'd recognise the voice less than half the time

4. You're with a group of married friends. Two of them are having a clandestine affair. Would you detect their relationship?

   (a) Nearly always
   (b) Half the time
   (c) Seldom

5. You're at a large and purely social gathering. You're introduced to five strangers. If their names are mentioned the following day how easy is it for you to picture their faces?

   (a) You'll remember most of them
   (b) You'll remember a few of them
   (c) You'll seldom remember any of them

6. In your early school days how easy was spelling and the writing of essays?

   (a) Both were quite easy
   (b) One was easy
   (c) Neither was easy

7. You spot a parking place but you must reverse into it – and it's going to be fairly tight squeeze:

   (a) You look for another space
   (b) You back into it . . . carefully
   (c) You reverse into it without much thought

8. You've spent three days in a strange village and someone asks you which way is north:

   (a) You're unlikely to know
   (b) You're not sure but given a moment you can work it out
   (c) You point north

9. You're in a dentist's waiting room with half a dozen people of the same sex as yourself. How close can you sit to one of them without feeling uncomfortable?

   (a) less than 6 inches (15 cm)
   (b) 6 inches to 2 feet (15 cm to 60 cm)
   (c) over 2 feet (60 cm plus)

10. You're visiting your new neighbour and the two of you are talking. There's a tap dripping gently in the background. Otherwise the room is quiet:

(a) You'd notice the dripping sound immediately and try
   to ignore it
(b) If you noticed it you'd probably mention it
(c) It doesn't bother you at all

Scoring the test

Males score		Females score	
(a) 10 points		(a) 15 points	
(b) 5 points		(b) 5 points	
(c) − 5 points		(c) − 5 points	

Unanswered questions count for 5 points

Most males will score between 0 and 60.

Most females will score between 50 and 100.

The overlap – scores between 50 and 60 – indicates a thought compatibility between the sexes.

Male scores below 0 and female scores above 100 point to a very differently 'wired' brain than that of the opposite sex . . . yet differences also attract.

Male scores above 60 *may* show a brain sex bias to the female. Females who score below 50 *may* show a brain sex bias to the male.

However, all such differences are average differences. A male might score above 60 and still possess a male brain. A female might score below 50 and still possess a female brain. There are deeper differences than can show up in such a simple test. It is those differences we must explore.

CHAPTER FOUR

Childhood differences

EACH SEX HAS a mind of its own at birth. Innate differences in brain structure mean that from infancy and through childhood, the male and female paths increasingly diverge. Biology – accentuated by social attitudes which may themselves have a biological base – makes the destiny of men and women different, gives them different priorities, ambitions, and behaviour.

As we have seen, the baby's brain is born sexually biased. Though it has some way to grow, the basic brain blueprint has been plotted out, the basic circuits set.

> He or she comes into the world with constitutional,
> genetic, and hormonally mediated . . . behavioural
> biases and innate patterning . . .

Inborn tendencies grow stronger as the brain responds to the world. As we grow up the interaction between our perceptions and the thinking 'muscle' of the brain affects the brain's structure, just as exercise transforms any other muscle. Rats develop bigger, thicker, and more complex nerve systems when kept in cages equipped with a variety of rat toys – running wheels and mazes. The dissected brains of other rats, who have been kept either in more spartan cages or in conditions of sensory deprivation do not show the same complex development of connections in the threads of the brain.

Conversely, when brain functions are not exercised, like underused muscles they become flabby and atrophy. Lacking sensory stimulation at a critical point in the brain's development leads to permanent disadvantages. Kittens reared in darkness will never learn to see after a certain amount of time.

In humans, too, the brain structure carries on developing after birth. All the basic cells are there from the outset, but up till the age of three new connections are being formed, new cell networks emerging. A growing child needs the right sort of stimulation to promote these growing strands of brain skill, such as speech and language. A sad case from the United States illustrates this need.

The Case of Genie

The story of this twelve-year-old Californian girl shows that brain functions, however inborn, depend on stimulation and exercise – in other words, that there is a relationship between biology and environment, neither of them being the sole determinant of behaviour.

Genie spent her entire young life locked up in a Los Angeles bedroom. She had never heard human speech, and in spite of several years of training after her rescue from isolation, never properly acquired it. At a crucial stage of brain development, lacking the necessary stimulation, the innate mechanism for speech had failed to develop normally.

Our brains develop in an active way in response to experience; they are not empty filing cabinets waiting for experience to fill them.

So how does this fit in with the innate differences in the brain structures of girls and boys?

The fact that sex differences show up from an early age – at just a few hours in the case of certain sensory perceptions – means that there must be an innate bias in the brain, an underlying sex difference which makes girls and boys see, feel, respond and react to different things in different ways. The world, in one sense, means different things to each sex.

54

This phenomenon can be observed at such an early stage – and is sometimes so obvious – that it further undermines the argument that society, rather than sexuality, conditions these inherent biases.

BABIES

Annie and Andrew

Gillian was determined to resist sexual stereotyping when she learnt that she was to be the mother of twins. She would bring them up exactly the same, with no nonsense about blues or pinks, pretty frocks or rugged dungarees.

That determination came under challenge, within minutes, from her own children. 'They were born within three minutes of each other; but as babies they could just as well have come from different planets.

'Andrew was impossible to get to sleep. Annie would drop off easily, though the slightest noise would wake her. We had two dangling mobiles hung over each bed, because we knew it was important to stimulate them. Andrew loved his, and lay gazing at it for hours, even when I was changing him. Annie was much more communicative, though, babbling away whenever I came into the room . . .'

At a few hours old girls are more sensitive than boys to touch. Tests between the sexes of tactile sensitivity in the hands and fingers produce differences so striking that sometimes male and female scores do not even overlap, the most sensitive boy feeling less than the least sensitive girl. When it comes to sound, infant females are much less tolerant – one researcher believes that they may 'hear' noises as being twice as loud as do males. Baby girls become irritated and anxious about noise, pain or discomfort more readily than baby boys.

Baby girls are more easily comforted by soothing words and singing. Even before they can understand language, girls seem to be better than boys at identifying the emotional content of speech.

From the outset of life, girl babies show a greater interest in communicating with other people. One study involves babies of only 2–4 days old. It shows that girls spend almost twice as long as boys maintaining eye contact with a silent adult, and girls also look longer than boys when the adult is talking. The boys' attention span was the same, whether the adult was talking or not – showing a relative bias towards what they could see, rather than what they could hear. From the cradle, baby girls like to gurgle at humans. Most boys are just as talkative, but are equally happy to jabber away at cot toys or looking at abstract geometric designs. Boys are more active and wakeful than girls – the male-wired brain of activity at work.

This female bias towards the personal shows itself in other ways. At four months old, most baby girls can distinguish photographs of people they know from photographs of strangers; boys usually cannot. A one-week-old baby girl can distinguish a baby's cry from a background of general noise of a similar volume. Baby boys cannot.

These discernible, measurable differences in behaviour have been imprinted long before external influences have had a chance to get to work. They reflect a basic difference in the newborn brain which we already know about – the superior male efficiency in spatial ability, the greater female skill in speech.

But even those who may accept the scientific evidence of a difference between the male and female brain may insist that the influence of conditioning, upbringing and the social environment is more potent than the distinctive arrangement of the brain. They will point to evidence that mothers tend to play more roughly with their male children than with their female; with girls, they spend more time cooing and talking. Little wonder, they conclude, that baby boys and girls behave, from the outset, in different ways.

Take another look, though, at that observation; could it be that the mother is not in fact moulding the sex stereotype – but responding to the needs innate in that infant? She knows she gets the best response from a girl with cuddling, and from a boy with more boisterous behaviour, and she wants to meet and satisfy those needs. She is acknowledging, and serving, those behavioural biases of the child's brain, the ones that predispose a girl baby to respond more to soothing noises and close, soft faces. The baby is exercising an infant Baby Power – if anything, it's the baby that is manipulating its mother to satisfy its innate needs.

How many mothers have noted a certain determination in some of their children from the very earliest days of suckling? No one has taught the baby determination. No one teaches the typical girl baby her typical, comparative reticence.

TODDLERS

We were so worried about Andrew. Unless you watched him all the time, he'd be in and out of cupboards, fiddling with the buttons on the cooker . . . He wasn't talking much either, though Annie was chattering away. We thought he might be backward, or something . . .

The brain biases persist and strengthen as children grow up, 'seeing' life through that particular filter of the brain which they find easier, and more natural, to use. That bias in girls towards the personal, for instance, shows up in experiments. A group of children was given a rather special sort of sight test. They looked through a contraption rather like a pair of binoculars, which showed the left and right eye two different images at the same time. One was of an object, the other of a person. The children had been shown exactly the same images, but when asked what they had seen gave different replies. Boys reported seeing significantly more things than people, and the girls more people than things.

Girls learn to speak earlier because they have a more efficient brain organisation for speech. This is located in the front of the left hemisphere, while the same function in male brains is found both in the front and at the back – a less efficient distribution. With better specialist centres to deal with speech, girls speak their first words at an earlier age than boys, and develop better vocabularies. In a study of 2–4-year-olds, girls are more likely than boys to be able to master the comparative subtleties of sophisticated grammar

– like the difference between 'I did this' and 'I've done this' – and the use of the passive tense – 'I'm being teased by Jimmy' rather than 'Jimmy's teasing me'.

At the age of three, 99 per cent of the speech of girls is comprehensible – it takes the boys, on average, a year longer. (It took Einstein five years to speak.) Girls form longer and more complex sentences, make fewer grammatical errors, and are better at tests which ask them to think of as many words as they can which include a certain letter of the alphabet.

As the months go by, and the child stands upright, the boys tend to show a greater interest than the girls in exploring the corners of their small world. Their greater muscle-mass helps them explore and range further than their sisters, and they make fewer journeys back to the reassuring base-camp of mother. Scientists have devised a test where a barrier is strung across the playroom, separating mother and child. The girls tended to stand at the centre of the barrier and cry; the boys made little safaris to the edge of the obstacle to see if there was a way round it.

Children will explore the world in the terms to which their brains predispose them, playing to their mental strengths, and so further strengthening that disposition, like the inquisitive rats whose explorations increased the muscle-power of their brains. Most children conform, mentally, to sex stereotypes, but not the stereotypes ordained by a liberal society. The children are, in effect, listening to themselves, to their own internal world, and what their brains tell them is important to them. And as they use those skills, and return time and time again to those natural and preferred ways of looking at the world, the inherent sexual bias is being reinforced.

> The boy more naturally involves himself in experiences
> that sharpen spatial skills; the girl involves herself more
> in experiences that strengthen inter-personal skills.

Boys want to explore areas, spaces, and things because their brain bias predisposes them to these aspects of the environment. Girls like to talk and listen because that is what their brains are better designed to do.

PRE-SCHOOL

I thought at one stage it wouldn't be safe to send Andrew to playgroup. It wouldn't be fair on the teachers and the other children. He was so destructive. It broke my heart, too, sometimes – the way he didn't seem to have any time for me, his mother. I swear there were times when he'd happily have swapped me for another toy truck.

The infant sexes differ in the way they play. According to one English study, having said goodbye to their mothers at the school gates (taking an average 92.5 seconds for girls, 36 seconds for boys), boys will wheel off into the playground. There, they will play more vigorously, and occupy a much larger play-space than the girls. In the playschool classroom, the boys will be much more interested in building structures out of blocks, playing with any kind of vehicle – indeed with anything which does something, be it a door handle or an electric switch. Girls will opt for more sedentary games, and, if they build, will tend to build long, low structures while boys go for toppling height in their creations.

A newcomer to the playgroup – of either sex – will tend to be greeted with friendship and curiosity by the girls; with indifference by the boys. There is irritation if the newcomer follows the boys about; girls will tend to welcome the stranger into their group.

By the age of four, girls and boys usually play apart, having instituted their own form of infant sexual segregation. Boys tend not to bother about whether or not they like any particular member of the gang – he's included if he's useful; girls exclude other girls because 'they're not nice'. Girls accept younger children into the group; boys tend to try to join groups of older children. Girls know and remember the names of their playmates; boys often don't.

Boys will make up stories full of zap, pow, and villainy. Girls' narratives focus on home, friendship, emotions; the

59

boy will tell the story of the robber, while the girls tell the same tale from the point of view of the victim.

Boys' games involve rough and tumble, bodily contact, a continuous flow of activity, conflict, a large space, longer periods of involvement, with success measured by active interference with other players, the outcome clearly defined, and winners and losers clearly identified. Girls' play typically involves turn-taking, methodically defined stages of a game and indirect competition. Hopscotch is the perfect girls' game, while tag appeals to the boys.

Of course we all remember, from the playground, girls and boys who did not conform to this pattern. Indeed, they stick in the mind precisely because they were so different from most of the other girls and boys. There is almost certainly a hormonal explanation for these exceptions to the general, sexual rule.

The Case of Mandy

Mandy was a pretty six-year-old who never really fitted in. She very soon got bored with the complicated rituals of skipping, and tried to join in with the boys' football games. Grudgingly, they agreed to let her keep the score because she was good with numbers, but Mandy wanted a more active role.

Like Jane, whose case we examined in Chapter Two, Mandy's was a case of adrenogenital syndrome, a condition caused by kidney malfunction, which results in the abnormal secretion of a substance chemically very similar to male hormone. Exposure to this hormone, at a particular time of brain development, had given Mandy's brain a more typically boyish bias.

Girls are much more likely to play caretaking games, with dolls; with boys, such dolls as they have may well become fantasy human dive-bombers or super-heroes. Faced with a new toy, boys have been seen to find more original and creative uses for it – the key word being 'uses'. Boys are interested in the function of things, and how they work;

that's why they will take them apart with infuriating regularity.

Interest in a new toy, but not a newcomer; there are hundreds of observations to support the conclusion of one of the first explorers of sex differences, that 'boys are primarily interested in objects or "things", and activities, whereas girls are interested in people'. In one study of nursery-school children many of the boys took toys apart; none of the girls did. This skill extends beyond mere destructiveness: boys were twice as fast as girls, and made half as many mistakes, in assembling jigsaws and other three-dimensional objects.

Even in the Israeli kibbutz, where deliberate attempts have been made to play down the differences between boys and girls, and where the engineered society proclaims a virtual interchangeability of the sexes, it was found that in all age groups, while girls co-operated, shared, and acted affectionately, boys engaged in more acts of conflict such as seizing other children's toys; in all but one age group they engaged in more acts of aggression, such as disobedience, violence, and verbal abuse. For a boy, the world is a thing to be challenged, tested and explored.

The discipline of school is deeply unnatural to boys . . .

SCHOOL

Andrew took such a long time to learn to read. Perhaps we should have noticed the signs earlier. Anyway, thank goodness we have now recognised his learning problems. But I wish he would help himself, and pay more attention, concentrate more. What the hell was the point of the sexual revolution if our children be sexual counter-revolutionaries . . .

Girls learn to read more quickly than boys, which, according to received wisdom, ought to undermine the thesis of boys' greater visual acumen. For years, it was held that reading was principally the trick of identifying visual symbols. But a few lonely educational pioneers have at last succeeded in establishing that the basis of learning to read lies in the experience not of seeing but of hearing.

Here, as with learning to talk, the structure of the female brain gives girls the advantage. This learning function resides in the left hemisphere of the brain – where females have the biological advantage, and which they call upon as their 'preferred cognitive strategy', their more natural mental strength, which is hearing, not seeing.

> Sex difference research indicates that females have a
> greater disposition to develop the kinds of auditory and
> motor skills important in learning to read.

Hearing tests reveal an intriguing qualification to this general rule of feminine superiority. Boys are actually better than girls at identifying animal noises – possibly the evolutionary result of those millennia of hunting. Boys are just as voluble as girls, but, as with what they hear, they show a preference for imitating the sound of animals or cars. Girls, on the other hand, make the choice of verbal, social, human communication. Look at the playground: the boys, arms outstretched, are aeroplanes, their engines whining as they bank out of the imaginary clouds; the girls are in a corner, perhaps discussing how silly the boys look.

It is not the relative immaturity of boys which results in their being, according to one test, four out of every five children with reading disorders such as dyslexia; nor is it that they are backward, though much educational damage has been done in the past by the assumption that a boy's slowness in learning to read must be due to stupidity or laziness. It is just that while the girls are using the right tool for the job – the 'hearing' skills – the boys are better endowed in the skills of seeing, not hearing. And that's not a good way of learning to read, says American psychologist Dianne McGuinness:

> It is clear that visual processing has little to do with
> reading, and in fact a strong reliance on the visual mode
> is often antagonistic to progress in learning to read.

Boys do better than girls in tests where they are told to circle or underline the written letters of the alphabet of a certain shape – like spotting all the S shapes in a paragraph – because that is a visual task, and their brain bias is appropriate for it. But girls will do better in a test where a list of words is read out, and the class is asked to identify which of the words contains an S, because this is an aural task which suits their brain-set better. It is difficult to find a sociological explanation for this phenomenon.

As long as education is principally an 'I talk – you listen' affair, it will be biased towards the technique of learning which suits the female brain up to a certain age. Little girls will also be comfortable in an educational framework where they receive information secondhand, interacting with the teachers; they'll ask questions – for that is part of their language apparatus – and accept the answers. Little boys, on the other hand, like those inquisitive male rats in the maze, want to exploit their advantage in seeing and relating. They are less interested in the relationship they may have with the teacher – just as they were less interested in people at one day old – and have a brain bias which makes them curious to explore and to find out for themselves.

The female infant's superior babble translates into higher verbal intelligence scores in later childhood; she has discovered, enjoyed, and reinforced the advantage of a better framework for the processing of language, while the boy is still enjoying his more mechanical world of things – their shape, the space they occupy, and how they work.

The boy will make up for his verbal inferiority later in the marked male superiority, common to all mammals, of spatial ability – working out the shape of a thing, or the correct route to take. At all ages between six and nineteen human males are better than females at moving a beam of light to hit a moving target. A study of nine- and ten-year-olds finds boys more adept at reproducing a pattern by walking it out on the floor. In an American assembly test, boys far surpassed girls in the assembly of objects such as spark plugs and bottle-stoppers. Any parent will recognise a son's curiosity, from early infancy, with things mechanical.

Meanwhile, let's go out into the playground again, to see

how our children, now nearly ten, are growing further apart from each other, as they practise, exercise, and strengthen those sexually distinctive aptitudes with which they were endowed six months before they were born.

The girls cluster at the side, listening, talking to their friends, exchanging their secrets. When they quarrel – though they quarrel less often than boys – disputes are settled by argumentative words, not pushes or punches. One of them is probably rather bossy; her male counterpart is a bully. But for the most part the play is co-operative, collaborative, uncompetitive. When they go home, they may write detailed personal diaries about themselves and their friends. They are growing up in their own familiar world of communication and relationships.

The boys race around, their hormonally inlaid aggression channelled into games of action, competition, dominance and leadership. Wider ranging, more independent and curious about the space he inhabits and the things in it, the boy, as a child, wanted to touch, assemble, disassemble, the hands becoming the extension of the eyes as he discovered for himself the world of things, through the agency of his specialist right-hand brain. As early as the age of six, this right-sided dominance can be experimentally identified: he can discriminate shapes much better with his left hand (controlled by the right side of the brain) than with his right. He constructs huts, forts, space stations. Back home, if he keeps a diary, it will be a laconic thing concerned with the loss of a penknife, or the score in a winning game. But he will probably make for the computer game; after a day of frustration – spelling and writing – he can hardly wait to use his own mental skills, and zap the Martian spacecraft.

His is a world of action, exploration and things. But school tells him to sit quiet, listen, not fidget, and pay attention to ideas; everything, in fact, that his brain and body are telling him not to do. We've already hinted how the bias in education favours the bias in the female mind – the passive acceptance of verbally communicated information, qualified by question and answer, suits the female well. Even manual tasks, such as handwriting, suit the fine motor skills

64

of the female, as opposed to the grosser mechanics of the boy. According to Dianne McGuinness, education is almost a conspiracy against the aptitudes and inclinations of the schoolboy:

> In the early school years, children concentrate on reading and writing, skills that largely favour girls. As a result, boys fill remedial reading classes, don't learn to spell, and are classified as dyslexic or learning-disabled four times as often as girls. Had these punitive categories existed earlier they would have included Faraday, Edison and Einstein.

Over 95 per cent of children diagnosed as hyperactive are boys. The condition is hardly ever found in girls. Given what we now know about the male brain and the female bias in education, the statistic of frustration is not surprising. Dr Dianne McGuinness maintains that for too long this has been the guilty secret of educationalists:

> Hiding the knowledge concerning sex-specific aptitudes in learning has done far more harm than good . . . it has caused a great deal of suffering in many boys who *normally* are slower to acquire reading skills when compared to girls. Even more pernicious is the spectacle of young boys on medication for a 'disease' that has no valid diagnosis.

Boys eventually catch up with the girls in their basic verbal skills, though they will never be quite as fluent. That ability now takes its place alongside the fully developed visual and spatial skills. With language and mathematics now in harness, the boy can successfully call on his greater powers of perceiving ideas and the relationship between them.

Meanwhile what has happened to the girl? She has had no encouragement of her visuo-spatial skills, and no reason to call upon them. As we will see in the next chapter, when mathematics becomes more than a question of mere computational skills, and has to do with the recognition of abstract

65

patterns of theory, she has to yield to the innate strengths of the boys sitting beside her. Their verbal skills have just about caught up with hers; but as for her higher conceptual skills – like kittens in the dark, she may find that that function has atrophied.

So the educational system which discriminates, in its early modes of teaching, against boys, turns at a later stage against girls. It's enough to make a social engineer despair – although many social engineers may prefer to reject the evidence and its implications. But how much can we change the pattern, how much should we? In theory, we could change it absolutely, by the manipulation of the foetal hormones – there's no little boy we can't make behave like a little girl, and vice versa, given the appropriate syringe. All it needs is the application of Nazi principles to late twentieth-century biochemical technology.

A reform in the method of education can compensate for comparative differences to some extent. It may even give us more women architects or male social workers. But that would involve an acknowledgement of differences which most educationalists have been reluctant to admit, and a degree of positive discrimination which brings with it its own philosophical and political problems.

We will not change the essential boyness of boys or girlness of girls. Each is exercising the sexual muscles of mental aptitude. They will enter a world which is designed not in accordance with some elaborate, political, social theory, but out of the history and experience of generations of people who were men and women before them. If the world is a sexist world, it is because the men and women who created it before us behaved in what we would call a sexist way. To reconstruct the world on non-sexist lines takes a positive effort, because it is an unnatural act; it is a social and political precept, but political and social precepts do not organise brains. Only hormones do that.

We are still at the school gates, and the children are already little women, little men; already, even though the great switches of the body have yet to be pulled. For puberty looms, and with it the discharge and circulation of the hormones. So far, we have seen the design and development of two separate engines; now we will see what happens when you put in the fuel and switch on the ignition. Great, distinct, and irreversible as are the differences between boys and girls, the greatest change is yet to come.

CHAPTER FIVE

The brains come of age

As CHILDREN, THE way the hormones set the minds of boys and girls apart put a certain distance between them. At adolescence, that distance becomes a chasm.

With the onset of puberty, the human mechanism is past the blueprint stage. Now the hormones take on their second role, fuelling, powering, and informing the brain and our subsequent behaviour as human beings. The changes will be so great that we'll look at them in two chapters – how male and female behaviour diverges, and how the hormones influence the respective skills and aptitudes of men and women.

Human responses to the action of hormones on the brain are more sophisticated than those found in rats, mice and monkeys. That is because human intelligence has evolved to a stage where we are more in control of our emotions, less slaves to our biology. But none of us can totally buck our biological systems.

Before puberty, in spite of all those infant sexual differences we have already documented, girls and boys have the same kinds of hormones circulating at the same levels in their bodies. Once the hormone levels increase, however, the changes are dramatic. In girls, at around the age of eight the level of female hormone begins to rise. The body becomes more rounded, the breasts swell, and at about the age of thirteen the menstrual cycle begins.

The hormones of boys come on stream about two years

later than girls, but they share with girls the psychological trauma of their physical change, as the voice wobbles down from its piping treble to a clumsy tenor, the hairline begins to recede, the testicles drop, and their sexual equipment, responding to conscious and unconscious urges, takes on a life of its own.

No one denies the psychological impact of this biochemical process as we become men and women. What we can now understand, though, is that while the bodily changes alter the psyche, the biochemistry itself alters our behaviour, perceptions, emotions, and abilities. Hormones are mind chemicals. Acting on the brain, they tell the brain to change the body.

In the case of boys, the hormone principally involved is testosterone. It's the same substance which was responsible for organising their developing brains into a male pattern in the womb. Testosterone, an anabolic steroid, helps to build up the body, beefing up the capacity to store calcium, phosphorus and other elements vital to the repair and growth of muscle and bone. It helps give the male teenager a body ratio of 40 per cent protein to 15 per cent fat. In boys, puberty comes with a rush. The testosterone levels soar to twenty times their level in girls. As you would expect of a body-building steroid, there is a sudden spurt in height. Boys also develop many more red blood cells than is the case with girls, and, as the red cells carry energy-burning oxygen round the body, they can enjoy the advantage of physiological superiority in leading a more active and strenuous life.

The principal female hormones are oestrogen and progesterone. They break down proteins and dietary fats, and redistribute the fat around the body. The girl will have a different ratio of bodily protein and fat – 23 per cent protein to 25 per cent fat.

Some athletes take the male hormone, which produces muscle, to increase their performance, while farmers know that pumping their stock with female hormones fattens them up and makes for better prices at market.

But few of us are athletes, and none of us are cattle. The mind-bending chemicals of the hormones are affecting our behaviour, by affecting our brains. As one study puts it,

> It is essential to recognise that the hormones which induce bodily growth, breast development and menstruation are, at the same time, exerting their influence upon the brain, and therefore the girl's emotional and intellectual reactions.

That brain, as the same study reminds us, has already been 'pre-wired' by the impact of the hormones which, in the womb, left 'a lasting imprint on neural organisation'. That imprint means that the brain has been structured to respond to specific male or female hormones in puberty. That is, female hormones have a much stronger impact upon a brain which is, by its very design, more sensitive to their effect, while a male brain is predisposed, again by design, to react to male hormone.

Traditional thinking was that the hormones did not invade the brain. Scientists were perhaps anxious to cut themselves adrift from the paramedical tradition of the Greeks, in which the 'humours', vaguely defined spiritual essences, made us by turn phlegmatic, sanguine, choleric or melancholy. We now know that, like the mythical humours, the hormones do enter the nervous system, and affect our behaviour.

The hormonal flow is regulated by that part of the brain which researchers first noticed was different in men and women – the hypothalamus. And, depending on whether you are a man or a woman, it organises your hormones in correspondingly different ways. Briefly, it tells the pituitary gland to give instructions to open and close the valve for the sex hormones. In men, its job is to keep the hormone levels fairly constant. It operates like a thermostat; if the bloodstream is 'hotting-up' with too much testosterone, the message goes out to 'cool it', and diminish the flow. Scientists call this process 'negative feedback', and it results in a fairly constant hormone level.

But in women, things are different. Operating on what is called 'positive feedback', the hypothalamus-pituitary command system sometimes seems to behave like a lunatic in charge of a flood barrier; when the water rises, instead of closing the gates he opens them wider. This leads to wide fluctuations in hormone concentrations in women – and sometimes great fluctuations in female behaviour. While the male hypothalamus is concerned with keeping things constant (though men, as we'll see later, have body rhythms too), that of the female is conspiring to create a system of phases, or cycles. These occur in regular patterns roughly every twenty-eight days.

Male and female hormones can be used therapeutically to alter behaviour. In nature, they do exactly the same thing. In some women, these drastic fluctuations are so severe as to leave them incapacitated.

Again, there has been traditional reluctance to accept that women's behaviour is affected by these hormones. Initially, in the early days when medicine was male, men didn't really understand what went on in a woman's body, although it was recognised that women were emotional sorts of chaps. Then, with the growth of feminism, there was an urge to deny this sex-specific difference, on the grounds that accepting biologically determined emotionalism might not be helpful to the cause of equality.

In fact, such significant things are going on in a woman's body during the menstrual cycle, involving concentrations of what are known to be mind-altering chemicals, that it would be absurd not to chart them and take account of them.

In the first half of the cycle, oestrogen alone is present, and its job is to promote the growth of the egg, secreted in the follicles of the ovary. Oestrogen reaches its peak when ovulation occurs and the egg breaks loose, and then its level begins to decline. Then the second key hormone, progesterone, is produced at the spot where the egg originally grew. Progesterone's job is essentially to promote the conditions for a healthy and successful pregnancy. Both oestrogen and progesterone levels then rise gradually until they reach another peak, together – to come tumbling down again at the onset of menstruation. If the egg is successfully fertilised, however, both progesterone and oestrogen levels stay high.

It is now accepted that regular changes in personality correlate with phases of the menstrual cycle, involving a swing in some women between 'elevated positive moods'

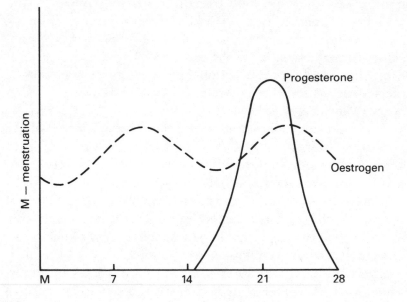

and 'elevated negative moods' in a manner independent of social factors. The sun may be shining, the job satisfactory, the house beautiful, the children sweet-tempered, the husband kind and loving – but the woman is prey to a biologically induced chemical gloom.

Oestrogen specifically promotes the brain cells to be more active. So during the first phase of the menstrual cycle, as oestrogen concentration mounts, the brain is more alert, and is capable of absorbing a greater amount of information. The senses are heightened, whether they be sound, touch, taste or smell. This stage is associated with a sense of well-being and alertness, high feelings of self-esteem, enthusiasm, pleasure, and sexual arousal. Evolution has equipped women with a chemical timetable which makes them feel pleasure and contentment at the optimum time for successful conception.

Progesterone, on the other hand, has an inhibitory effect. Experiments show that it produces 'a profound reduction in cerebral blood-flow, oxygen and glucose consumption comparable to that of barbiturate anaesthesia'. The brain becomes more sluggish, compared with the bright, receptive phase induced by oestrogen. Libido drops, and anxiety conspires with tiredness to produce depression. At the same time, progesterone seems to have a calming effect, stabilising the emotions. This seems to be typical of the second half of the cycle, as progesterone reaches its peak.

Four or five days before menstruation, the levels of both progesterone and oestrogen plummet. Withdrawal symptoms can be dramatic. In this premenstrual state, with suddenly much less progesterone to calm the mood, and much less oestrogen to promote feelings of well-being, behaviour can swing between hostility, aggression (hitherto suppressed by the soothing effect of progesterone), and severe depression, occasionally spilling over into the psychotic.

The Case of Susannah

Susannah, and her family, have become accustomed to her monthly moods. Tension builds up for a week beforehand. She becomes tired, and has a general feeling of lethargy. Sometimes, Susannah suffers from a dull headache. She is irritable, mildly depressed, physically clumsy and occasionally tearful.

Because she and the family recognise the symptoms, Susannah manages to remind herself that her behaviour is not strictly rational, and her husband and children accept that she 'is not herself'.

In evolutionary terms, this is a relatively modern problem. Prehistoric woman, with a shorter reproductive lifespan, and more time spent in nursing her young, could expect a total of ten periods of menstruation in a lifetime. Today's woman can expect between three and four hundred; four hundred months when her emotions, perceptions and sensations are pulled by the tides of her internal chemical sea.

The symptoms of severe premenstrual tension, or PMT, were first described in Hippocrates' *Diseases of Women*, but were only fully documented and accepted in the 1960s. The

Monthly Hormonal Effects: Normal	
MOOD CHANGES	Mild depression
	Irritability
	Tearfulness
	Lethargy
PHYSICAL CHANGES	Tiredness
	Headache/sore throat
	Dizziness
	Muscle aches

condition is placed in the category of temporary insanity under the French penal code. In Britain, the PMT defence has twice been successfully pleaded, reducing murder charges to manslaughter.

For most women, like Susannah, it must be said, it's little more than a monthly squall, but 25 per cent of women find that the symptoms can be more severe, and for one in ten the symptoms can be devastating. One study has found that during the premenstrual and the menstrual period, nearly 50 per cent of acute psychiatric and medical admissions are made to hospital. Half of female prisoners committed their crimes during the same stages. A barmaid with twenty-six convictions was found to have committed all but a handful of them at times which corresponded with the premenstrual phase of her menstrual calendar. Most female prisoners involved in violent behaviour requiring removal to maximum security quarters are found to be in the premenstrual phase. Incidents of suicide, violence, and, among pilots, plane crashes are markedly higher. As a key study on the syndrome reports,

> The psychological changes that occur during this phase of the menstrual cycle can have serious consequences for a susceptible woman and also for society at large, and should not be looked upon as a minor nuisance.

Monthly Hormonal Effects: Severe	
MOOD CHANGES	Irrational and uncontrollable anger Hatred of loved ones Violent reaction to trivial provocation Uncharacteristic social deviance – shoplifting, physical assault

The Case of Moira

Moira was a charming, intelligent and attractive girl. As a child she was sweet-natured and loving.

At fifteen her character changed radically. She became dramatically and irrationally bad-tempered, had no energy and stayed in bed for two weeks of the month. She developed a spite and loathing for her parents. In the worst two weeks of her month she tried on several occasions to kill them by setting fire to the house.

With police action threatened, her parents took her to Dr Katharina Dalton, Britain's leading expert on PMT.

Moira was prescribed progesterone, the female hormone normally present in the second half of the menstrual cycle.

All symptoms have now disappeared. But they are only held at bay by regular injections of progesterone.

The existence of biochemically induced differences in behaviour between men and women does not need to be laboured further. What is strange is that, these differences having been accepted in the context of the menstrual cycle, few people have thought to enquire further; are there other biologically determined and biologically explicable differences between men and women?

The most obvious difference between boys and girls is male aggression; and it has an overwhelmingly biological rather than social cause. For while girls are beginning to have to cope with the effect on their behaviour of the ebb and flow of their female hormones, boys, in their own way, begin to experience swings of mood which are directly influenced by their own endocrine system.

> From mouse to man, with few exceptions, the male of the species is the more aggressive.

> Human aggression is essentially a problem for men, not women. It is men who wage wars, engage in bitter competition, fight each other individually, and maintain vendettas lasting for years or even centuries . . .

Now the scientists know why. And, once again, they followed the clues yielded by animal experiments and human accidents of nature.

First, they induced antisocial behaviour in mice, which is rather more difficult than the layman might think. One trick is to keep the mouse lonely for a while, and then introduce a stranger into the cage. Adult male mice make the stranger unwelcome; they attack it. But this behaviour can be controlled. If the male is castrated, he is altogether more placid. But then if you inject the neutered animal with replacement male hormone, he returns to his old aggressive ways.

It's not just a matter of the hormones: to produce aggression, the hormones have to have a developed male brain to act upon. If, for instance, the male mice are castrated before the hormones have finished their work of arranging the brain into a male pattern, no amount of extra injections of male hormone will produce this synthetic aggression. The brain has not been exposed to male hormones during its development phase, and so has not been organised to respond to the hormonal stimuli which produce aggressive behaviour.

Similarly, if you dose female mice with male hormone – provided it is given early enough in life, at the time that the brain is developing – they will become as ratty and aggressive as the males.

76

As we have seen, it's quite easy to play around with the brains of rodents, because they do not acquire their distinctive male or female patterns until some time after they have been born. But with rhesus monkeys, as in humans, the brain is 'wired-up' into a male or female pattern before birth. But we can affect the aggression of unborn female rhesus monkeys by injecting their mothers with male hormone while their offspring are developing in the womb – and while their brains are taking on their male and female structure. Changing the behaviour of these rhesus females involves two distinct stages. First, doses of male hormone in the womb give a male cast to the brain, and then, once they have emerged into the world, booster doses of male hormone trigger the brain into aggressive action.

The manifestation of masculine behaviour in otherwise fully female women is a much-debated subject. There are, however, clinical findings which point the way to a possible explanation. Most of them concern women who have been exposed to an abnormal level of male hormone in the womb during the critical period of brain development.

Boudicca was not the embodiment of tender femininity. Could it be that she was dosed in the womb with male hormones? In ancient Roman accounts, for instance, she sliced the breasts off her living, female prisoners, stuffed them into their mouths, sewed the lips together, and waited for them to die. Neither Joan of Arc nor Florence Nightingale were entirely passive people.

The Case of Erika

Erika's mother had had two earlier miscarriages, and was prescribed a course of synthetic progestins, which are similar in effect to male hormones. When Erika was born, she was somewhat anatomically virilised, but not to any great degree. The greatest difference between her and her sisters who were born after her is in her excessively boisterous play. She likes rough-and-tumble games, chase games, and activities involving climbing – and trespassing. She dresses in boys' clothes, and prefers their company. She has only once taken her doll out of the nursery cupboard, and that was to put it into the bath 'to see if it would float'. Her schoolteachers complain of her rowdiness. She frequently starts fights, and is known to have a frequent, and violent temper. She is more self-confident, self-reliant, domineering and ambitious.

Another case study shows the syndrome working in reverse; this time the intervention of female hormone at a critical time of brain development has left an abiding, but gentle, imprint.

The Case of Colin

Colin is a quiet boy. He is studious, shy, and tries to avoid games. There's nothing particularly effeminate about him, and he's quite rugged and stockily built. His classmates don't bully him – in fact they largely ignore him. He has no interest in contact sports. If there's a free-for-all in the playground, Colin simply walks away from it.

His mother, who tells him he 'should stand up for himself', says that in sixteen years he has only once been involved in a fight.

Colin's mother, it transpires, took doses of synthetic female hormone during pregnancy – a treatment commonly prescribed for diabetics over the past twenty years.

Extra female hormone has the effect of neutralising the activity of male hormones. This, almost certainly, occurred at the time that Colin's brain was at the crossroads of its sexual development in the womb.

June Reinisch, Director of the Kinsey Institute in America, another of the pioneers of research into sex differences, has studied behaviour patterns in children exposed to additional male and female hormones. Boys 'washed' in additional male hormone, as babies in the womb, had aggression scores twice as high as their unexposed siblings, and the girls were roughly 50 per cent rougher than theirs.

It is not just aggression that is influenced by prenatal exposure to hormones. Another of Reinisch's studies adds an extra behavioural dimension, a range of characteristics concerned with independence and self-assertion. The mothers of girls who had been bathed in male hormones while in the womb 'reported high levels of self-assertive independence and self-reliance, and correspondingly low frequencies of dependency and demand for succourance'.

Both boys and girls whose mothers had taken extra male hormones during pregnancy were found to be more self-sufficient, self-assured, independent and individualistic on a standard personality questionnaire. Those whose mothers had taken female hormones preferred group activity and were more reliant on others.

The most placid of all are those girls who have never experienced the effect of any male hormone at all – the Turner's syndrome girls, born with only one half of the pair of sex chromosomes. Lacking the gonads which produce both the male and female hormone, they have never been exposed to male hormone in the womb. They are markedly milder than other girls, and their behaviour is exaggeratedly shy and retiring; none of the subjects or their mothers describe them as girls who would start fights, and they were much more likely to withdraw from attack than to defend themselves.

The evidence is incontrovertible that the male brain pattern is tuned for potential aggression; that the action of male hormones acting upon a predisposed male brain network is the root of aggression. In the opposite direction, hormones play an important part in making woman the less aggressive sex. Oestrogen, for instance, has a neutralising effect on the aggression hormone, testosterone. Several clinical studies show how the female hormone can rescue violent males from extremes of aggressive behaviour. It has been used to control the behaviour of male sex offenders.

Scientists have not yet been able to identify the precise neural networks in the brain which are responsible for degrees of aggression and assertiveness. The research scientists are sure that such differences exist, in the same way that exposure to hormones in the womb has been shown to alter brain structure and behaviour in other ways.

Male hormone increases	Female hormone decreases
AGGRESSION	
COMPETITION	
SELF-ASSERTION	
SELF-CONFIDENCE	
SELF-RELIANCE	

The level of the male hormone, testosterone, soars during puberty, which is when the full forces of aggression come into play. It is no coincidence that the age group with the highest crime rate is 13–17 years, for the male hormone has an effect on aggression even greater than the influence it plays in more obvious forms of sexuality.

Most criminals who have committed violent offences during adolescence had high testosterone levels – in much the same way that the irrational and over-emotional women had high secretions of female hormones. One study reveals 'a highly significant relationship between testosterone production rate and a group of hostility and aggression indicators in normal young men'. It is, then, worth considering how far the turbulence of male adolescence is as much to do with coming to terms with unaccustomed aggression as with unaccustomed sexuality. The law has begun to recognise PMT as a source of problems for women. Maybe one day men will be able to advance the mitigating plea of VMT – violent male testosterone. This is not to denigrate the problems that women with severe premenstrual tension suffer, but to point out that some men suffer a similar severe reaction as a consequence of their biology.

What's crucial, as we've seen, is the effect of the hormone on a brain structure which is pre-wired to react with it. A normal woman, for instance, will not become as aggressive as a man if you inject her with doses of testosterone, because her brain, not being 'programmed' to react to the chemical, will not respond strongly to it. But unaggressive men can be made more aggressive with a booster injection of testosterone, because they still have brains which are sensitive to the hormone. Adult men castrated for sex offences in Norway can retrieve many of their masculine attitudes by injections of testosterone – to the extent that one exasperated researcher reported that they had resorted to 'all their old antisocial tendencies, attacking small children, starting fights, breaking windows and destroying furniture'.

With men, the impact of the hormones on the receptive brain not only produces aggression, dominance and assertiveness, it also tends to trigger the release of further testosterone, reinforcing those initial aggressive tendencies. Among sportsmen, testosterone levels are higher at the end of a match, or a season, than at the beginning. Competition raises testosterone levels. Rivalry fuels aggression.

The capacity for aggression is imprinted very early, before the increase in levels of hormones at puberty. Psychologists have long noted the fantasy stories of infants, in which, for the girls, everyone lives happily ever after, whereas one young lad brought his story to its conclusion with the words, 'So he put Mommy on the stove and fried her in the frying pan 'til she was all burned up.'

In another test, children were rewarded if they could persuade their friends to eat a particularly nasty-tasting cracker. Both girls and boys accepted the challenge, but while girls tended to be apologetic about the task ('It's their idea, not mine'), avoid direct lies, and cajole their victims by offering to share the tainted snack, boys were more robust – lying, threatening and challenging their victims to submit to the ordeal. One commentator says that the test shows girls to behave like insurance salesmen, boys like used-car dealers.

Boys, as they grow up, exhibit much more rough-and-tumble play. There is sometimes a cruel edge to this aggression; boys were found to be much more hostile to the weak and the disabled, and their response to hearing cries of pain was one of annoyance with the victim. The girls tended to feel more sorry for the person in pain.

When watching television, it has been recorded that boys'

faces more readily light up at scenes of violence. They have much better recall of the violent episodes in a film than do girls. Boys and girls enjoy different sorts of books. The attempts to produce sexually neutral children's books is unlikely to have any effect on their behaviour.

According to a study of British youth, fighting is part and parcel of male adolescent life. Girls tend to be aware of situations involving possible conflict, like gatecrashing or gang meetings, but avoid them. Boys, on the other hand, tend to seek out dares or challenges to flex their adolescent muscles in obedience to the dictates of their adolescent hormones. A study of responses to a hypothetical situation of conflict showed that 69 per cent of males chose the option of aggression, physical or verbal, while exactly the same percentage of women chose either to remove themselves from the situation, or cope by other, unaggressive means.

It has been found that, when driving, men will sound their horns more readily at any delay at the lights by the car in front of them. At the extreme of behaviour, men are five times more likely than women to commit murder, and twenty times more likely to commit a robbery.

Only in verbal aggression do the two sexes match each other – a reflection, perhaps, of the feminine compensation of verbal facility. In one study, a sample of students were asked how they would react to someone coming up to them in the street and hitting them. The sample was offered a variety of responses, verbal and physical. Those who chose the verbal option were equally divided between men and women. But of those who opted for an aggressive physical response, the majority was clearly male. Women put the physical option lowest, after verbal aggression, 'nonaggressive coping' (e.g. reporting their assailants to others in authority) and simply walking away from the situation.

Part of the explanation for male aggression may lie in evolution, where it was a necessary reaction to safeguard vital resources, settle squabbles in the tribe, and defend the encampment.

Another, and to our view, less than total explanation is, of course, the argument of cultural conditioning: we expect boys and men to behave like that, so they do. Actually, we do not seem to accept this sort of behaviour – boys are punished much more often than girls. Parents tell both their sons and their daughters to avoid theft, drunkenness, drug-taking, promiscuity, or fighting – yet these activities are overwhelmingly indulged in by men. As Walter Gove, American psychologist, comments drily,

> Sociologists have no good explanation for why deviance
> is primarily a male phenomenon.

The differences between the way men and women see the world and react to it go beyond mere aggression. Dominance, assertiveness, and the drive which sustains ambition belong to the same behavioural family and have the same biological roots. Throughout the animal kingdom, the top dog arrives at the summit through aggressive determination.

When it comes to dominance, top monkeys

> show clear-cut positive correlation between plasma
> testosterone levels and social rank and degree of
> aggression . . . there can be little doubt that a
> spontaneous, high level of testosterone secretion is a
> decisive factor for the attainment of high rank.

Scientists can wreak havoc on the social order, and stage manage a political coup among the monkeys by injecting a lower-order animal with booster testosterone.

Young male humans mirror these findings. Boys who mature earlier – i.e. those who have higher concentrations of male hormone – enjoy greater peer-group prestige. A study of conflict shows that teenagers 'form stable dominance hierarchies based on verbal and physical aggression'. One need look no further than the rowdy terraces of the soccer stand. The younger, weaker fans (all of the tribe, it goes without saying, were male) are charged with the menial chore of chanting abuse; the older, stronger ones, with testosterone coursing more freely below their scarves, were the 'natural' leaders, first in with their fists.

At the University of Chicago, male and female 'dominance hierarchies' were minutely examined in the context of a teenage summer camp. With the boys, fights and squabbles broke out in the first few days, before a clear-cut hierarchy had had time to establish itself. Then, the early-maturing youngsters assumed their position at the top of the heap. Among that elite, relative rank was decided by factors such as comparative fitness or sporting prowess. As time went by, and the power structure became more apparent, there was less need for any physical or verbal demonstration of dominance. The boys knew their place. Friendships grew up mainly between boys of equal unofficial rank. Studious, talkative, or socially skilled boys only enjoyed dominant positions if they were also strong, mature, and athletic.

With the girls, it was another story altogether. Theirs was a more liberal and fluid regime. Few girls exhibited any overt display of dominance, either verbal or physical. There was no obvious 'leader of the pack' – one girl might be respected as the best practical organiser, while another would be recognised as the group's supreme emotional mentor. (The boys didn't have any nonsense about emotional mentors.) Both roles attracted equal respect, because it was accepted that social wellbeing was just as important as drawing up the roster for the camp chores. The girls' group was an informal coalition of individual relationships. There was none of the boys' self-conscious striving either for dominance, or for the knowledge of where they fitted into the hierarchy.

Take that lesson into the office or the boardroom – as we will do later – and the implications are important.

The girls at the camp didn't seem to care as much about what was all-important to the boys – a dominant superiority. And, when the sexes came into contact, the girls mostly left it to the boys to contest their relative position in the hierarchy.

Another study had groups of pairs of friends competing against each other in a simple verbal task – unscrambling anagrams. Each subject was told – quite falsely, for researchers seem to delight in these methodological pranks – that his or her partner was in another room. Once the contest was under way, bogus messages were passed, purporting to be requests from the partner to slow down, so that the other could win the contest. Most men refused the request. Many women complied.

The pursuit of power is overwhelmingly and universally a male trait. American expert Dr Stephen Goldberg, in his *Inevitability of Patriarchy*, likened it to iron and the magnet; iron has no inherent 'need' to respond to a magnet, but the tendency to respond to the magnet is inherent in its physical make-up. Similarly, because of our biology, the average man is readier to display aggressive behaviour than the average woman.

There is more to male dominance, assertion and aggression than the mere exercise of existing muscle-power. To achieve the end of their ambition, males, if denied the resort to brute force, will use other means. If election to public office involves kissing babies, men will kiss babies with greater alacrity, and less sense of personal embarrassment, than women. To rise in the hierarchy, men are much more prepared than women to make sacrifices of their own time, pleasure, relaxation, health, safety or emotions.

Those who remain unconvinced by the biological evidence may still call upon the influence of conditioning to explain women's comparative passivity. Men are dominant, that argument goes, because women are less disposed to 'achieve', or 'dominate', because of the sexual role with which they are endowed: giving birth to children of itself leads to a greater emphasis on defensive, compliant, nurturative virtues. Yet in a key study of academics, it was discovered that even those women who had no domestic ties tended to play the 'success' game with less dynamism and commitment than men. In the academic world, success is measured to a great extent by the number of papers published; women academics published less. When this raw finding was analysed, it was found that such women attached a greater importance to factors which counted less in their academic advancement – for instance, the welfare of their students, the fostering of scholarship, and service towards the college.

Simone de Beauvoir put an elegant gloss on the selfish/self-less differentiation between the sexes when she wrote that women, as the child-bearing sex, 'with the species gnawing at their vitals', had to live for all mankind; men simply had to live for themselves. Interestingly, this male desire for dominance fades in old age, as indeed do most of the manifestations of gender difference; how often have we heard of men 'mellowing' with age? They may have become better people, but the truth is that they have become less masculine men. The process is a gradual one, caused by a slow decline in the level of male hormone from the age of about fifty, which makes them less aggressive and assertive.

Women, however, experience a rapid and sudden decline in hormone levels at around 45–50 years of age, when the menstrual cycle ends. Most women suffer some discomfort, but it is usually short-lived. They experience mood changes, becoming irritable and anxious, and suffer from headaches, hot flushes, palpitations and dizziness. Female hormones protect women against strokes, and their vulnerability increases at the menopause. The bones become more brittle, and the skin loses its elasticity. Many women at the menopause have turned to synthetic hormones to replace the disappearing natural ones and hold age at bay. Skin texture and the joints retain their suppleness. The danger of strokes does not increase. But Hormone Replacement Therapy (HRT) is still controversial, carrying with it the suspected danger of a higher vulnerability to cervical cancer.

An interesting behavioural effect of the menopause is that women no longer produce the female hormones that counteracted the small amount of male hormone produced by their adrenal glands. In consequence, they may become more aggressive and assertive, as well as producing more facial hair.

In old age, men and women increasingly resemble each other in behaviour, as the influence of the hormones fades away.

Anger and placidity, aggression and appeasement, sociability and individuality, dominance and compliance, obedience

86

and assertiveness – taken together, these make up a fair amount of what we can call the personality. And in each of these aspects of personality, marked measurable differences have been observed between girls and boys, men and women, which we know have an underlay in the wiring of the brain.

Men and women *are* different; the society we grow up in does affect us, but essentially in reinforcing our natural differences. These differences are stamped into us by the intercession of chemistry. For most of us, they are not absolute; different doses nudge our male minds towards some aspects of the female, our female minds into a degree of maleness. In all of us, the brain has been fashioned in a specific way which affects behaviour long before the influence of society's values, or the teenager's hormones, have come into play.

CHAPTER SIX

The ability gap

JUST AS PUBERTY dramatically sorts out the girls from the boys in their behaviour and social attitudes, the hormones play their part in accentuating differences in mental abilities and aptitudes. We know that chemistry largely dictates the structure of our brains and the disposition of the functions in it. It should not be surprising, then, to find that differences in the organ of thought affect the things we choose to think about, and how well we apply our minds to them.

A leading Danish psychologist believes that the sex hormones, acting on the brain and the rest of the central nervous system, bear the 'ultimate biochemical responsibility for producing gender-related differences in interests, cognitive style, gender role differences . . . all these traits would depend on whether or not the sex hormones were present at the right place, and at the right time, and in the right amount.'

We already know how important the hormones are in organising the brain by being present at the right time and place and in the right amount. With puberty, the sex hormones complete their role. Not only do they make the sexes behave differently, as we have seen, in terms of aggression or emotionality; they also make the sexes better and worse at different tasks, for each sex has different brain strengths and strategies.

Ideally, everyone would have the opportunity to do what

he or she wants to do, and the chance to do it as well as possible. Many people believe that we live in just such an ideal world, and that either sex can achieve anything. They insist that we are born not equal but identical in potential. But we also know that, even given equal opportunity, some will fail to excel. Sexual inequalities will persist, however much we may wish them away. We ascribe this unequal achievement to basic biology. The brains of each sex are, on the whole, better suited to different tasks.

As we have seen, boys do not do particularly well at school initially. Come puberty, though, and the boys accelerate dramatically. They catch up with the girls on the verbal and writing scores, and surge ahead in mathematical ability. Male IQ scores soar between the ages of fourteen and sixteen while girls' scores tend to level off, and even sometimes fall.

The most dramatic difference, which the pre-adolescent years have already hinted at, is in mathematical and scientific aptitude. The academic shorthand for this is 'visuo-spatial ability'. As we know, the area in the male brain which deals with this is more tightly and exclusively organised than in females.

Although girls learn to count earlier than boys – they learn to do most things at an earlier age – boys soon show a superiority in arithmetical reasoning. The early female advantage in maths begins to fade, as the nature of mathematics changes from computation to theory.

A talent search for gifted children has been carried out since 1972 by Johns Hopkins University in Boston. Thousands of children, between the ages of eleven and thirteen and in the top 3 per cent of verbal IQ or mathematical ability, participated.

On the maths part of the test, boys do significantly better, and the success ratio of boys to girls increases with the level of difficulty. On a score of 420+ out of a possible 800, boys beat girls 1.5 : 1. At 500+, the ratio is more than 2:1. At 600+ it is over 4:1. And at the very highest range, of 700+, the ratio is 13:1. The sex difference becomes even more pronounced with age. The male hormone enhances the visuo-spatial skills and female hormones depress them; so the differences in higher maths become more marked when the boys reach full maturity – a couple of years later than girls.

The principal researchers involved, Camilla Benbow and Julian Stanley, admit that any hypothesis involving biological differences between males and females will be 'unpopular and controversial'. Accordingly they went to great lengths to iron out any alternative social or environmental factors.

They investigated the proposition that boys do better in reasoning, and girls in simpler computation, because schools adapted the maths syllabus differently for boys and girls – but they found that the differences in skill between the sexes appeared before the sexes had been streamed into different disciplines. They looked at a possible explanation that because maths teachers are mostly male, and the language and attitude of maths teaching is correspondingly masculine, girls would conclude that maths was not their 'thing'; yet by definition this could not be true of the female high-achievers who had made a conscious and deliberate choice of this mathematical discipline – in which, overwhelmingly, the boys outperformed them.

Clearly, the prejudices of society may reinforce natural advantages and disadvantages – though we find it hard to believe that the parents of those mathematically gifted daughters conditioned them to accept a sexual inferiority. It becomes ever harder to deny that the male brain, with its right hemisphere moulded for, and more specifically dedicated to, comprehensive spatial processing – or, in this case, higher mathematical reasoning – exploits that natural strength.

Intriguingly, many of these gifted children had not been taught any formal algebra, yet were solving problems by intuitively algebraic means – the mathematics, one might say, of the imagination. Most boys seem to approach maths in a way not found in most girls: they are able to see and think in concepts and patterns, finding abstract relationships between different areas of study, and linking them. Girls tend to treat each area of work as a separate entity, master it, and then move on to the next. There is a much smaller difference in ability when it comes to the more self-contained disciplines, and specific problem-solving such as is involved in algebra and the computational elements of mathematics.

Men find it easier to concentrate on an abstract idea or theorem, dissociating it from other, distracting information, just as they can more easily disentangle a hidden geometric figure from a larger pattern – findings which are reinforced from research studies in America, England, Holland, France, Italy and Hong Kong.

Research into human beings suggests that girls with the highest oestrogen levels seem to be at an intellectual disadvantage, while those girls with high levels of male hormone tend to do better than the female average in all academic disciplines. Boyish girls do particularly well in the field of spatial skills – the traditional area of male advantage. And there is growing support for the belief that girls with male character traits such as aggression, independence, self-confidence and assertion tend to achieve higher academic success than the norm for their sex. Those stern and mannish bluestockings may owe their success in some part to the influence of male hormones upon them months before they were born.

Teenage girls whose mothers took male hormones during pregnancy have higher overall IQs, and are more likely to pass university entrance examinations. They also seem to be disproportionately interested, for their sex, in science subjects. Of 79 children with above average school grades, the girls exposed to the male-like hormone showed a consistent statistical advantage over their peers.

Such hormonal abnormalities may occur, as we've seen in Chapter Two, either from the mother's artificial therapeutic hormone injections or from kidney malfunctions in the developing child in the womb.

The Case of Catherine

Catherine was always a lively girl; sometimes, indeed, a bit of a handful at home and school. Unlike her sister, she liked strenuous outdoor activity, and would often come home with her jeans torn after a morning scrambling up trees and through the briar patch. At school her grades were in general average, though her teachers were convinced that she would do better were she not so hyperactive and 'fidgety'. In two disciplines, however, Catherine did superbly well: wood-work, and mathematics.

Catherine has a kidney disorder called congenital adrenal hyperplasia, or CAH, which means that her body produces too much male hormone.

Previous studies of CAH patients in the 1970s had not revealed any significant differences in the spatial abilities of these affected girls, but they had mostly been carried out on pre-adolescent CAH subjects. As we now know, the major differences between the sexes only appear once the hormones of puberty have 'activated' a sexually differentiated brain. A new study in 1986 concentrated on adolescents, and carefully compared the skills of male hormone dosed girls with control groups of unaffected brothers, sisters or cousins.

All the participants were tested for spatial ability. Females who had been dosed with male hormones got significantly higher scores than normal females in tests to measure their skills at discovering hidden patterns, or mentally rotating an object and describing how it would look from different angles. The higher the concentration and the earlier the dose of male hormones the female foetus was exposed to the greater the improvement in spatial skills in the adult. The more the brain is exposed to male hormones the more it takes on the male structure, and the better the spatial skills.

So what happens in those women who have no male hormones at all?

We have already looked at the phenomenon of the Turner's syndrome girls, who have no ovaries, and so do not even produce the small amount of male hormone as ordinary women do. With none of the hormone which we know tilts the mind towards mathematical and spatial ability, we would expect Turner's syndrome girls to score very badly indeed on measures of these skills.

They do. Typically, such a girl fails to make the proper mental relationships, such as identifying the shape of an object in her hand, looking at a picture of an object and working out what it would look like from other aspects, or determining her position in relation to what she sees. She confuses left and right, scores low in mental arithmetic and in mathematical/spatial IQ tests.

When matched against their twin sisters who were unaffected by the syndrome, the Turner's girls, while doing less well on the spatial tests, held their own in tests involving verbal intelligence. This finding once again ties the presence or absence of male hormone to specific spatial ability.

The Case of Ginette

Ginette was a seventeen-year-old Turner's syndrome (TS) girl. Like most TS girls, she had romantic ambitions. Ginette wanted to be a kindergarten teacher, and, for the time being, was applying to become a mother's help. While a little shy, sensitive and introverted, her IQ was reckoned to be perfectly normal.

In spite of a good verbal fluency, she became confused when tests involved a spatial as well as a verbal dimension; that is, she could read and write perfectly well, but floundered when faced with a jumbled-up sentence such as 'forest-went-and-into-wood-cutter-the-some-got-a-wood' and asked to re-arrange it to make sense.

In normal girls, the wiring of their brain puts them at a disadvantage in problems involving spatial perception and mathematical ability. When the female hormones are released at adolescence, they interact with the brain circuitry and further affect that area of ability. The variation is related to the menstrual cycle; puzzles that test spatial ability prove easiest when oestrogen is at its lowest, and most difficult when it is at its highest. In general, though, exposure to the adolescent hormones depresses the mathematical skills in the majority of girls.

The studies show that high levels of female hormones in women depress the skills that men are better at. These very same high levels, however, enhance, the skills that women are good at.

In one crucial area of observable differences in abilities between the sexes the hormones hold the key. Most girls are at a natural disadvantage with things involving a spatial component; girls with no male hormone particularly so, girls with an abnormally high male hormone level less so. We should also examine if the process operates in reverse – with boys exposed to female hormone. It does.

Boys with XXY genes – an extra female chromosome – have abnormally high levels of the female hormone; they also have spatial skills below those of the average male, and at the same level as the female average.

And boys whose mothers had taken female hormones as part of their treatment for diabetes also scored below the male average. At the age of six, this disadvantage was not noticeable. By sixteen when the male hormones had been released, but failed to 'switch on' a feminised brain, the low spatial scores became apparent.

In normal adult males, their brains already pre-natally biased to give them an advantage in spatial ability and mathematical skills, the level of male hormone affects those skills, just as the amount of female hormone affected the skill of women. Very low male hormone levels depress male spatial ability. The very highest levels of the male hormone testosterone do not, however, produce the very highest scores in tests of skill; the optimum amount for success in spatial and mathematical tests seems to be one notch down from the highest testosterone level.

To most of us, spatial or mathematical ability doesn't matter very much. Most of us are not mathematicians, physicists, architects, or molecular biologists, so it may seem that we have written at inordinate length about this particular difference between men and women. We've done so for two reasons – first, to show that there is an experimentally demonstrable difference between the average male and female brain; secondly, because the worlds of mathematics, vision and space are not confined to the academic cloisters. They play a part in everyday life. If men are more interested in the structure of things – which they are – they are not just interested in isosceles triangles; they are interested in new cars. If men are interested in matters of geographical space, they may be the sex more likely to become concerned by the encroachment of a neighbour's garden on their own territory. If men are more interested in the relationship of mathematical concepts one to another, and better at finding such relationships, they may be more adept at discovering other intellectual connections – the simple stuff of genius.

Meanwhile, with the hormonal sap of puberty rising, you'd have thought that boys would be busy charging about and exercising their aggression at the expense of their capacity to concentrate in the schoolroom. But testosterone has another advantageous effect, which by now is clinically well documented. It's a hormone which seems to make the brain less liable to fatigue – more single-minded.

Experiments have been carried out on men and women volunteers injected with extra testosterone and a placebo. Both groups were set a task of working out a number of mathematical subtractions. This is the sort of behaviour which doesn't involve great mental or physical effort, once learnt, but where performance tends to drop off after a certain amount of time as a result of boredom, distraction, and weariness. Other activities in the same category – known as automatised behaviours – include walking, talking, keeping one's balance, maintaining observation, and writing. The experiment showed that the group injected with testosterone suffered a significantly lower decline in their skills as the day wore on. Those who were not given the added male hormone were more likely to make mistakes and become tired.

That study points to a broader role for testosterone – and there is, after all, more to life than doing subtraction sums. Generally 'individuals who naturally excel at ... automatised tasks are more male in appearance than individuals with less ability on such tasks'. More male hormone means more 'automatisation' skill, and more 'automatisation', in one study at least, seems to spell success.

> Strong automatisers had higher level occupations and
> greater social status than weak automatisers, matched

for age, education level, and general level of intelligence.
The strong automatisers were also more upwardly
mobile than weak automatisers.

Testosterone gives men a particular advantage in that it is focusing and galvanising a brain that is already, by its very structure, more focused than the female. Remember that the male brain is a tidier affair, each function in its special place; already, the male brain is biased towards a more single-minded approach – he is less easily distracted. Add the hormone, with its mind-concentrating and fatigue-resistant qualities and the differences between the male and female brain-performance are accentuated.

Women's capacity for concentration and application seems to vary with their menstrual cycle, high oestrogen levels apparently suppressing these specific skills. Certainly, in girls between the ages of eleven and fifteen, when the female hormone is in full flood, these aptitudes begin to decline, while boys' seem to improve.

Biology, then, every bit as much as social conditioning, militates against a strongly feminine role in areas traditionally regarded as male preserves.

Other tests, while confirming the female disadvantage during high-oestrogen periods, have also revealed a corresponding advantage. High levels of female hormone seem to enhance co-ordination skills in women. From early on, girls are superior in tasks requiring rapid, skilful, fine movements, as well as, of course, in everything requiring verbal fluency and articulation.

The way the brain was organised in the darkness of the womb creates the mechanism, and the potential, for a specific skill. But the mechanism is only fully activated, and the potential fulfilled, at puberty. Clearly genetic and environmental factors have a part to play; equally clear is the underlying importance of the biology. These factors, indeed, often overlap. It is the maleness of the brain that makes the young boy explore the world through things and the space they occupy, and this in turn is reinforced at puberty by the interaction between the hormones and the central nervous system.

With puberty, the full differences between the male and female brain are made manifest; differences in behaviour, emotion, ambition, aggression, skill, and aptitude. The much-lamented sexual stereotyping of boys and girls, men and women, comes from themselves at least as much as it does from society. There are limits to the 'ideal' of non-sexist child-rearing.

The boys want to play with things, and the girls want to chat with people. The boys want to achieve, and be dominant. The girls will accommodate to this not as a result of some fierce repression, but because most of them are not as interested in reaching the top. Studies of school-age children have shown that, for girls, popularity is more important than success or achievement. This cannot be explained by the theory that clever girls are less popular, because in fact research shows that in girls brain-power is closely associated with social success. More often, the girls expressed a concern for what others thought about them. The boys had begun to define their life aims in terms of the occupations, and the prestige of those occupations, that lay ahead. They were asking, 'What is my work to be?' while the girls were wondering, 'Who will my husband be?' Social conditioning certainly reinforces the bias, yet artificial efforts to reverse it do not seem to succeed. For instance, when girls were given specific lessons in leadership, as a sort of social orthodontism, their leadership aspirations did not increase – except when that leadership function could be linked to some form of social responsibility and acceptability.

As time goes by, this tendency becomes reinforced. The importance of academic achievement increases for a boy, decreases for a girl.

Leaving school, in spite of all the best intentions of equal opportunity employers, the sexes stubbornly continue to opt for the sort of work that appeals to them. The boys, overwhelmingly, go into jobs with a mechanical or theoretical bias, the girls into jobs which, for the most part, involve some form of human interaction, like catering, social, or secretarial work, or teaching. Social determinists will argue that a second-class sex is doomed to second-class jobs – but we would turn this assumption round on itself: girls opt for a certain sort of job, and, given male dominance, aggression, and sense of hierarchy, those jobs come to be regarded as second-class. Biology steers them towards a particular sort of job. Mere prejudice devalues the nature of that work.

The pattern is already taking its predetermined shape. Men, preoccupied with things, theories and power, women more concerned with people, morality and relationships.

With such different priorities, the potential for mutual misunderstanding is great; which is what makes the relationship between the sexes – subject of the next chapters – so fascinating and frustrating.

CHAPTER SEVEN

Hearts and minds

Hoggamus Higgamus, men are polygamous,
Higgamus Hoggamus, women are monogamous

(Insight recorded by the philosopher-scientist William James while under the experimental influence of nitrous oxide.)

PHYSICALLY, MEN AND women are generally attracted to each other because of their differences. Ask any group of men from any culture to assess the attractiveness of a female, and they will tend to opt for the figure which curves where they are flat, is soft where they are strong and – though this may be a matter for aesthetic as much as scientific debate – swells where they are narrow. The same, in reverse, is true of women, who will tend to express a preference for men with broad shoulders tapering to narrow hips. The rule has many exceptions – non-drinking males seem to prefer women with small breasts, according to one eclectic study – but the rule, in its generality, holds.

Yet in every other respect, we expect the sexes to be attracted to each other because of their similarities. Any computer-dating questionnaire will try to match intellectual like with like. We tend to say, approvingly, 'They were made for each other.'

So, although we were attracted physically to our partner's difference from us, it seems to come as something of a disappointment – indeed may perhaps induce a sense of failure – when we find how different he or she is in every other respect. The computer, after all, matched us ideally – we both like good food, opera, and hate smokers, yet here we are, after a few weeks . . . strangers.

But we always were.

As we've seen, the sexes are born with brains wired in different ways. They think in different ways, have different strengths, value things in a different way, and use different strategies in their approach to life. These brain biases are accentuated and refined throughout life, particularly when spurred on by the hormonal surge of adolescence.

A women is more sensitive than a man in her very being. She is more alert to touch, smell and sound. She sees more, and remembers, in detail, more of what she sees. The bias of her brain leads her to attach much more importance to the personal, and interpersonal, aspects of life. Ever since that early eye contact, at a few hours old, she has been more interested in people. She is better at imparting, and receiving, the social cues of body language. She smiles more than men when she is not happy, and is nice, more often than men, to people she may not like – possibly a defence mechanism to compensate for her comparative physical weakness. She maintains closer, longer, and more regular links with her friends, to whom she confides more about her hopes and fears. She has a better memory for faces and characters. She understands, better than a man, what a man or a woman means, even when he or she is apparently saying nothing.

That's because her brain is specialised for this very function. As we described in Chapter Three, the right hemisphere of her brain that controls the emotions is better connected to the left side of the brain that controls verbal expression than it is in men. The intuitive, if you like, is more in touch with the communicative skills. Not surprisingly, she has spent most of her life so far with like-minded people . . . that is, people of her own sex.

He, meanwhile, is ploughing a very different furrow. His brain, even before he was born, has been changed from its natural female form. In most of the key senses, he hears and feels less. He is more single-minded because his brain is more compartmentalised. He does not notice distractions. His, since birth, has been the world of things – what they are, how they work, and the space they occupy.

His brain strategy leads him to tackle problems in a practical, overall, and inherently self-interested manner. Invited to a party which clashes with another date he will calculate the comparative benefit to himself, or investigate the time and motion possibilities of attending both. A woman is more likely either to honour her initial commitment, or opt for the social situation in which she, and others, will be happiest. His relationships are those of power and dominance. Hers are those of interplay, complement, and association.

He has spent most of his life with like-minded people . . . that is, people of the same sex.

Suddenly, these alien species are thrown together by their biology – a biology which attracts them physically, yet, in so many other respects, is mutually antagonistic. No wonder being in love is so confusing.

Should we not leave it, then, a matter of mere wonder? Senator Proxmire clearly felt so, when, in opposing a grant request from the National Science Foundation into the nature of love, he said,

> 200 million Americans want to leave some things a mystery, and right at the top of those things we don't want to know is why a man falls in love with a woman and vice versa.

All right, Senator; we promise we will not reveal the secret of love (even if we knew it). But we do feel that if the two sexes understood each other a little better, why – the path of true love might even be a little bit smoother. We love each other's physical differences, but we can only love each other's differences of character, mind, values, and sensitivity once we actually recognise and understand them. There are thousands of marriages beached on the bleak sands of mutual incomprehension – why on earth does he or she react so differently from me? Most teenagers receive manuals on how to plug in their respective genitalia, yet none explain the different, yet complementary, apparatus of mutual perception.

Some marriages may, of course, be doomed for the opposite reason – that the partners have come to understand how fundamentally and irreconcilably incompatible they are.

For the most part, however, mutual sexual ignorance prevails.

> We know more about the maze-running activities of
> rats, or the learning of nonsense syllables by
> sophomores, than we do about the psychology of sex.

Yet what we do know, and what we can surmise, fits in clearly with what we now know about the difference between the male and the female brain.

We are nature's sexiest species. (In response to those who will protest that we are already confusing love and sex, we will explain how that very confusion is also a matter of sex differences.) Unlike the apes, a female human being is always sexually accessible even during pregnancy and nursing. The female baboon is only available for one week of her monthly cycle. The male *Homo sapiens* has not only the longest, but the thickest erect penis of the 192 species of apes. Woman, incontrovertibly, can experience orgasm. She is endowed with a unique multiplicity of erogenous zones which undergo physical transformation during the sexual act. Man alone can fantasise an erotic image to the point where, sometimes without physical stimulus, he can ejaculate. The human sexual act is capable of greater intricacy, variation, and duration than that of any other species. Freud, Marie Stopes, and Kinsey have all played their part in heightening sexual awareness in modern times. In many surveys men are quoted as complaining that they cannot get enough and more women that they may be getting too much.

And that's one hint that, below the surface of a mutual,

human enthusiasm for sex, lie two separate submerged continents of appetite, attraction, appreciation and desire.

So much has been written, academically, about sex, and so much of it, academically, is of doubtful value. That's because sex, in every culture, is a private affair. Sexual anthropology can be little more than subjective pattern-weaving, in terms of 'pathological simile, of mythological parallel, and other more or less literary or artistic ways of intuition'. Professor Hans Eysenck, the British psychologist, deplores the fact that the field has been left mainly to the sociologists and the psychoanalysts: what do sexual averages mean, he asks, when Georges Simenon boasted of having slept with ten thousand women, while the philosopher Kant never slept with one?

This chapter will attempt to relate our new knowledge of the sexually different minds to sexual behaviour. There is, after all, enough proven science, in our new knowledge of the male and female brains, to make it unnecessary for us to spin off into mythological fantasies.

Testosterone, the aggression and dominance hormone, is also the sex hormone – in both men and women. Women who lose their ovaries – which produce female hormones – still retain their full capacity for sexual arousal. At menopause when the female hormones cease women do not lose their appetite for sex. But if they lose their adrenal gland – which produces and controls the flow of testosterone – their libido collapses. It can, however, be restored by testosterone injections, which may also be used in the treatment of frigidity. Testosterone is the key sexual activator for both sexes.

There are two important differences, however. First, man's brain is better tuned to the effects of testosterone upon it, because it has been so made – through testosterone – in the womb. Secondly, after puberty, man has twenty times more of the substance in his body than woman.

As you might expect, this makes a difference.

It means that this mix of aggression, dominance, and sexuality is a headier mixture in men. The more testosterone, the greater the sexual urges already present, be they homosexual or heterosexual, orthodox or deviant.

In a woman's menstrual cycle, libido is at its peak when testosterone levels are at their highest. This is also the time of maximum fertility – one of nature's helpful nudges towards the survival of the species.

In men, testosterone secretion has a rhythm, reaching peaks six or seven times a day. It is high in the morning, and on average 25 per cent lower in the evening. During sleep, high testosterone levels correspond with 'active' sleep and rapid eye movements. Testosterone levels also change with the seasons. In the spring the level is at its lowest. The high point comes in early autumn. We may have to rewrite the poetry books, and abandon all those metaphors about the sexual sap rising with the greening of the year. But then, a lot of sexual folklore is overdue for revision.

Sexual awareness comes earlier in boys and is almost always more important to them. And, as with women, the brain plays its part with the other sex organs. As we've said, boys can achieve orgasm through the mental exercise of sexual fantasy, even without physical contact. They have erotic, and wet dreams. Most girls do not have erotic dreams. This, of course, could be explained by culture, conditioning, and comparative psychology. Some girls, however, do dream erotically, and they are the ones who have a male brain pattern. These are the girls we have seen earlier who were exposed to higher doses of male hormone in the womb, and therefore had their brains wired in accordance with a more masculine blueprint.

Sex is, to a great extent, in the brain.

High concentrations of male hormone, acting on a male brain, mediated through the hypothalamus, mean that boys are much more sexually active than girls. They masturbate more frequently, seek sexual gratification with a greater appetite, and, while maturing later, have sexual intercourse earlier. It is a pattern set throughout life – until, at the age of fifty, the hormonal tides in men begin to subside.

A male-voice choir provides an informative control group. Testosterone is a key factor in body build and vocal register. Basses experience more ejaculations per week than tenors.

Testosterone can be burned off during vigorous physical exercise like combat training – another link between sex and aggression. Hence the traditional advice from the schoolmaster to Jones minor that he should go for a long run to purge himself of profane thoughts, which is well founded in biophysical fact. But a word of caution: the exercise should be specified, because the expenditure of energy in short bursts actually increases the testosterone level – just as participating in the brief energy bursts of an ice-hockey game increases aggression at the end of the match. Jones minor should not practise his 100-metre sprints. He needs a long run . . . a very long one.

A difference in sexual energy is not the only sexual difference between men and women. Men are born to be more promiscuous.

> There seems to be no question but that the human male would be promiscuous in his choice of sexual partners throughout the whole of his life if there were no social restrictions . . . The human female is much less interested in a variety of partners.

Mothers have forever warned their daughters that men are after only one thing, and they are usually right. Brain, body, and hormones conspire to make the male sexually aggressive. In an American questionnaire the majority of boys reported that they would like to take part in an orgy, that they 'believed in taking their pleasures where they found them', and that 'it doesn't take much to make me sexually excited'. The majority of girls surveyed said that the very idea of an orgy was disgusting, nudes did not interest them, and that sex without love – impersonal, functional sex – was highly unsatisfactory.

Men, deprived of sex, are much more likely to become morose and irritable. Women rarely experience the same feeling of deprivation in a celibate state. What they miss is the companionship of sex. Men just miss sex.

In spite of their greater sexuality, men do not live in a state of permanent erection. What 'turns them on' is a matter of perception – the processing of sensory information through the brain.

In men, the key perceptual sense is vision. More men than women like making love with the lights on – seeing sex excites them. Pornography – the graphic depiction of sex received through the eye and transmitted to the brain – is essentially a male industry.

Women are not, in the main, turned on by pictures of nudes. When they are, the sex of the nude seems to be irrelevant – they are interested in the picture for its beauty, or by identification with the figure featured. Women may be aroused by pictures of couples coupling – because what they are seeing, in however sterile a sexual context, is a relationship in action. They are not excited by a picture of a penis, while close-ups of the female genitalia do arouse men.

Women rightly complain that men see them as sex objects. Rightly, because to men sex is largely a matter of objective things and actions. Their whole world, ever since infancy, has been a world of things. In the cot, they as readily coo at a balloon as at a human face. At play, they want toys rather than relationships. Later on, they achieve satisfaction from making models of battleships or mending cars. Macho men sometimes celebrate themselves as 'sex machines' – completely missing the point that, for women, impersonal sex is the ultimate turn-off. Men like a genital close-up in a porno mag because it is a thing to which they can imagine doing things. Sex for men is vastly more impersonal – pornography is simply meat for men. Do they ever wonder who that nude is? Not for a moment – they wonder what they would do to her.

Two magazines designed primarily for a female readership conducted an intriguing survey, after featuring nude, male centrefolds. *Playgirl* and *Viva* discovered that their women readers were not particularly interested in the centrefold. *Viva* dropped the feature. *Playgirl* continued it, its readership including a high proportion of homosexual men.

The same findings are mirrored in the commercial massage parlour. Women who massaged and masturbated their male clients admitted that they were rarely aroused sexually in the process. When arousal occurred, a quick glance at the man was usually enough to dissipate the sexual urge. Not that the man was necessarily unattractive – but sex just for its own sake was a turn-off.

A woman is more excited by those senses to which her brain's priorities predispose her. She prefers to make love in the dark, because the absence of visual distractions heightens her other superior senses – of taste, smell, touch, and hearing. Remember how women are equipped to hear so much better than men? Then you can understand the wisdom that the best way to a woman's heart is through her ears. Pillow talk, allied with gentle fondling of a body much more alert to tactile sensation, pays, for the male, sexual dividends.

While men are turned on by the glossily reproduced pubic regions of the impersonal pin-up, women achieve moderate erotic stimulation from something very different – the imagination of a sexual relationship. Just as they are more likely to be aroused by the pornographic depiction of a couple coupling, they find gratification in the bodice-ripping romances of popular fiction, which have an overwhelmingly female readership. Publishers would make a fortune if they could find a brand of fiction which was equally arousing to both a male and a female readership. They never will, because there is no such thing.

Men want sex, and women want relationships. Men want flesh and women want love. Just as the boys wanted balloons, toys, and carburettors, the girls have always wanted contact, and communion, and company.

All this, the magazines assure us, is no longer true. This is the age of the new woman, equally capable of, and disposed towards, taking her impersonal pleasures where she finds them and when she needs them. The new man, meanwhile, has rededicated himself at the altar of greater sensitivity, banishing his sexual brutishness, and bewitched by his beloved's brains rather than her bosom.

Neither the new age, nor the new man, is likely to last.

The sexual revolution is largely built upon the misapprehension that each sex has an equal appetite and is equally receptive. It will be seen as a mere blip of social fashion in the history of our evolutionary selves. It happens that we live in an age when greater freedom of expression has led to a greater awareness of our differences, and the social need to suppress them. But how long will it be before we revert to type, how long before those same magazines are talking of the New Romanticism – 'At Last, We Can Be Feminine Again' – or running features on 'The Return of The Macho'?

Preoccupied with shape and form from birth, it is in men's nature that the beauty and shape of the opposite sex matters more to them than it does to women. Mr Universe contests have never commanded the same female interest as Miss World competitions do for the male half of the population. Preferences tend to be testosterone-linked: submissive men, with lower male hormone levels, prefer small-busted women, while extroverts go for a bigger bosom.

The general pattern seems to hold across the cultures.

> In most societies the physical beauty of the female
> receives more explicit consideration than the
> handsomeness of the male. The attractiveness of the
> man usually depends predominantly upon his skills and
> prowess rather than upon his physical appearance.

Nancy Kissinger knew what she was talking about when she said that that power was a strong aphrodisiac.

Love, or at least male lust, is blind. High testosterone, acting upon a male brain, increases, as we saw in Chapter Six, the single-minded approach to a problem. The same is true of sexual opportunity – high levels of male hormone propel the male towards the object of his desire. When the testosterone levels subside – when passion is spent – the brain at last begins to receive a wider input of information. The girl who seemed so sensational last night now appears, on the cold pillow of dawn, to have bleached hair, dirty fingernails, and, now he comes to think of it, rather limited intelligence. This is the biochemical background to those feelings of post-coital male remorse – Shakespeare's 'expense of spirit in a waste of shame'.

108

With these inbuilt differences in attitude, it is not surprising that men misunderstand what women find attractive. Top of the men's list of what women find sexy is a muscular torso. One per cent of women rate that as their favourite male physical feature. Fifteen per cent of men think that a big penis inspires female admiration. They have the support of only two per cent of women. Women prefer wide shoulders and slim hips.

And so to bed, that battlefield of mutual misconception.

Men like sex because they are guaranteed gratification. Hardly any men are incapable of orgasm, while only one-fifth of women can claim an automatic climax. Male ardour cools abruptly after ejaculation; the non-orgasmic woman experiences a much longer — and lonelier — decline in the level of excitement.

Sexual gratification matters less to women than it does to men. An overwhelming number of women cite affection and intimacy as their primary reason for liking sex. Men, too often mistaking their partner as the sexual mirror of themselves, may pump and thrust with the energetic misapprehension that 'this is what she really wants', when essentially, and not even sexually, she wants to be gentled. This is also, for women, the surer route to pleasure — the positive role of affectionate and intimate love may explain why the female orgasm rate is 17 times more likely in marriage, while for men it is 9 times more likely.

The affectionate and social side of sex matters less to a man. One interesting study asked college students to rate their sexual pleasure, on a scale of 1–5, with a variety of partners — acquaintances, friends, and lovers. Men awarded points of 4.2 to sex with acquaintances, 4.4 to friends, and 4.9 to lovers. Women rated sex with friends high, and with lovers highest — but sex with mere acquaintances scored 1.0 — defined as very little or no pleasure. Women's liberation has surely increased the number of women having casual sex with acquaintances — if he does it why shouldn't she? — but it cannot be assumed that she derives as much pleasure from the experience as he does. She just isn't made that way.

Her mind is organised so as to place a primacy on relationship – his, on achievement. He keeps a tally of his sexual conquests. The female brain, the mind of a woman, is not organised so as to keep sex in a separate mental compartment. That is more the male model – it is as if his brain has a specific filing cabinet for sex, completely unrelated to emotion. Hers connects sex with a far wider variety of emotional information, against a background where the importance of relationships is paramount. Women are much less 'hit and run' lovers than are men. For them, to have gone to bed with a man is not just another sexual scalp, but a manifestation of an intimacy which cannot be abruptly shed.

Yet women end romantic attachments more often than men. But this, too, fits in with our knowledge of the female brain. Seeking romance, they can judge the success or failure of romance because relationships are the subject they know, and can therefore judge, best.

> Women do tend to be more practical with respect to
> matters of the heart than do men . . .

After all, women are not the ones blinded by testosterone-fuelled desire. They can tell whether or not a relationship is a true and durable one, because they have always known the real nature and value of such a bond. Heartbroken, the man will say how he wants, and needs her; sadly, the woman will know that want and need are no basis for a relationship. Physically, in the female brain, the centres of reason and emotion are better connected. She is better equipped to analyse and rationalise her emotions. Young men fall in love more frequently than women, because their hearts have less communion with their heads . . . or, more accurately, because their brain functions have less communion with each other.

Men are less able to understand why women break off a romance, because for them romance itself is more of a mystery. It's significant that when men try to be romantic they invoke the mental strategy which is more appropriate to them – they do it less by words, than through things. Not for nothing are chocolates and jewellery described as 'tokens' of affection.

Not for nothing does he 'say it with flowers' – he cannot say it with words. Many men may send their loved one a birthday or anniversary card – that's no problem; the trouble arises when it comes to wondering what to write on the darned thing. Men do not have such easy access to the language of love.

Men, indeed, sometimes see love as an essentially female contribution to the domestic economy of a sexual relationship; they 'provide' the sex and women can look after the emotional side of things. They certainly need love – premature death is higher among unmarried or widowed men – but this romantic division of labour obviously creates problems. She truly wants him to express himself, share with her his hopes and fears. He wishes she wouldn't press him. It is a familiar male attitude – 'She always says that I don't talk to her. I don't understand. I'm sure she knows what I'm thinking, but that isn't good enough for her.' While, from the female point of view – 'Sometimes he listens, but he hardly ever talks back. It's hard to talk to a drunk, and yet it's the only time he shows me any real feelings.' Alcohol breaks down the barriers between the discrete compartments of the male brain.

Another man, told by researchers to show more affection towards his partner, decided to wash her car. Again we see the stilted male language of love, defined as doing things, sharing activities. Men show their love by invitations to dine, sail, ski or even go to the football match together. Women's friendships involve sharing confidences.

It is hard to understand nature's plan in arranging this inherent incompatibility between the two sexes of the species. Maybe if we all felt and thought alike we would soon get bored with each other. But sex would surely be less of a disaster area if these differences were recognised and understood. Science is doing what it can, by producing the evidence that the minds of men and women are different. The rest is up to us.

We could start by recognising that men do take a more objective and selfish interest in sex than do women. This is not the product of pornography or some socio-economic plot to subjugate women and establish male superiority. Sex, aggression and dominance are simply in the nature of the beast, in his brain, his hormones, and the interaction between them. Banning pornography has as little chance of tempering the male appetite as would a ban on appetite itself.

Women could recognise, then, that men are very easily aroused and easily misconstrue the slightest hint of friendship as a sexual invitation. Recognise, too, that men do see women largely as sex objects – acknowledging, accommodating, and even trying to find some form of shared enjoyment in the fact, rather than trying to deny and eradicate it.

Men, in turn, while not denying their own natures – how can they? – could acknowledge more the need for communication in a relationship. It does not come easily to them, because the language is unfamiliar and the expression may be somewhat awkward. But as a means of communicating love, it's better than washing her car.

Little progress seems likely from the much-trumpeted demands for a sexual revolution. Male and female attitudes – with their biological rather than social basis – cannot be as easily altered as attitudes which have social roots alone. We can, however, come to terms with the reality of our sexual natures, and those of others, respecting the differences rather than decrying them, stretching out to one another across the chasm rather than bellowing insults across it in the rage of blind, frustrated ignorance.

Knowing how different we are could be the first step in becoming a little less alien from each other.

That, in itself, would be a sexual revolution. And one worth fighting for.

CHAPTER EIGHT

Like minds

ONE OF THE most dramatic differences between the sexes is that overwhelmingly more men than women are homosexual. In men, the figure is probably around 4 per cent – although Kinsey put it as high as 10 per cent, while only one woman in a hundred is a lesbian.

Indeed, sexual deviancy – be it transvestism, voyeurism, exhibitionism, or sado-masochism – is almost entirely a male preserve. In 48 cases of sexual fetishism studied in 1983, all but one were male. An American study on erotic preference states bluntly, 'We will discuss males throughout because the majority of sexual anomalies apparently occur only in men.'

This book addresses itself to the brain-derived differences between the two sexes; in fact, assessed on brain sex and behaviour rather than on simple anatomy, there are many more sexes than the traditional two. And the evidence now points overwhelmingly to the conclusion that sexual deviance is as much a function of biology – as much a product of nature – as the orthodox sexuality which society accepts as 'natural'.

We make no value judgements on sexual 'deviancy' – the word itself may seem to imply disapproval, but we use it in a statistical sense – because it seemm pointless to judge the outcome of a biological process in moral terms. It would be equally absurd to disapprove of the fact that tadpoles turn into frogs.

First, we have to put to one side that psychological literature which obscures, rather than illuminates, our understanding of sexual deviance. There is much to be said, and enough has been written, about the significance of parental relationships, gender-stereotyped play, the perception that our parents had actually wanted a child of the other sex, order of birth, early sexual experiences, attitudes towards siblings, and so on. Of course some adult sexual orientation is caused by early social conditioning. We cannot, for instance, claim a biological basis to explain why some people are aroused by the sight of red handkerchiefs or reach orgasm only when coated with whipped cream and showered with the contents of vacuum-cleaner bags – the alleged speciality of one anonymous client of a well-known London brothel. These cases we are happy to leave to the psychiatrists, and good luck to them.

But now we can link most abnormal sexual behaviour to our new knowledge of how the male and female brains develop, and the biological interaction of hormones with the developing, and developed brain.

The East German scientist, Dr Gunter Dörner, has devoted his life's work to the theory that exposure to certain hormones before birth determines sexual inclination. He claims that potential future homosexual behaviour can be detected through amniocentesis, the test of the uterine fluid which can reveal Down's syndrome in the unborn child. Dörner further claims that, with pre-natal injections, homosexuality can be prevented.

Dörner has, not surprisingly, attracted anger from homosexuals, who see his theories as equating homosexuality with disease, or as a 1930s-style sexual totalitarianism involving 'the endocrinological euthanasia of homosexuality'. Scientists, too, were initially sceptical. But gradually, the weight of scientific opinion has shifted towards Dörner. His theories may need some refining and qualification – but Dörner is increasingly gaining the status of a respected pioneer of sexual science.

As we have already learnt, the chromosomes instruct the developing foetus, around the sixth week of pregnancy, to develop female ovaries or male testicles. These in turn produce hormones. Male hormone masculinises the mind.

Dörner finds that the brain is not masculinised, as it were, all in one go. The classic experiments with rats described in Chapter Two have shown how behaviour can be modified in the male by castration and injections of female hormones. The male rat will be sexually attracted to other male rats and behave in a female manner when mounted by them – wiggling the ears and arching the back.

But the degree of femininity in the male rat depends critically on the stage at which it was castrated. Castrate it early and, with no male hormones to change its direction, the brain is more likely to retain its original, female pattern. The later castration occurs, however, the less feminine the behaviour.

What Dörner concludes is that the maleness of the brain in rats is laid down in a gradual sequence. With normal females, in the absence of testosterone, the brain develops along a naturally female pattern. But should the brain be accidentally dosed with male hormones during development, this natural female pattern can, at any stage, be upset. The more frequently, and the earlier, the brains of females are dosed with male hormone, the more male their sexual behaviour. The later, the less.

Dörner suggested that in men and women too it is the presence or absence of male hormones that build the structure of the brain bit by bit into a male or female pattern of sexual identity. It happens, he says, in three stages – the development of what he calls the sex centres, the mating centres, and the gender-role centres of the brain. First, with the 'sex centre', the hormones set to work on creating typical male or female physical characteristics. The next, and to some degree overlapping stage, is the transformation of the 'mating centre'. This Dörner identifies as the hypothalamus which, it is now known, is arranged differently in men and women, and controls sexual behaviour in adult life.

The last stage is when the hormones get to work on the 'gender-role centres' in the brain of the unborn child, laying down the networks in the brain which determine our general behaviour like the level of aggression or lack of it, our sociability or individualism, our adventurousness or timidity – characteristics which get fully expressed under the hormonal influence of puberty.

Dörner believes that each of these centres can be independently upset at each stage of development. Indeed, we've seen how at the first stage – the development of primary sexual characteristics – genetically female foetuses exposed to an abnormal level of male hormone may develop male-like organs.

The development of the mating centre, the hypothalamus, Dörner argues, can also be upset; in a male, the lower the concentration of androgens, or male hormones, the greater the likelihood that the eventual child will have homosexual tendencies. In girls, a higher level of androgens moulds the hypothalamus in a manner which will produce same-sex attraction.

Finally the gender-role centres, the wiring up of the brain, and the way the functions are distributed, may follow a male pattern in the female, or a female pattern in the male, depending on the abnormal presence of male or female hormones.

The beauty of this theory is that it explains how, for instance, obviously physical males, with obviously male identities and mannerisms, may be attracted to same-sex partners; in that case, only the second stage, the development of the hypothalamus, and the mating centre, has been upset. Similarly, it explains how some boys, effeminate in looks and behaviour, may still be robustly heterosexual in their sexual preferences; their sex centres and gender-role centres have been hormonally unbalanced at a key stage of development, but during the development of the mating centre, nothing untoward occurred. In short, it explains why not all sissies are homosexuals, and not all homosexuals are sissies.

A British psychologist, Glen Wilson, the author of *Love's Mysteries*, agrees with Dorner that the pre-setting of the brain before birth may sometimes be 'inappropriate, in that the gender of the child is male and his anatomical appearance is male, but for some reason or another, his brain has not received the necessary hormonal instruction that would cause it to be masculinised.' He reminds us that we are dealing with very fine and critical amounts of testosterone, measured in thousand-millionth parts of a gram; a possible explanation of how, in non-identical twins, developing in – virtually identical – conditions in the womb, one may be homosexual and the other not.

Another American scientist, Dr Milton Diamond, also comes to the same general conclusion as Dörner, but believes the development of sexual brain tissue involves four, not three, stages. First, basic sexual patterning, e.g. aggressiveness or passivity; second, sexual identity – what sex people ascribe to themselves; thirdly, sexual object choice, which is the same as Dorner's mating centre; and finally the control centres for the sexual equipment, including the mechanisms of orgasm. If something goes wrong during the development of each or any of these stages, they will eventually be 'out of phase' with each other. So a man may be assertive and aggressive – typically male – yet have a homosexual choice of sexual object; he may have effeminate mannerisms, yet have a high, heterosexual drive. The brain is not sexed in one 'big bang'.

The hormonal theory would explain why sexual deviancy is so much more common in men. Men have to go through a hormonal process to change their brains from the natural female pattern present in all of us, whatever our eventual sex, from the first weeks of our life in the womb; they have to be soaked in extra male hormone and restuctured – so in the process of reconstruction the chance of mistakes is much greater than in the female, who doesn't need any reconstruction of her brain.

This explanation of the biological key to human sexual deviance is not universally accepted by scientists. Some say that there simply isn't enough human evidence – though obviously the necessary experiments would raise vast ethical problems. Dörner, it is sometimes argued, does not pay sufficient regard to social, rearing, and cultural factors. And why do some women, exposed to high degrees of male hormone in the womb, become homosexual, while others similarly exposed do not? What is the nature of the interaction between the biological and environmental cues to sexual deviancy? There is much still to be understood.

To back up the general thesis, we must return to accidents of nature in the human species. Some men are born with three, instead of two, sex chromosomes. They have an extra female chromosome – XXY men have both the female XX pattern, and the male XY. They look male, are raised as males, but suffer a lack of libido and a loss of potency. In adult life they have low testosterone levels – something which has been correlated with low testosterone levels during development in the womb. These XXYs report confusion about what sex they are, and how they ought to behave. They are hesitant about assuming a masculine role, and this confusion and diffidence often expresses itself in transvestism, transsexualism, homosexuality, bisexuality and non-sexuality. What seems to have happened is that, with a confused genetic message giving contrary instructions to the gonads, not enough masculine hormone has been dispatched to the developing brain to make it match its male body. In particular, Dörner's mating centre seems to have been muddled or misinstructed, and allowed to develop along female lines.

Then, there are those males who, in the womb, were exposed to high concentrations of female hormone. A long-term follow-up study of 136 children has revealed that those whose mothers took high doses of therapeutic female hormone were twice as likely to be unmarried as children whose mothers had not taken the drug. Dörner's mating centres, and the influence of hormones upon their development, now become altogether more credible. So do his gender-role centres: another study of six- and sixteen-year-olds, again exposed in the womb to female hormones, demonstrated a lack of general masculinity, assertiveness, athletic ability and aggression.

Some girls, as we have described in Chapter Two, experienced high male hormone doses in the womb. They are reported as more frequently exhibiting bisexual or homosexual behaviour. From early infancy, they have resisted the normal sex-stereotyping – not playing with dolls, and preferring the competitive company of boys.

In a fascinating experiment, Dr Dörner has actually made a key brain centre in the male homosexual brain demonstrate female characteristics. The hypothalamus, which is the brain's mating centre, has different functions in men and women. In men, it regulates the flow of hormones in a way which ensures that levels are kept steady. In women, the hypothalamus can respond to high hormone levels by triggering still further secretions of hormone, with dramatic behavioural consequences, as we have seen in Chapter Five.

Dörner found that the male homosexual hypothalamus did exactly the same thing when injected with female hormone – it reacted in the manner of the female mating centre. It responded to oestrogen dosage by producing more of the female hormone. The homosexuals' brains had been wired in a female response pattern. Heterosexual men showed no such rise in female hormone levels after being dosed with female hormone. Dörner concludes that

> Homosexual men may possess – at least in part – a
> predominantly female-differentiated brain, which could
> be based on androgen deficiency in prenatal life . . .

Although an American team has confirmed this finding, it is more cautious about the cause and the explanation. Indeed, other researchers are openly sceptical, some claiming that Dörner's methodology is suspect, some failing to replicate the phenomenon, and some disagreeing on other factors, such as the levels of male hormone found in homosexual men and women.

One reason for the confusion could be that homosexuality – like any other form of sexuality – is a complex and varying form of behaviour. There is not one single homosexual type. A sophisticated British study endorses much of the general theory that the homosexual die is cast *in utero*, but makes a distinction between primary homosexuals, and secondary subjects who may have some heterosexual experience, psychologically a less female view of themselves, and who respond better to contra-homosexual therapy. This secondary group may have weaker biological roots than the primary homosexuals, and their homosexuality 'may arise more from psychosocial influences acting in accordance with learning theory'. The primary homosexuals when injected with oestrogen had a female pattern of hormone response – just like the one Dörner found when he tested homosexuals. The secondary group had the male pattern of hormone response when injected with female hormones. This type of homosexuality could have some environmental or political cause.

All the complications and qualifications tie in with the idea that different stages, levels, centres – call them what you will – of our mental sex make-up develop at different times, leading to subtle differences in the eventual sexual psyche: if only the mating centres have been exposed to the 'wrong' hormone, then people may be attracted to the same sex, yet display few abnormal sex traits in behaviour or outlook.

Testosterone levels in homosexual men are certainly high enough to make most of them think and behave in a male manner. They have, for instance, the same somewhat unromantic and promiscuous view of sex as most heterosexual men. At the same time their specific mating centres are female. So they have all the same sexual drives as other men, but channelled in a different direction, which is partly why – in pre-AIDS days at least – male homosexuals might number their sexual partners in thousands over a lifetime.

A minority of homosexuals are effeminate, and display stereotypically 'female' behaviour. In these men, the behaviour centres as well as the mating centres have been feminised. In their relationships they will display much more of the caring tenderness associated with women, as well as a lower interest in sex for sex's sake.

Female homosexuals seem to follow the normal female pattern of wanting fulfilling social relationships. In female homosexuals, the natural female hormone not only inhibits the impact of testosterone, but also acts upon the overall brain mechanism to turn on the more tender, typical female attributes.

Homosexual or heterosexual, male or female, 'among men, sex sometimes results in intimacy; in women, intimacy sometimes results in sex'.

There are other sorts of sexual confusion where there is now general agreement that there is a biological explanation. Transexuality is the feeling of being trapped in the body of the opposite sex, or as Jan Morris puts it, 'the realisation that I had been born into the wrong body'. Jan Morris, the British author, had a sex change operation and is now happy and content as a woman. She pondered a number of explanations for this phenomenon, and it is intriguing, in her book, *Conundrum*, to find the germ of what we now know to be the explanation. 'Was it just that something had gone wrong, during my months in the womb, so that the hormones were wrongly shuffled . . .?'

That's almost certainly what happened.

The classic male transsexual is not particularly feminine as a child, but is withdrawn and gentle. He has little sexual interest and often a loathing of maleness. There is an early, abiding, and increasing desire to be female. As Jan Morris put it, 'For forty years . . . a sexual purpose dominated, distracted and tormented my life: the tragic and irrational ambition, instinctively formulated but deliberately pursued, to escape from maleness into womanhood.'

An American scientist has found that there is no discernible evidence that an aberrant upbringing is responsible for this phenomenon. The subject seems literally to defy his or her environment, persisting in opposite-sex behaviour in spite of the attempts by the parents to suppress it.

Some psychologists, of course, would say that this parental opposition in itself aggravated – or even created – the aberrant disposition. But most studies of sexual abnormality which seek to find parental, social, or environmental roots and causes – nurture rather than nature – have proved unsatisfactory.

The book *Sexual Preference – its development in Men and Women* was the most exhaustive American survey of homosexual attitudes and behaviour. After interviewing 500 homosexuals, the authors found 'the role of parents in the development of their sons' sexual orientation to be grossly exaggerated'. They were also unconvinced by the notion of the unresolved Oedipus complex, the responsibility of cold, detached fathers, peer-group pressure, labelling as 'being a sissy' at an early age, or bad experiences with the opposite sex. Even among non-homosexuals, early same-sex experiences, interestingly enough, seemed not to play any role – 'the popular stereotype that homosexuality results when a boy is "seduced" by an older male, or a girl by an older female, is not supported by our data.'

Single-sex boarding schools and prisons may be hotbeds of homosexuality, but they probably do not create the condition. At school, homosexuality may be part of adolescent curiosity, while in prison it may be a functional necessity. Both institutions may reveal, or bring out, the natural homosexuality in a boy or a man, but are unlikely to implant it.

What most clearly signalled whether or not a boy or a girl was going to be a homosexual was how they behaved as children – withdrawn, unathletic and shy boys; rowdy, active girls. For, although the hypothalamus hadn't yet been primed by the hormones of puberty, the general wiring of the brain had a 'wrong'-sex bias.

The biological explanation may even explain where some of the psychological explanations went wrong. For instance, it has long been thought that a hostile or indifferent father could be a cause of homosexuality – the boy reacting against the main male role-model of his early years, and rejecting traditional masculine attitudes and behaviour. Yet it is perfectly possible that the father *became* hostile for the very reason that the child was – naturally – unmasculine, and not 'the son I always hoped for'. Fathers who have looked forward to the day when they could go to the football match with their sons are likely to be disappointed, if not downright disapproving, when those sons, for whatever reasons, prefer more typically feminine pursuits.

So what is the original, biological cause of sexual deviation? If it's the hormones in the womb which so affect the sexuality of the child and adult, what happens to upset those hormones in the first place?

The first clues came from those rats again. It is known that high stress levels in mothers lower the level of male hormone in the womb. Experiments showed that when pregnant rats were subjected to severe stress, the resulting male offspring were attracted to other male rats – indeed that the rats were homosexual, apparently as a consequence of the stress endured by their mothers.

Dörner was intrigued by the news. Understandably, he could not put a laboratory-full of pregnant women under severe stress, but he could examine the results in the laboratory of history. He looked at the years of the Second World War – a time when the inhabitants of his country could be said to have been living under more than usually trying circumstances.

Dörner found that out of about 800 homosexual males, significantly more were born during the stressful war and early post-war period than in the years before and some time after the war. The highest number corresponded with the last months of the conflict.

Two-thirds of the homosexual men and their mothers reported experience of severe, or moderate, maternal stress during their pre-natal life – with factors such as bereavement, bombings, rape, or severe anxiety. On the other hand, none of the mothers of heterosexual men in a control sample had been the victims of severe stress, and only 10 per cent of moderate stress, during pregnancy.

Low pre-natal, male hormone levels can be affected by factors less drastic than major global conflict. Taking inappropriate medication is one of these. Barbiturates, one of the most widely prescribed and abused classes of drugs, are thought to have been prescribed in as many as 25 per cent of pregnancies between the 1950s and the 1980s. In animal experiments involving exposure to barbiturates the drug acted directly on the neural tissue, and indirectly through the brain-sexing substances secreted by the foetus. Among the observed results was an 'alteration of behavioural and physiological sex differences'. In humans the predicted results would

123

include 'psychosocial maladjustment, and demasculinisation of gender identity and sex role behaviour in males'.

The implication – and it is true of many drugs – is that pregnant women would be well advised to avoid barbiturates; it is comforting to know that they are no longer being prescribed as readily as they used to be.

So convinced is Dörner of the link between hormonal levels in the womb, and subsequent sexuality, that he believes it would be sound medical practice to monitor and correct those levels. It is even rumoured that behind the Iron Curtain's cloak of secrecy, East German doctors have already embarked on such a clinical practice.

Our new understanding of the biology of sex raises profound questions about our attitude to, and treatment of, homosexuals. If biology – or nature – is at the root of it all, how can homosexuality be condemned as 'unnatural' – any more than, say, left-handedness? Or is the appropriate comparison some other biological manifestation, such as a congenital disability? Then again, is it right to label what is, in effect, a non-genetic 'race' of people as 'disabled'? Is the clinical correction of the syndrome all that far removed from the grotesque medical malpractices of the Third Reich which perverted medicine in its pursuit of racial purity – while, as we've seen, ironically provoking, in war, the very conditions in which homosexuals were more likely to develop?

We trust that the very knowledge of the natural and biological springs of sexual abnormality will bring about the recognition that the syndrome is natural, and may change our perceptions of what is normal. After all, the principal problem homosexuals face is not of their making; the problem derives from the rest of us, and our intolerance that they do not conform with what we decree is normal gender identity and sexual behaviour (though even that intolerance may be biologically wired into our brains, as a part of aggressive behaviour to the outsider).

Meanwhile, surely, it is time for an armistice in the battle between those who seek a biological, and those who look for a psychological, explanation for human behaviour. The terms of such a treaty were suggested decades ago, when a psychologist wrote to his colleagues that they should

> bear in mind that some day all our provisional
> formulations in psychology will have to be based on an
> organic foundation . . . It will then probably be seen
> that it is special chemical substances and processes
> which achieve the effects of sexuality . . .

The psychologist was Sigmund Freud. And that 'some day' has surely dawned.

CHAPTER NINE

The marriage of two minds

MARRIAGE, THE OLD comedians used to say, is a great institution; but who wants to live in an institution?

Most of us do, in fact. In spite of the great increase in the divorce rate – due in large part to modern legislation and female financial independence – in the West 93 per cent of us, with varying degrees of optimism, take our vows binding us to our beloved stranger. Seventy-five per cent of marriages survive, and even when marital shipwreck occurs, most of those involved defiantly opt for hope over experience and get married again.

Our new knowledge of what makes us tick, and tick to different rhythms, is not of itself going to revolutionise the complex design of marriage – we will present no new marital blueprint. But we do believe that much of the stress in this most vital of relationships stems from the misconception that men and women are essentially the same people. The contradiction between this assumption and the facts can lead to exasperation, bitterness and recrimination.

It could all become a little easier once we acknowledge how different we are from each other. We could even be a little happier. There is, after all, scant evidence that the gospel of feminism and the denial of sexual differences have made marriages any more blissful either for women or men.

An appreciation of sex differences is more likely to
promote a cease-fire in the battle of the sexes than are

naive promulgations of the 'good news' that there are
no important differences.

One problem is that for the first time in history we are
educating girls and boys in a virtually identical manner. The
school syllabus reflects, and encourages youngsters to believe
in, the assumption of sameness. Marriage, then, comes as
something of a shock. 'We don't seem to be bringing up the
two sexes to get married to each other,' says the author of a
recent study of marriage; 'it is hardest for all of us to admit
today that the two sexes come to marriage with very different
expectations, talents, and emotional training.'

A woman brings to the relationship emotional sensitivity,
a capacity for interdependence, a yearning for companionship and for sex to reflect that emotional intimacy. A
man, if not totally blind to the importance of emotions, has
a less-demanding emotional nature. He has the capacity for
independence, and sees his duties in the marital contract
largely in terms of providing financial security. He wants a
'good' sex life, as a result of which his wife will 'people the
small state of the family he heads . . . and make solid his own
foundations in life'. He probably does not know that her
biology will subject her to inexplicable and irrational changes
of mood. She does not realise that his biology brings with it
a lower threshold of anger and frustration. As a result, the
domestic crockery, if nothing else, is vulnerable.

Men are usually held responsible for the problem. 'It's not
us,' said Shere Hite, after pondering the conclusions from a
poll of 4,500 American women, 'it's men's attitudes towards
women that are causing the problem.' The problem apparently manifests itself in 95 per cent of respondents claiming
to suffer from 'emotional and psychological harassment', 98
per cent frustrated at the lack of 'verbal closeness' with their
partners, 79 per cent questioning whether they should continue to put so much energy into love relationships, and 87
per cent admitting that their deepest emotional relationship
is with another woman.

The value of Hite's work has been questioned because of
the survey techniques. There is the suspicion of an unrepre-

sentative grinding of sexual axes. But her findings do not surprise us in the least. We are only surprised that anyone thought it worthwhile to produce such a resounding statement of the biologically obvious. This failure of communication is one of the basic facts of life. In the light of our new understanding it seems absolutely predictable that women should fret at men's lack of communication – because men's brains are not structured that way. It seems to us quite natural that the closest friend of most women should be another woman, because women's biology places a premium on relationships, and like attracts like. We remain unamazed at the frequent complaint that men want to 'star' in the relationship, that their priority is 'being' while women's is 'giving'.

Raging at men's innate maleness is as useful as raging against the weather, or the existence of the Himalayas; we believe it is rather more sensible to put on a raincoat, and abandon plans to bulldoze Everest. Yet some women believe that the only salvation lies in relandscaping our entire social and sexual planet. We have the technology, some extremists argue, to wipe out the biological differences between the sexes. Menstrual extraction, test-tube conception, and laboratory breeding will make pregnancy, sex and marriage redundant – men, too, except as a corralled herd of pedigree spermifers, though refrigeration techniques may have the answer even to that.

That's fine, as long as we are content to limit the biological differences to the fact that women lactate and bear children and men do not. But the differences, as we now know beyond peradventure, go deeper than that. They lie in the brain, its structure, priorities and strategies. These in turn inform our hopes, ambitions, skills and abilities. They are at the core of our being. Reducing the differences simply to those of reproduction is a denial not only of the scientific truth, but of the very essence of our humanity, be it male or female.

The problem is that it is the apostles of sexual sameness who set the agenda; they would enact the laws and ban the sexist books in a vain attempt to divert children from their

128

natural sexual identities. But the idea that we are all born with a clean slate of a mind, a *tabula rasa* ready for society to print its message upon, is a totalitarian's dream. And if, after all, we are what we are because of our biology, is it not as monstrous and hopeless a task to eliminate our differences as it was to create a master race? There is a disturbing whiff of sexual fascism in the premises and prescriptions of those who advocate sexual neutrality.

Biological diffidence has meant that thousands of books have been written, statutes enacted, and studies undertaken on the subject of marriage which ignore the central import- ance of sexual difference. Dr Alice Rossi, an American and one of the few sociologists to accept the biological roots of society, tries to incorporate this knowledge into her own work. She has warned her fellow sociologists that without this perspective their theories 'may be doomed to irrelevance against the mounting evidence of sexual dimorphism from the biological and neuro-sciences'.

The problem arises from the confusion of sex and equality. Where sex is concerned, Alice Rossi writes, 'Diversity is a biological fact, while equality is a political, ethical, and social precept.'

At the turn of the century, even a generation ago, women were not so confused. They had come to acknowledge their own sexuality, and, as far as equality was concerned, they knew that power takes many forms. For men, power tradi- tionally consists in dominance and aggression – the male definition of status that some women's liberationists have uncritically adopted. Women's power was something subtler, the force that creates relationships, binds families, and builds societies. Women who understand this, and do not deprecate the value and power of this intrinsic, invaluable, and essential quality of their sex, have fewer qualms about their status. That's not to say that these women accept the frequent prejudice afforded them in the home or the workplace – a subject we'll return to later at greater length; but they know that they have certain skills denied to men.

This difference between the sexes' definition of power is

just one aspect of an overall difference in the attitudes of men and women to life. Many studies have revealed how men and women perceive and value their lives, and all record a difference between the sexes. In a survey of six modern cultures men and women were asked to describe the 'kind of person I would most like to be'. Overwhelmingly, the characteristics chosen by men included being practical, shrewd, assertive, dominating, competitive, critical, and self-controlled. Cross-culturally, women were more likely to describe their ideal selves as loving, affectionate, impulsive, sympathetic, and generous.

In another survey, in which the sexes were asked to assess the value of different interests and pursuits, girls gave higher ratings to social, aesthetic and religious values while the boys preferred economic, political and theoretical values. Women valued 'having interesting experiences' or 'being of service to society', while men's priorities were for power, profit and independence. Men value competition, scientific toys and principles, prestige, power, dominance and freedom, while women value personal relationships and security.

Studies of married couples show that men's marital happiness is related to their wives' performance of 'services' such as looking attractive, cooking and shopping. Women's ratings of marital satisfaction related directly to how affectionate their husbands had been on the day they answered the questionnaire. Intriguingly, women are found to be happier than men between the ages of eighteen and sixty-four, when the men, at last, come into their own. This is around the time when the hormonal tides recede ... and men and women come more to resemble each other in their behaviour. Women become more bad-tempered, selfish and assertive, while men become gentler, discovering the value of intimacy and relationships.

Women show a greater sensitivity to emotional stimuli than males. Women are naturally more affectionate than men, just as they were as girls, welcoming the newcomer to the playgroup. 'Women's sense of integrity appears to be entwined with the ethic of care, so that to see themselves as women is to see themselves in a relationship connection.'

Do these findings merely confirm that we are the cultural victims of our social stereotypes, or could the simpler answer be that we are the products of our distinctive biology? The almost ubiquitous, not to say eternal, nature of these differences argues for biology; that, because of the way our brains are formed, we 'see' the world in different ways, attributing different values to matters differently perceived.

Those who argue for the sexual status quo – mostly men – will be mightily relieved by this analysis, while sexual revolutionaries – mostly women – will not be pleased. They will argue that the acceptance of biologically based differences dooms women to their traditional roles, tending the family, submitting to their dominant husbands to whom they render those 'services', sacrificing career to domesticity, uncomplainingly accepting roles and values that are deemed inferior to masculine ones.

But deemed inferior by whom? By men, of course – although men and women, as the evidence has shown, are different, and have different values. It is only when women judge their own worth at men's valuation that the problem arises. A woman isn't as concerned with status and the pecking order. That is man's obsession. So, at the risk of literary inelegance, why should any woman consciously adopt a male value system which devalues her own female values? For a woman to try to be 'more like a man' seems almost by definition to make her a less-happy woman.

Now, as we strive towards a greater mutual understanding between the sexes, by means of a greater awareness of our differences, the past has some of the answers to why we are different, how history has reinforced our separate, innate, attitudes, and the problems we now have in adapting them to the circumstances of the present.

We live in a technological world, but are still

> genetically equipped only with an ancient mammalian
> primate heritage that evolved largely through
> adaptations appropriate to much earlier times.

These last two hundred years of industrialised society are a mere blip in our evolutionary development. For most of our past, we lived in communities which depended for their very survival on hunting animals and gathering plant food. Men, with their greater strength and stamina, their roving tendency, and their greater skill in relating the spear to the space occupied by the prey, did the hunting, an unpredictable and dangerous activity. Women gathered nuts, grains, and grubs – a safer and surer pursuit. This was a division of labour unique among higher mammals, and a pretty fair division – women's foraging work contributed about half of the calorie intake, and two-thirds of the dietary bulk.

This division made sense, because the woman stayed closer to home and could suckle the young, which, in humans, are uniquely dependent on their mothers. A chimpanzee orphaned at six months will survive; a human baby cannot even toddle until it is at least one year old.

With the baby so dependent on the mother, and the mother so fully occupied with the child (even today, in spite of millions of years of evolution, women are still often caught unawares by the sheer volume of work involved in bringing up a baby) it is not surprising that both mother and child developed a relationship of dependency on the hunting male.

In other words, for millions of years, we have lived in a sexist society. We cannot buck our evolution overnight.

Male promiscuity, for instance, has an evolutionary pedigree. It made sense to add to the number of the tribe at every opportunity. The greater the number of offspring, the greater the chance of passing on his genes to the next generation. Promiscuity is encoded in the male genes and imprinted on the male brain's circuitboard. Every farmer knows that each time a bull ceases to copulate with a cow, interest can only – but immediately – be re-aroused with the introduction of another cow, the bull's sexual response to the seventh cow being as strong as to the first. A ram presented with the same ewe will not ejaculate more than five times – but if new ewes are substituted he mounts each one with the same sexual gusto as he did with the first. You can't fool them, either – when sacks are put over the heads of their erstwhile partners, or they are disguised in other ways, both rams and bulls tend, as it were, to turn up their noses.

This has been happily described as the Coolidge Effect, because of remarks made when the American President and his wife visited a government farm. Passing the chicken coops, Mrs Coolidge enquired how often the rooster copulated each day.

> 'Dozens of times,' was the reply. 'Please tell that to the President,' Mrs Coolidge requested. When the President passed the pens and was told about the rooster, he asked 'Same hen every time?' 'Oh no, Mr President, a different one each time.' The President nodded slowly, then said 'Tell that to Mrs Coolidge . . .'

The desire for sexual novelty is innate in the male brain, a combination of that desire to explore which we saw in the pre-school children, hormonal testosterone levels, dominance, and the lower priority on long-term, fulfilling personal relationships which is part of his brain bias. Madame Bovary's handsome lover muses on 'the eternal monotony of passion, whose forms and phrases are forever the same'. Only sexual variety can redeem the barren desert of lust.

All the research shows that men desire sexual diversity. Kinsey concludes that the human male would be promiscuous all his life if there were no social restrictions. Another author writes perceptively, 'Where marriages are founded on love, women may give sex for love while men give up sex for love.'

The novelty factor can be seen at work every Christmas in the lingerie department of the stores. The men sheepishly rummage through the sheer and exotic nightwear. They, apparently, are more capable of kidding themselves by disguising their partners than are those bulls and rams, who weren't fooled by the sacks over their partners' heads. The male brain places a high priority on the visual when it comes to arousal. Come the New Year, and the same lingerie counters are thronged with women returning the love tokens. 'It just isn't me,' they say, returning the scarlet satin suspender belts, the flimsy erotic negligees. They find them embarrassing, and perhaps a little silly. They may well wish that their men had chosen gifts to reflect the different female sensory priorities – body oils, for instance, to enhance and reflect women's greater sensitivity to touch and smell.

So different are the needs of men and women in a long-term relationship, argues one American anthropologist, that a conscious effort is demanded by both partners to acknowledge, accommodate, and reciprocate those needs. This means that the women should perhaps think again before returning that dreadful lingerie . . . while men should realise that intimacy and affection are perhaps more important for women than mere sexual athleticism. As we have noted in an earlier chapter, intimacy, security and fidelity are an erotic turn-on for a woman, the orgasm rate rising five-fold in the marital bed.

The pill, and other forms of female contraception, may have changed the politics of sex but they have not erased the fundamental, and different, philosophies of sex to which each sex adheres. However, it is still true, as a British psychologist, Glen Wilson contends, that 'women want a lot of sex with the man they love, while men want a lot of sex'. Men can separate sex and love – those neat and tidy compartmentalised brains again. Hence the inevitable disparity between the emotions of the married man and his lover. Women nearly always take an affair with a married man more seriously than the man does, however vehemently he denies the fact.

The happily married woman who has an affair is a rare creature. The happily married male adulterer is not. Men are three times more likely than women to instigate an affair.

Sexual liberation is doubtless increasing the number of women seeking the same sort of casual male sexual relationships. Pre-liberation, we can understand that there must have been a reservoir of female sexual frustration and an unfulfilled appetite for promiscuity. But the depth of that reservoir is not bottomless – unlike men's. There is a natural limit to the female desire for mindless fornication. Overwhelmingly, surveys show that women want sex with feeling, not sex for its own sake. And why, in the name of liberation, should women ape the male initiative, follow the male script?

Liberation condemns the sexual double standard – why should sex outside marriage be 'all right' for men, all wrong for women? The standards are indeed double, in that an extra-marital affair does mean different things, and has a different level of importance, for men and women. 'It didn't mean anything,' mutters the man, when his indiscretion is revealed – and it almost certainly didn't. He says that he loves her just as much as ever, and he probably does. But the wife sees his affair as an assault on what is to her most precious – intimacy and fidelity. If she were to embark on an affair, you can bet that it would 'mean' a lot to her. She cannot forgive him; for she cannot even understand him. Their brains and their hormones have made them strangers to one another.

Understanding, even within marriage, of each partner's different sexual appetite might also calm the marital waters. Kinsey sees the difference in the sex drive between men and women as one of the major causes of unhappiness. His is higher than hers in the early years – hence her complaint that he is all too often merely 'using' her. In later years, as his drive lessens, it may fall below the lower, but more constant level of her desire, and the boot, as it were, is on the other foot; he resents having to 'perform' for her.

In spite of all this, 70 per cent of couples surveyed claim to have happy marriages. Happy marriages, we are told, have to be 'worked at'. We would simply suggest that the work would be easier once we fully understood the nature of the task, and the differences to be overcome, instead of bringing up our children either in ignorance of those differences or in the erroneous belief that there are none.

Sex apart – though intimately bound up with it – marriage's biggest bugbear is the inequality of the emotional contract. Because of the differing priorities in the brain of each partner, the contract is an unequal one. Ninety-eight women in a hundred, according to an American study, wanted men to talk to them more, about their own personal thoughts, feelings, plans, emotions, and questions, and to ask them about their own. Eighty-one per cent of women say that it is they who initiate most deep conversations, trying very hard to get men to express their innermost thoughts and feelings. But most wives meet great resistance when they try to push their man to talk about feelings; they have come to the conclusion that the men in their lives are afraid of expressing emotion. Nearly three-quarters of the women in long-term relationships or marriages had finally given up trying to achieve a closer emotional bond. Eight out of ten say men often seem not really to hear, and about half that number say their male partner often tells them not to feel what they are feeling, or at least not to express it.

The conventional explanations are that men are conditioned not to acknowledge their feelings – the 'big boys don't cry' syndrome. But we now know that the reluctance men have with feeling and with communicating emotions has a biological root. Their capacity to feel is, to a greater degree than in women, physically divorced from their capacity to articulate; further, the emotional centres of the male brain are located far more discretely than in the woman. It's not that he 'bottles things up' – more that his emotions are in a separate box, in a separate room, a room not routinely visited. The language of the male is more in the vocabulary of action – doing things, sharing activities, expressing feelings through inarticulate gifts, favours, and physical courtesies. Holding a door open, or carrying in the groceries is not mere social convention; it is the masculine for 'I care for you'. Yet verbal self-disclosure, and the sharing of confidences and feelings, is inextricably part of the intimacy a woman desires.

Put another biological perspective to that difference, and the problem is accentuated – because of their hormonal fluctuations, women may be more extreme in the manifestation of their feelings, which may seem more 'irrational' to the male mind.

This greater female priority on the emotions is a product of the 'wiring' differences in yet another way. We have examined the primacy of personal relationships for the female brain. Women are more emotional because they are

136

more specifically designed to care about people. They experience other people's distress as their own. Men, with their 'doing' brains, will respond to another's distress by searching for a practical solution to it. To the mother, the baby's crying reaches her heart. The father goes to the baby book to scan the useful catalogue of cause and cure: wetness – change the nappy, hunger – feed the child, wind – burp it, tiredness – rock it. Men often express the caring side of themselves by playing with children – again, doing things.

The circuitboard of the male brain is programmed for action rather than people. It ignores megabytts of personal information, such as the delicate visual cues to which women respond so much more readily in conversation. Men have to ask, for instance, 'Am I boring you?' Women know. The male perceptions leave him with less information to go on. Men find things, rather than people, are easier to deal with: car stops, carburettor blocked. He carries this approach into the personal sphere: baby cries, nappy needs changing. The man cannot understand why the woman spends so much time agonising over a relationship any more than she can comprehend why he spends so much time tinkering with the car.

Women rarely understand another reason for this male remoteness from intimacy; men simply need more 'space' in every sense. On ships at sea, there is an unspoken (it would have to be unspoken) acknowledgement that one tiny corner of the vessel 'belongs' to a particular seaman; it is his territory, somewhere where it is recognised that he has the right to be, think, smoke, or whatever – alone. It is no coincidence that that favourite male pastime – fishing – involves solitude, space, and the freedom from any human intercourse.

At Boston University 48 male, and an equal number of female, students took part in an experiment. Rather forbiddingly, they were told to 'interact' with each other. Observers found that eye contact was greatest when both parties were female, and least when both were male. Men also stood further apart from each other, and leaned back further in their chairs than the women did. They were all allowed to move their chairs; the women moved the chairs closer than the men.

One explanation of the male need for greater space is that it is an aspect of his need to dominate – space as status. More likely is the fact that his brain is not tuned for intimacy, from which he physically shrinks. A woman's is, and her desire to get closer is a reflection of that.

Women, then, see, hear, and feel more, and what they see, hear and feel means more to them. Women cry more often than men perhaps because they have more to cry about – they are receiving more emotional input, reacting more strongly to it, and expressing it with greater force. It could be that a man cries less not because he's been conditioned against such a display of emotions, but because he hasn't actually registered the hurt or the insult, either at all or to the same extent. It literally means less to him.

If a man does cry, something is badly and deeply wrong, while there is a degree of hyperbole in much female expression, whether physical or verbal. Women choose and stress words exaggeratedly – 'If the kitten's been sick, I'll simply *die*,' or 'There's *nothing worse* than a clumsy hairdresser.' This can annoy the man: 'No, you won't die, it will be merely rather annoying,' and 'Yes, starvation in Ethiopia is worse than a clumsy hair-do.' Women, in turn, see these male responses as an infuriating and sarcastic 'put-down'. They are, in fact, a clumsy reaction to the gulf of perception and communication that divides them. Why doesn't she get things 'into proportion'? Because her sense of proportion is different from his. His is literal, objective; hers is approximate, subjective.

But how does that square with that particularly male irrationality, his quickness to wrath? Anger is a function of high testosterone levels. Just as the man is more easily roused to lust, he is more easily roused to frustration and anger. And, just like passion, that anger is soon, explosively, spent.

Anger is also another reflection of the male bias of the brain. To be angry demands a certain depersonalisation of the object of one's rage – indeed, that person becomes an

138

'object', and so fits more easily into the male mind set. Anger and violence demand a more abstract, impersonal view of the world – people become things to shout and yell at. The female view of the world, based essentially on people and her relationships with them, means that the depersonalisation necessary for rage comes less naturally to her.

The very fact that marriage is, for humans, the norm throughout the world – when, as we know, men are naturally disposed against the institution – represents a remarkable triumph of the female brain, and will. It is a truly stunning victory for female power and control over the naturally promiscuous biology of the male. In starkly sexual, and evolutionary, terms, there is nothing in marriage for men, given their rooster desire for novelty and the widest possible distribution of their seed. Yet most men enjoy and respect marriage and fidelity. Partly, it is because they recognise the havoc that would result from wholesale promiscuity; their own wives, after all, might be seduced by other men, and throughout history men have dreaded the public ridicule of being cuckolded. It may also be because marriage is a contract, and the male brain places a high premium on rules. There may also be a degree of straightforward self-interest; home is usually a safer and more comfortable place.

Women, mistresses of personality, are the experts when it comes to the politics of marriage and social relationships. Their diplomacy and social skills give them the crucial edge in maintaining this – to men – unnatural institution. We have already mentioned their greater sensitivity to non-verbal behavioural cues; they study faces more closely, indeed research shows that they have a better general memory for faces. Power, in any state, depends on the possession of information. In the married state, women have more of it.

Errant men are baffled by how their wives seem to know – 'intuitively' – what they have been up to. Intuition has nothing to do with it. Women simply notice more things, and it's not simply that strand of blonde hair, or the fact that he is paying more attention than usual to his personal hygiene (though men would never pick up such clues from women). They can see from a man's demeanour, the way he looks, speaks, and stands, that something is up. Husbands are an open book to wives, not because of any magic or witchcraft, but because of their greater acuity of perception. Men often don't realise what women notice – a quick erasure of truant lipstick seems to them to be subterfuge enough. It is not.

Marriages work, against all the odds, not because women are submissive, and accommodate their domineering males; marriages work because women's natural social skills – it's been called 'social intelligence' – enable them to manage a relationship so much better than a man. Women can predict and understand human behaviour better than men, can sense the motives behind speech and behaviour; so, if he is the engine of the ship, she is the rudder. She is also the navigator, because she alone has the chart and knows where the rocks are. If women are worried about their status in a relationship, or indeed in life, they could recognise, and build upon, those skills specific to their sex.

Marriages go wrong when men and women fail to acknowledge, or begin to resent, each other's complementary differences.

CHAPTER TEN

Why mothers are not fathers

NOTHING IS SAID to bring men and women closer to each other than the shared experience of parenthood. The truth more often is that, because of the different perspective each partner brings to it, few things more dramatically define the difference between men and women.

However disappointing the fact may be to a devoted father, there is something unique in the relationship between a mother and a baby. No known society replaces the mother as a primary provider of care. Social scientists have conducted experiments in which fathers were encouraged to become much more closely involved in natural childbirth classes; and babies were exposed to a multiplicity of 'care-givers'. In the first case, the results showed that within a few weeks, in spite of the fathers' greater involvement, mothers were none the less measurably much closer to the children; in the second, that the children were confused and wanted their natural mothers back.

Female attachment to an infant seems to be innate, male attachment a function of social learning. Mothers are natural parents; men, with the best will in the world, are not.

This bias towards care in the female brain can be proved by experiments with animals, and by observation of human accidents of nature. In animals, maternal instincts can be accentuated by injections of female hormone; in women, the natural progesterone levels rise one-hundred-fold during pregnancy. At an early stage in its life, before its brain has been sexed, a male rat can be treated with female hormone to induce typically female parental behaviour. Conversely, if you tinker with the developing brain of a genetically female rat, and thwart its natural female design by dousing it with male hormones, the rat will exhibit little maternal behaviour.

In most primates, parenting is exclusively a female occupation. The pattern of female caring for the young emerges early; pre-adolescent males and females display marked sex differences in their reaction to a new-born of the species. Young females show strong affection for the infants, while young males are either indifferent or positively aggressive towards it. Those rare species where the male shares the parental duties are also characterised by physical and other behavioural similarities between the males and females. In man, too, the more apparently feminine the man – a result of pre-natal exposure to female hormones – the greater his involvement in infant care.

Physical intimacy, which, again, we have found is a female characteristic, is essential to the process of infant bonding. Baby monkeys were offered two 'surrogate' mothers – mere feeding mechanisms. One was made out of wire, the other out of cloth. The youngsters 'reared' by the softer machine turned out to be better adjusted than those brought up by the more spartan apparatus, 'proving', says a British psychologist, 'that cuddling is a more important role of the mother than feeding'.

Fathers are, at last, beginning to learn the importance of the cuddle, but 'learn' is the key word here. There is little in their brain pattern to predispose them naturally to such intimacy. They cannot 'switch on' that extra surge of female hormone and, anyway, it would have little effect on a brain whose pre-set structure is immune to its influence. They can only switch on conscious, caring behaviour; and switch it off.

Once the child is born the levels of female hormone, progesterone, in the mother decline rapidly. The sudden cut-off of these female hormone levels after birth can temporarily upset the natural female pattern of care, with results that may sometimes baffle the male. This, he reasons, should be a time of happiness. But according to a recent study 84 per cent of new mothers experience 'baby blues' immediately after giving birth as a result of the abrupt cessation in the calming flow of progesterone.

Nearly one in four report 'clinical depression'. To the proud father, the new baby is an exciting new 'project': he cannot understand why the mother suddenly despairs at her capacity to cope with the new arrival, or behaves in an emotionally volatile manner while her body readjusts to normal hormone levels.

Parenthood means different things to the different sexes, and that difference is a reflection of the sexually distinct brain biases. Four out of five marriages go through a severe crisis at the birth of the first child. All the literature suggests that once the novelty factor of the new child has worn off, the father tends, to a greater or lesser extent, to resent the newcomer. His brain teaches him to see the world in terms of competition and dominance, and so he feels that he has in some sense lost the competition for the mother's affection, and has been replaced in the social hierarchy by this demanding young pretender. Studies on both sides of the Atlantic show a steady decline in 'marital satisfaction' between the time when couples were without children and their children's teenage years; satisfaction returned when the children had left home and, presumably, when men felt that they had come back into their own.

But woman's brain emphasis on the personal and the emotional enables her to embrace a wider variety of relationships without denying or diluting any of them. Her love for the child is not 'at the expense of' anyone else. Only men would see affection as such a finite commodity. In fact maternal affection can be seen not as an alternative to sexual love, but as an extension of it. Lovers coo and indulge in 'babytalk' during their courtship, and kissing may echo a primitive past of mouth-to-mouth feeding. Both men and women need to understand and acknowledge these different

143

perspectives if the crib, like the marriage bed, is not to become another sexual battlefield.

The female hormones are profoundly and inextricably bound up with the need to care for her child. The high levels of female hormone at birth have a crucial influence on mother-infant attachment. The mother's response to these hormones is dependent on having a female brain network. As described in Chapter Two, the brain takes on a female structure as the foetus grows in the womb provided male hormones are absent. The female brain is what determines certain maternal behaviour in the adult.

The evidence for this – as with the rats – comes from studies of women exposed to high levels of male hormone in the womb that were described in Chapter Two. This exposure occurred because their mothers were taking male hormones or because the foetus had an abnormality and was producing male hormone itself. These women display little or no maternal behaviour, whether as children refusing to play with dolls, teenagers indifferent to baby-sitting, or as adults unconcerned with children. Meanwhile the Turner's syndrome girls, with the extra female chromosome and no exposure to male hormone at all, show an exaggerated interest in dolls, babies and mothering.

The roles of the hormones and the female brain are accentuated by the interplay between anatomy and evolution. For example, infant crying stimulates the secretion of a substance called oxytocin in women, which triggers nipple erection preparatory to nursing.

The difference between the attitude and proficiency of men and women as parents again reflects those basic differences of the brain. In this most intimate of relationships, between parent and child, it is the mother rather than the father who is more alert to the nuance and the non-verbal hint, more naturally responsive to the baby's needs. A woman is better equipped in all her senses for the task of child-rearing, better able to hear and identify the cry of the baby, more sensitive to touch, sound and smell. Taking one of those rare evenings off during the early months, sitting in a restaurant or a cinema, a mother will feel that she has left part of herself behind at home. Fathers, however devoted, will be relieved to have escaped the domestic menagerie for a while.

Men may fret at their biological exclusion from the most intimate mysteries of parenthood. But they must accept that this bond of the mother is innate. The stronger engagement in the care of babies has been empirically proved, and cannot be explained away by socialisation alone. Evolution, of course, plays its part – the defence of the tribal encampment would suffer if the soldiers were forever shirking picket duty to dandle their offspring on their knees – but the difference is rooted in biological fact.

Even in the most self-consciously 'role-sharing' families, mothers will note, as a British expert writes, that a father is not so well attuned to his baby's needs as the mother is. He will decide to 'jolly along' the infant, just at the moment when it is about to drop off, at last, to sleep; "his timing" is off . . . he fails to pick up subtleties of mood or mesh his approaches to the child's moment-to-moment states of mind as easily as she does.'

Fathers come into their own when the child begins to grow up. Or, perhaps more accurately, children come into their own when they are old enough for fathers to 'do' things with. Right from the beginning the father's interaction with the baby was a matter of 'doing' – tweaking the nose, pedalling the feet, swooping the small bundle in infantile aerobatics. While mothers deal with the child-as-it-is, fathers' concerns are with the child as-it-will-be, preparing them for ocean surf and horse-riding through those carpet romps on father's back, presenting them with their first, enormous football shirt, promoting world-title babyweight prize fights in mock pugilism. American sociologist Dr Alice Rossi writes of studies which show that fathers act towards infants as if they were things rather than persons with whom they can interact. At best, communication from the father is based on the need to teach.

> I give him a bottle; he's just learning to hold it up for
> himself now. I continually will teach him things or try to;

how to hold his bottle, how to get it if it's fallen over to one side. Right now I am trying to teach him how to roll over. Also . . . I will interact with him by trying out new toys . . .

Compare that description from a father with an account of the silent, or at least non-verbal, communion between mother and baby:

> During a feeding, dozens of events occur. The baby sucks, winces, squirms, relaxes, lets go of the nipple, burps, falls asleep, hiccups, smiles, roots, cries, opens his eyes, tenses his face or softens his expression. His mother rocks, sits still, hums, is silent, adjusts her position, tenses, relaxes, gazes, smiles, talks, pats, strokes, lifts the baby, puts him down. *Each event is a remark* . . . Through such dialogues a mother and baby negotiate a feeding, each trying to accommodate to the other's style . . .

Men bring their maleness to parenting, says Dr Alice Rossi, as women bring their femaleness. Fathers hold babies to play with them, mothers to soothe them. When babies do not respond to the repertoire of male games, it is father, not baby, who gets bored. And when he gets bored, and wants to read the newspaper – this is Dad, not the baby – the child is returned to constant, dependable, mother, who may have fewer games . . . but then she has less need to play them. She knows her child and its needs, while the father, in parenting as with sex, simply switches his fathering on and off to suit himself.

One divorced mother we know dreads and resents the father's access visits to their child. 'He immediately assumes he is The Treat, The Star, The Magic Man. He doesn't notice whether Jimmy is tired, whether he's got a cold, or if he's in one of those "leave-me-alone" moods. No, it's got to be ten brisk rounds of "Here we go round the mulberry bush", then a multiple pile-up on the freeway with his toy cars, and "Why does he have to go to bed now when he's obviously enjoying himself?" When Jimmy doesn't want to play, his father sulks or pretends to cry or smothers him with great globs of affection, toys, sweets, whatever. It undermines the whole relationship I have with him, and it takes days to get back to normal.'

Marriage styles can be made to accommodate the differences between two adult personalities. Parental roles are less amenable. It is harder work for a man, except, intriguingly, for a grandfather; male grandparents have an observably more affectionate and feminine relationship with their grandchildren than they had with their own children. Again, this coincides with an age-related decline in their male hormone levels.

Being a parent is no pushover for a mother, but at least she comes with all the right equipment – perceptual, cognitive, emotional as much as anatomical. And, whatever the new liberationists may teach her, she usually wants to be a mother.

Yet just at the moment when women are freest to enjoy and exploit their natural, superior, skills in motherhood, a stern sisterhood tells them that this is an unnecessary, low-value, and socially regressive role, predicting that the future will see the abolition of the traditional roles of parenthood, to be replaced with a communal Utopia such as the one outlined here:

> By always having some children in our unit, we will be
> able to assume parental roles when and for as long as
> we want . . . Our children will have an advantage in
> that from the adults they can select their own parents,
> brothers, sisters, friends . . . our special ties will not be
> forced nor strained by the mandates of kinship and
> marital obligations . . .

Well, we have seen the future and it does not work.

The Israeli kibbutz was not designed specifically to abolish the Jewish mother. But in these forcing-houses of social engineering, girls and boys grew up with virtually interchangeable roles. Children were reared communally, and the household duties of cooking and laundry were a community,

147

rather than a family, responsibility. The expectation was that, with the passing of several sexually neutral generations, sexual differentiation would evaporate, and sexist stereotyping would become a memory as remote as slavery is to the newest generation of America's blacks.

But that has not happened. Three or four generations later, the children of the kibbutz are still stubbornly clinging to their traditional roles. The women are returning to maternal roles. 'They have acted against the principles of their socialisation and ideology,' write the authors of a study of women in the kibbutz, 'against the wishes of the men of their communities, against the economic interest of the kibbutzim, in order to be able to devote more time and energy to private maternal activities rather than to economic and political public ones.' It is a reassertion by women themselves of their fundamental, innate bio-grammar against a system which, like most Utopias, has been created by men.

Psychologists may attempt to explain this turnaround in the kibbutz as a subconscious rebellion by women against their own non-maternal mothers, who themselves denied their children traditional female care and comfort. But if that were to be the case, where did these new women learn their motherly skills, and acquire their motherly ambitions? No, it is much more likely to be a case of the inherent, biological imperative. 'It is far more likely, and more respectful of their dignity, to say that these women know their own minds and act accordingly.'

Other studies of neutrally reared children suggest that the artificial elimination of the mother-child bond neither reduces sex differences nor promotes the healthy development of the child. Where communities take turn and turn about in parental duties, the child becomes confused. 'Communally reared children, far from being liberated, are often neglected, joyless creatures.'

'Modern' mothering, a result of social, political, and economic pressures on the woman to play a fuller part in the world, may provoke signals of infant stress 'resulting from environmental demands alien to our biological needs'. Alice Rossi is aware that such an analysis could be seen as a conservative justification for the status quo, for traditional family and work roles for men and women. Nevertheless, she believes that any redrafting of the sexual charter should be built on the foundations of the fundamental biological root of parenting, rather than upon 'the shaky superstructure created by men in that fraction of time in which industrial societies have existed'.

But just as we cannot buck our biology, we cannot ignore the fact that we, as men and women, do live in changed times – and times when time itself is at a premium. Studies of primitive peoples show that 70 per cent of a woman's day is spent in close physical contact with the infant, while in modern societies the figure is closer to 25 per cent.

Never before in our history have we been so eager to tear up the blueprint of biology and redefine our roles as men and women, mothers and fathers. It is an awkward time, as the sexes struggle against the differences in their mental make-up, while at the same time denying the existence of difference. Men are said to feel threatened by the 'new' woman, while many women feel that they have somehow failed their sex when they maintain traditional roles.

This female guilt shows itself in a forty-year-old, non-working – or should we say 'unwaged?' – mother of two. She knows that it is by her efforts, primarily, that family life runs smoothly: she collects the children from school, arranges the family's social schedule, cooks, cleans, launders, irons. Yet . . . 'I sometimes think I'm a complete failure. I feel I'm making no contribution to the family. I feel helpless when my husband worries about the bills, because I don't do anything to help the family finances. I just spend his money, at the grocery store, buying the children's school uniforms, getting the vacuum-cleaner serviced. I look around at other mothers who go out to work, and I can see what a difference it makes to their sense of worth. OK, they may not be earning as much as their husbands, but at least they can buy a new dress without feeling guilty . . .'

Many women, when asked 'what they do' – a typically male question, defining character and value through employment – shamefacedly admit that they are 'just a housewife'. Most women still do most of the housework – for every two hours that a man puts into domestic chores, a woman invests five. Even women working full-time refer to their husband's 'helping' around the house, acknowledging their own primary responsibility for the organisation of the home and the delegation of duties. When there is a self-conscious concept of equal sharing, women still find themselves in the position of managers – having to remind the men of their obligations. Even in Scandinavian countries, where sex roles have been de-emphasised, feeding the family, washing, cleaning and child care are done by wives in 70 per cent of families, while husbands pay the bills and undertake routine household maintenance.

In the self-consciously sex-neutral kibbutz, the notion of 'women's work' stubbornly persists. And the women's work is defined by women themselves. More than nine women in ten initially engaged in men's work reverted to a more typical female work pattern. 'Sex-typed work is widely attractive for both sexes,' concludes a recent study, 'especially for women . . . The movement of the women is towards more polarisation, that of the men towards less polarisation' in stereotyped sex roles.

That 'movement of the women' seems to be at odds with the ambitions of the women's movement. Further, women's demand to return to womanly work seems to be stronger among the young. 'Some powerful pervasive force or forces intervene between the intentions of kibbutz ideology and the reality of kibbutz social structure . . .'

That 'pervasive force' lies in the very nature of the male and female brain. Men do not, indeed, 'see' the dirty glass partly because of a less perceptive eye for detail, but mostly because clean glasses have a relatively low priority in their view of the world. To a woman, where the home is less of a motel, and more the backdrop to the relationships that matter to her, the dirty glass stands as an implicit rebuke to her own values.

This next comment may be a female complaint against men's attitudes, but it could just as well be an illustration of the difference in male and female perceptions.

> I feel it is a personal insult to me, his attitude about the
> house. He says I am 'obsessed' with cleanliness, but he
> could let the whole house go until the cockroaches run
> over the piles of dirty underwear by the bed . . .

In the kibbutz, women do most of the cleaning because they
are not impressed by their husbands' ability in this sphere.
One husband admits, 'I do what I can, but her standards for
cleaning are too high. I'd do more, but what I do isn't good
enough for her. She says that if I did it, she'd just have to do
it again.' Perhaps this explains why, with the best intentions,
the husband who tries to 'cope' with his wife's 'irrational'
menstrual behaviour by taking on the household chores gets
into trouble by misstacking the dishwasher, in however tri-
vial a manner, or misfolding the tablecloth; the hormones
are accentuating a basic sex difference in attitudes and perceptions.

'Women's work' is only inferior work on the male value
system, and that difference in values is the result of different
brain biases. It matters to women whether or not their
homes are pleasant and hygienic places to be in, because
what matters to women – love, affection, relationships, security – takes place more in the home. For men, the office or the
factory floor is just as important as the home – and the
workplace is cleaned, magically, mysteriously, invisibly, by
an anonymous workforce of cleaners before he arrives for
work. Sharing chores, one of the planks of the egalitarian
platform, is no answer, because most men attach less importance, and apply lower standards, to domestic chores – thus
tacitly demeaning these tasks and resenting the natural fastidi-
ousness of the female.

In the same way a man attaches less importance to personal
appearance – either in his wife, or in himself, not noticing
her new dress, or stubbornly resisting her demands that he
should buy himself a new pair of trousers.

It is yet another example of the basic differences in the way
we, men and women, see the world, and see each other. We
have innately separate approaches to each other, our children,

our jobs, and the values we attach to them. Different perceptions, brought to bear either upon the child or the washing-up, may cause stress and strife. Denying the differences devalues the perception, and causes further conflict – 'Oh, all right, I'll do it your way if it's so darned important to you' – is annoying because the presumption is that 'your way' is not important.

As in most of the differences between the sexes noted in this and other chapters, the key to peaceful coexistence, as in the political sphere, is diplomacy, and, to a lesser extent, negotiation; a lesser extent, because negotiation may succeed in diminishing nuclear stockpiles, but it cannot erase basic ideological differences. There is not a war between the sexes, not even a cold one. But there is, in key respects, a basic incompatibility. The success of many marriages is a tribute to women's superiority in social diplomacy. Perhaps more marriages would be more universally successful if men, too, acquired at least that one female skill.

CHAPTER ELEVEN

Minds at work

> The car skidded off the road, and the two occupants, a man and his son, were badly injured. In the ambulance, on the way to the hospital, the father died. The son was taken straight into the operating theatre. The surgeon took one look at the patient and gasped, 'Oh no . . . it's my son.'

We have a wicked friend who poses the tale as a riddle to his feminist friends – if the real father is dead, how can the patient be the surgeon's son? He takes delight in the fact that many of them *accept* it as a riddle: is the surgeon the boy's step-father? is the son married to his own ex-wife? they ask, constructing all sorts of elaborate relationships – until they realise that the surgeon is a wife, a mother, a woman.

We live in a world where we are no longer surprised to find a female prime minister, a female judge, a female rabbi or a female pilot. But there are still remarkably few women in top jobs, considering the large increase in the number of well-educated women.

That is likely to remain the case.

This, of course, is heresy to those idealists who maintain that, since the sexes are identical, identical education will lead inevitably to an equality of achievement. With the best will in the world, the sexes, when given the choice, don't choose to study the same subjects, do better or worse at particular subjects according to their sex, and, even when men and women achieve equal academic success, do not always maintain an equal momentum in success at work.

This decade, in Britain at least, as many girls as boys took mathematics at intermediate level, and nearly as many sat the chemistry examination. At the higher level, girls represented about a third of the passes; in physics and chemistry the figures were 21 per cent and 37 per cent. It was a significant advance on the situation ten years earlier; so it was hoped that we could soon – and at last – expect to see rather more than the present 5 per cent of architects as women, rather more than 3 per cent as air traffic controllers.

It takes more than one generation for the seeds of equal opportunity to flower, but we can hazard an informed guess at the answer, again by looking at the experience of the Israeli kibbutzim. Social engineers worked hard to iron out classic gender stereotypes at an early age: 'All children are dressed in the same work-clothes . . . there is no sex difference in the style of haircut. Children take whatever they want from the pool of toys; girls are not encouraged to play with dolls, boys are not encouraged to play with cars and trucks. The children do not hear such sex-typed injunctions as "It isn't nice for girls to . . ." Girls often climb trees, play very energetic ball games, and engage in fights. Boys cry without shame, handle dolls, learn to cook, and sometimes knit.'

Even so, data on ability and achievement in kibbutz high schools show 'conspicuously superior performance on the part of boys'. Boys and girls themselves chose to study sex-specific courses; and went on to careers which were typically male or female. The boys went on to study physics and become engineers, the girls to study sociology and become teachers. It is telling proof of what we now know – that the minds of men and women are different, that ultimately boys and men live in a world of things and space, girls and women in a world of people and relationships.

> Our data about education and careers confirm what the psychological studies have always told us – that women are more interested in interpersonal transactions . . . and that men prefer impersonal and very broad activities.

The pattern is repeated elsewhere. More than three-quarters of US college entrants majoring in foreign languages are female, while women represent only 14 per cent of students planning to major in engineering; while in the American world of work 'by and large, the labor market is still quite segregated'. In fact, some of that sex-segregation has become even more acute; in 1960 women represented nearly 70 per cent of bank tellers in the US: by 1979, nearly 93 per cent of bank tellers were women – while 99 per cent of bank managers were men.

Sylvia Hewlett, an economist who has written extensively on the economic status of women in Britain and America, sums up how the hopes of the 1970s that the social ethic of women's equality would be translated into economic terms, have been only partially fulfilled, and at what cost.

> The spirit of the decade was to pretend that there were
> no differences between men and women. Well, the
> results are in. More women than ever are working
> outside the home, and at least some of them have
> broken into the previously closed ranks of executives
> and professionals. But despite all of this 'progressive
> change', most women are in worse economic shape
> than their mothers were.

In Britain, women's earnings stick stubbornly at about two-thirds of men's; the difference has proved 'remarkably difficult to reduce'. Equal pay legislation seems to have had 'little impact on the earnings gap' in hourly earnings. In the US, 'across the board, women earn less – far less – than men'; even at the top of the corporate ladder, the bright achieving woman very often receives less than her male counterpart.

Power in the professions is overwhelmingly male. In 1980, 99 per cent of company directors, civil engineers, surgeons, local authority chief executives, and even driving test examiners were not women. Ninety-eight per cent of British university professors are male. There are only nine women on the boards of Britain's top one hundred companies. In the law, women have fared better. There has been a big increase in the number of women lawyers and solicitors, but they remain at the bottom of the legal spectrum. The voice from the Bench is still almost universally male – and more likely to be so the higher up the judicial ladder you go.

In 1979, Britain elected a female prime minister – but the proportion of women in British politics is lower than it was in 1945; a reunion of post-war female Cabinet ministers could be held in a couple of taxis – only in two administrations have there been more than one.

If politics is really about 'serving the community' or 'helping people' (as the male candidates proclaim) then it might seem women are better equipped to do the job. But back in the kibbutz, in spite of complete formal equality in political rights, women have become less active in the kibbutz parliament, and while well represented on committees dealing with social, educational and cultural matters, they are 'seriously underrepresented in committees dealing with economy, work, general policy-making, and security'. The higher the level of authority, the wider the gap between men and women; six men in every hundred reached the highest levels of power, but only six women in every thousand.

Even in a trade or profession where women are in the majority, the higher career levels are usually overwhelmingly occupied by men. So, 96 per cent of nurses are women, yet almost all the people in charge of the hospitals are men; in the US, 83 per cent of elementary school teachers are women, yet 81 per cent of school principals are men. A recent British survey of women in the medical profession showed that although women represented about half of all medical students, only 2 per cent of medicine's higher jobs were held by women. The proportion of women in top gynaecological and obstetric positions has actually fallen since the 1960s.

Something has clearly gone wrong to cause this shudder in the progress of female emancipation. Why, in spite of equal educational opportunity, and even in those cases when men and women score equal academic results, is there so little equality of achievement?

One obvious answer is that many women have to do two

jobs – one at home, looking after the children, and one in the world of paid work. That's clearly an important consideration. But there's another element as well: work, success, and ambition simply mean different things to the different sexes.

A key study investigates the success rate of people working in colleges and universities. Male academics scored higher than women in the conventional measurement of academic success – getting more papers published, for instance. Intriguingly, the men did better than their unmarried, and childless, female academic colleagues. The explanation that women are handicapped by their role as mothers and wives is not, then, a convincing one.

What other explanation could there be? Two, probably – first that the academic world is incorrigibly sexist (which it very probably is) or that women may not actually subscribe to the same definition of conventional success as do men.

An early British pioneer in the study of sex differences, Corinne Hutt, favoured the latter explanation. 'Male and female academics,' she says, 'conceive their professional identities differently. Men are more concerned with academic prestige and institutional power, women with developing students, fostering scholarship and promoting institutional service.' In another study, women faculty members see their job more in terms of teaching and service, while men are more oriented towards research and publication – the academic fields where there are laurels to be won.

The male need for achievement emerges in experiments which show that, when asked what made them happiest, more men than women cited simply achievement. Women tended to fuse success at work with a sense of personal achievement; the notion 'I'm happiest when I can succeed at something that will also make other people happy' was endorsed by 50 per cent of women, but only 15 per cent of men.

Throughout the world of work, differences between the sexes echo the differences in the bias of their brains. Women gravitate towards work which has a socially fulfilling and personal dimension, in the same way that they are demonstrably more interested in people from their earliest

157

hours. Men, for the same biologically determined reasons, are interested in the worlds of things and of power. Women may predominate numerically in a trade or a profession because it reflects their priorities, but when men enter it they will demand and achieve a disproportionate amount of authority – because, as we first saw in those studies of summer camps, hierarchies and dominance are in the male scheme of things.

Again, the elaborate efforts to re-engineer the traditional male/female division of labour have not been successful. In the kibbutz, work roles began by being completely interchangeable. Women drove tractors, men worked in the laundry. But slowly the women drifted back to the traditionally female pursuits, and their jobs in the fields or the engineering sheds were taken over by male refugees from the kitchen. Women ended up in an even worse condition – 'Instead of cooking and sewing and baking or cleaning and laundering and caring for children, the woman . . . cooks *or* sews *or* launders *or* takes care of the children for eight hours a day . . . This new housekeeping is more boring and less rewarding than the traditional type.'

A more recent study reports: 'We found increasing with each generation a traditional distinction between women going into the management of morale, health, education and so on, and males into economic management, security planning, and the business that in our own culture is traditionally associated with male persons.' Today, the sexual polarisation inside the kibbutz is even more acute than in the outside, unengineered, society of Israel. Intriguingly, this could not be accounted for in classic political terms – that women were being pushed into the lower-paid jobs – because income in the kibbutz is irrelevant.

We really should not be so surprised that men and women gravitate to sex-specific jobs. We have always, as a species, divided labour. In evolutionary terms, the woman was contributing just as much as the man to the survival of the species, though they went about the affair in different ways. In economic terms, almost every society has consciously or unconsciously allotted certain tasks to certain sexes: in a cross-cultural survey of a hundred societies, for instance, boat-building is a uniquely female occupation in only one. A study of work patterns in California led the authors to gasp, 'We were amazed at the pervasiveness of women's concentration in organisational ghettoes.' They estimated that as many as seven people in ten would have to change jobs – from women's work to men's and vice versa – in order to achieve an equal sexual division in work.

The motivation of men and women is different both in degree and direction. There is an inherent difference between men and women in the values either sex assigns to specific achievement, and the effort worth expending in its pursuit. The early patterns persist with women preoccupied with the personal element of life – their own identity, and their relationships with others – while men are more preoccupied with competition and achievement. In the words of an American psychologist, 'Women continue to perceive the world in interpersonal terms and personalise the objective world in a way men do not. Notwithstanding occupational achievements, they tend to esteem themselves only insofar as they are esteemed by those they love and respect.'

By contrast the bias of the adult male brain expresses itself in high motivation, competition, single-mindedness, risk-taking, aggression, preoccupation with dominance, hierarchy, and the politics of power, the constant measurement and comparison of success itself, the paramountcy of winning – everything which we found in the male as an adolescent.

To the woman – to the average woman, that is – this all matters rather less. Men who fail will often offer the excuse that 'Success isn't worth the effort.' To the female mind, this is not so much an excuse as a self-evident truth. Her conceptual horizons are wider, just as she is more receptive in most other respects of her sensitivity. A woman's wider perspective means that a specific failure at work is less catastrophic; women try to comfort men by explaining that 'It's not the end of the world' if there has been some career setback. Men are not so easily convinced.

There was a startling illustration of the different attitudes men and women have to work when a prominent US company – one of the so-called Fortune 500 companies – was attacked for not promoting enough women as managers. This stung the company, as it prided itself on its vigorous affirmative action policy, in which it went out of its way to favour women for corporate advancement. To find out what was going wrong, the company hired analysts Hoffman Research Associates. After weeks of study, Hoffman concluded that the gender difference in promotion rate was due entirely to differences in motivation. Women clerks, they found, were less willing to relocate than men, or work longer hours, and were less inclined to see their job as the first rung on the corporate career ladder. Forty-four per cent said that they would prefer a part-time job, more than twice the figure among male clerks. Work was important – but not as consumingly important as it was to men.

Another study of women at work confirms this different female attitude.

> To reach the top, as apart from reaching an interesting
> and responsible post at middle level, would, as the
> women see it, call for a maximum commitment of time
> and energy, and so a sacrifice of other interests which
> they are not prepared to make.

Such wisdom will for ever be denied to most men at work, and they pay the penalty. The bias of the male brain is at the root of the occupational duodenal ulcer and the heart attack.

There is a specifically masculine appeal in competitiveness. A study of college men and women – both with a high need for achievement – found that men responded better to competition in class work, while women performed better in non-competitive situations. Masculine, too, is the correlation between career choice and risk-taking. American studies of college males show that a majority of them do not choose fields in which conventional success is assured: they choose one where there's a risk of failure – but the chance of much greater success. Females usually had different priorities: the nature of the occupation was much more important than formal achievement or financial success.

Talking of money – and men talk about it more than women – it is time to take a fresh look at the supposition that the low pay of women is part of a dastardly male framework of exploitation. In the male perception, success, ambition and money are all bound up together, because money is a symbol and a confirmation of his success. With women, just as prestige at work is less important, so, to a degree, is the level of salary. Women have other satisfactions at work – in particular the personal relationships fostered there. Could it be that women are paid less to some extent because money matters less in their scheme of things? Women may like money just as much as men – but maybe they do not need to insist on earning money, and to be seen to be earning money, as much as their male counterparts. One psychiatrist claims to have seen several men 'to whom great losses of money represented such a great loss of self, of ego, and ultimately of masculine image that life no longer seemed worth living'. Would a woman stockbroker jump out of a Wall Street skyscraper if the market crashed?

For men, success, aggression, dominance, status and com- petition find a focus in money. Successful women consistently allocate themselves less salary than do males. They tend to spend less than men on expense accounts, seeing no reason why they should live higher on the hog while involved in the company's business than they would if they were at home. Typically, they will hire a small car – while the men will go for a model more expensive than the one in the garage at home. A 1979 study found that females perceive less connec- tion between their work and monetary rewards. Women, to this extent, discriminate against themselves in the compara- tive sexual earnings league.

Putting these two aspects together – the fact that males attach more importance than women to occupational suc- cess, and that they see, and insist upon, money as being the symbol of that success – the widespread lament about women's low pay takes on a different complexion; though perhaps American Professor Michael Levin is unnecessarily acerbic when he remarks,

> There is no cosmic cashier dispensing wages for having a virilised brain. Nobody gets paid without performing. But because men try harder more often, they will, if not forcibly prevented, succeed more often than women in attaining highly-paid positions.

Little of this is surprising in the light of what we now know about the biological springs of aggression and dominance, the biological roots of personal or material preoccupations, the wired-in predispositions of the male and the female brains.

'To have power,' writes the Canadian psychologist Sandra Witleson, 'like riches or lovers, one has to want it, work for it, and strive to maintain it.' Men will make the most extraordinary sacrifices of personal happiness, health, time, friendships and relationships in the pursuit and maintenance of power, status and success. Women won't; most of them simply are not made that way. (Genius may have a lot to do with the greater male facility for exclusive single-mindedness.)

In great measure men's pursuit of conventional, publicly recognised and applauded success at work is central to their self-esteem. Indeed, you could say that it virtually defines it, when you consider that the role of work is central to a man's sense of worth, in a way that is more important than, for instance, his family. The connection between masculinity, prestige and status is a dynamic one; when traditional male jobs come to be filled by women, the jobs lose their status in men's eyes.

The job of a bank teller in the US used to be a fairly high-status, male, occupation; now that the counter staff are mainly female, it is downgraded as a merely clerical job. Schoolmastering used to be a respected profession. Now that most teachers are women, the profession commands less public respect. Margaret Mead, the American anthropologist, shrewdly observed how men – with the endorsement of their societies – have always assumed the commanding heights of status. 'Men may cook, or weave, or dress dolls or hunt hummingbirds, but if such activities are appropriate occupations of men, then the whole society, men and women alike, votes them as important. When the same occupations are performed by women, they are regarded as less important.'

Just as lower pay for women's work was to some extent a reflection of the lower priority women place on money, so the comparatively low status of women's jobs may be the result of men's desperation to colonise those jobs which confer status. 'If there are sex differences in the extent to which individuals are oriented towards the attainment of status in groups which they enter, and if males are usually more desirous of the attainment of status goals, it follows that whatever occupations or professions bring status in a given society would be those which attract most males.' In other words, men do not bring some grand masculine status to work – they identify it and seek it in work itself. Women find a sense of value in a much wider range of activities and relationships, in which they do not need to be dominant to achieve satisfaction.

No one would deny that some women are more intelligent than most men, nor their superiority in sensitivity and verbal ability, which could make them better doctors, priests, legislators and judges than men. There are probably only two ways to change women's inequality of achievement; the first is for women, in so far as they can, to mimic men. This would involve a conscious effort to take more risks, be more aggressive, suppress the value of personal relationships, acquire a fascination with status, office politics, competition, and achievement, with the comparative neglect of health, happiness and personal well-being.

The second, and it's an idealistic aim, would be to change the very definition of conventional success from its present, predominantly male, nature to something which involved a wider and more catholic set of achievements. But it may be some time before we see a man or a woman whose achievement lies in being a perfectly decent citizen, doing a socially useful low-paid job, and being an excellent parent on the front cover of *Time* magazine.

Meanwhile, there is evidence to support the success of the first alternative, the strategy of male mimicry, whether artificial or innate. A study of twenty-five women in top management positions revealed a common childhood background as tomboys. Corinne Hutt noted this same combination of tomboyishness, activity, and aggression in the top women she studied, a comparatively male personality pattern which suggested a pre-natal organisation of the brain into a male mould. Many clinical studies show that women whose mothers took male hormone therapeutically during pregnancy are much more likely to be competitive, dominant, and career-oriented. Many women who do best in a man's world seem to have a man's brain; it could also be that the women who succeed in a male world are exactly those who behave as 'honorary' men.

Towards the end of their meticulous compilation, *Sex Differences*, Professors Katharine and Kermid Hoyenga, American scientists, understate the conclusion: 'Given the sex differences we have discussed so far, it would not be surprising to find that men and women value events and objects differently.' As we have seen, in adolescence men and women do attach different values to different aspects of life; women outscore men in their emphasis on the aesthetic, social, and religious; the world of men is theoretical (interest in the intellectual pursuit of truth), economic (interest in useful, practical things), and political (interest in power or influence over people).

Men and women bring different, often complementary skills to the jobs they do. It would make sense to put these combined talents to good use.

164

CHAPTER TWELVE

Bias at work

As THINGS ARE arranged at present, women are only going to get a halfway equal chance in the male world of work if men choose voluntarily to emasculate its predominantly macho ethos. And if you can be sure of one thing about the macho ethos, it is that it isn't going to emasculate itself voluntarily.

Yet sheer commercial common sense may dictate such a change – and, painful as it may be, there will be advantages for men, women and the companies in which they work.

But nothing's going to happen until we clear away some of the misconceptions about the sexes at work, and start again from the basis of sex differences.

The *Wall Street Journal* once spoke of female careers being 'sabotaged by motherhood', demonstrating, in a few words, several misconceptions. First, many women do not see their retirement from the world of paid work as a disaster – home and family are a fulfilling and rewarding occupation. Secondly, motherhood is a career in itself, as any single-parent journalist will soon find out; and finally, even the most reluctant mothers, holding their new-born baby, find the notion that they have been somehow 'sabotaged' simply does not arise.

If there is any question of sabotage, it is women who sabotage their own self-esteem. Too often they have defined career success and achievement in male terms, and set off, in Sylvia Hewlett's words 'to clone the male competitive model'. That male model involves a relative degree of obsession, egocentricity, ruthlessness, a relative suspension of social and personal values, to which the female brain is simply not attuned. To succeed on male terms, by male methods, also makes successful motherhood an impossibility; there simply are not enough hours in the day. No matter how supportive the husband, there are some things that – mostly – only a mother can do. So today's woman too often finds herself in a career competition to which she is personally and biologically disinclined, and is further burdened by a sense of guilt and failure as a woman, a careerist, and a mother.

There is a fundamental difference between the sexes in terms of one crucial dimension – the importance attached to personal relationships; at the moment, as the world of work is presently constructed, such personal attachment is a handicap. But, as we will show later, it should be regarded as an asset; women won't have to change (they couldn't, anyway) but businesses could – and would profit by it.

Self-esteem is equally important to men and women, but studies conclude that levels of self-esteem in men and women are affected by different things: by 'affiliative success' in women – that is the depth and strength of their relationships – but by 'occupational success' in men. In one important study of sex differences at work, three principal types of women were identified. In each, the common factor was the need for a successful personal relationship.

First were the 'traditional' women, who put their families and husbands first, giving up their jobs if there was the slightest danger of compromising the family's welfare. Then, there were the so-called 'double-achievers', who tried to reconcile masculine and feminine characteristics as good wives and competent professionals, but often showed strain in the process. (There's a telling statistic that divorce is two-and-a-half times more likely for female scientists than it is for male scientists.) Yet these women, wives with a career, also put their families first, even if it meant sacrificing a career goal. They also needed the approval and encouragement of those dear to them before they felt free to pursue their own success. Finally, the 'role-innovators' tried to succeed by denying women's traditional roles and adopting a typically masculine strategy. But even these women often felt an excessive need for some form of companionship at work, to the extent that they often alienated their colleagues by constantly seeking their encouragement, approval and friendship.

In every case, then, the woman's sense of career is to some extent bound up in, qualified by, or in conflict with, the importance of personal relationships, while 'the conflict does not exist for men, at least not in the same form'. In the end, the secret of male achievement in the world of work probably lies in the relative male insensitivity to the world of everything – and everybody – else.

Women would flourish better, then, in a work environment where the emphasis on the personal is seen as an advantage rather than a handicap. In a man-made world of work such an environment does not, on the whole, exist. Women have had to create it: they may not be properly represented at important levels of big corporations, but they are now doing remarkably well in the firms they have set up themselves. Here, they don't have to play the male game according to male rules. They are free to make up their own rules, make relationships rather than play games, run their businesses more on a basis of trust than of fear, co-operation rather than rivalry, exercise their own intellectual strategies and make the best use of their natural skills. Listen to three female proprietors:

> . . . you have to act as a mother, a confessor. Someone that they will come to and who will understand. But someone who will also be able to judge the people you have to 'carrot' and those you have to 'beat' . . . to get the best work out of them.

> We don't believe in a hierarchical structure . . . we're not a rigid and inflexible organisation. We have to know how much a person is going to work well with a small team. You can see why women do well in this. Women tend to be very good at interpersonal relations.

167

I certainly don't think a man would be so sympathetic
or sensitive to the day-to-day domestic needs of these
people. They don't have to explain anything to me . . .
they don't have to tell me a rigmarole to justify their
leave . . . Women have a greater degree of people
sensitivity and men tend to have a greater degree of
thing sensitivity . . .

Women are nature's best personnel managers; too often,
they seem to have to set up their own businesses in order to
get the job. They are also naturally better organisers in any
job involving attention to detail and good memory (the key
aspect, incidentally, to success in organising the home). But
many of these jobs involve being the personal assistant of a
male boss – clearing the undergrowth for him so that he can
see his way to those grand, strategic decisions, unimpeded by
unnecessary detail.

And that's another area of work – decision-taking – where
a woman's brain seems to put her at a disadvantage, and
where the male society of work wastes a potentially important asset.

Men and women have different approaches to decision-
taking. For the female, it is a more complex business, because
she is taking in more information and taking account of
more factors than a male. A woman's strength, and her
weakness, is her capacity to perceive, for example, the human
dimension of a business decision. Her mind, with its greater
sensitivity to personal and moral aspects, and the greater
facility with it which connects the elements to be considered,
makes the decision altogether more complex than it is for the
man, who relies more on calculated, formulaic, deductive processes.

The difference between the sexes in their approach to
problem-solving was explored by confronting men and women
with the following moral dilemma: a man's wife is dying,
and cannot afford to buy the life-saving drug – should the
man steal the drug?

The quick answer is yes – life should always have a higher

priority than property. But intriguingly men and women tackled the problem through two different strategies. The men saw it as a simple matter of justice – what was the *right* thing to do. The women asked other questions based on the principle of caring – what was the *responsible* thing to do. Couldn't the man discuss the matter with the pharmacist? Couldn't he borrow the money? What would happen to his wife if he were caught stealing the drug and sent to prison?

The questions the women raised showed that they perceived different dimensions to a problem, including the moral aspect, theft; they may come up with a less snappy answer, but it is almost certainly a more comprehensive one.

Yet the 'masculine' ethos of management insists on blunt decisions – echoing the linear organisation of their intellectual processes. It takes 'guts' to take a 'tough' decision. Yet sometimes it requires brains to realise that a decision does not actually need to be taken, or that a problem does not actually exist – and they are more likely to be female brains.

Take, for instance, the famous managerial dictum, 'If you can't stand the heat, stay out of the kitchen.' This, after only the most cursory intellectual glance, is a fatuous thing to say. Logically, it means that you should only employ chefs who don't mind sweating into the gravy. It would be a lot more sensible – though perhaps a bit less macho – to suggest that if you can't stand the heat in the kitchen, the management should install an extractor fan or an air-conditioning unit.

Yet men at work will often misinterpret as indecisive the process by which women arrive at their conclusions or demand that the question be changed, and may characterise those eventual decisions as compromised by irrational emotion. It is difficult for the male mind to comprehend the greater input of data – factual as well as emotional – which makes female decision-making a more elaborate, lengthy, and balanced affair. For men, taking decisions is actually quite a simple matter, because they are divorced from many of the human and personal dimensions of the choice, and it is easier to arrange a smaller number of things in order than a larger number.

*

The difference in their approach to a problem, or a decision, is part of an overall difference in the thought processes of the sexes. Men tend to be more analytic, extracting the essential from the circumstantial detail. Women take in the larger picture. 'Women are concerned with the context; men are forever trying to ignore it for the sake of something they can abstract from it.' A wide range of studies leads to the inevitable acknowledgement of 'clear-cut differences in attentional styles' between the sexes. Men concentrate more intently on a narrower range of items; they are capable of ignoring distractions because, with their full sensory faculties expended on the work in hand, they are deaf or blind to them. One researcher concluded that there is a life-long male predisposition towards problems which can be analysed and compartmentalised, while women are more open to 'take in' a problem in all its complexity rather than to 'attack' it at key points. All this may lead to a male superiority in providing a 'solution' to a problem; but women may be better at actually understanding the problem.

Women, because of the way their brains are wired, bring an extra element of emotional sensitivity into the equation. This ought to be an advantage in terms of the eventual decision – after all, the ultimate judgement of the law is meant to be tempered with the emotion of mercy. But the element of emotion is, in male terms, still seen as a sign of weakness. In truth, males are disadvantaged in being less well equipped to explore, acknowledge, and express their feelings. And while men feel women show their emotions too readily, women feel frustration at the way their male colleagues seem comparatively deadened to true feeling, or, at best, suppress its expression.

This sexual emotion-gap causes other problems at work. For example, men cannot understand why a female colleague should be upset; stoicism is the order of the day in man's world of work, where any display of emotion undermines the ideal of professional detachment. The great mistake men make is in assuming that, when a woman cries, she is in the same emotional state as would reduce men to tears. In fact, a woman will cry much more readily than a man, who will not 'surrender' to his emotions until compelled by extraordinary circumstances. So when a woman bursts into tears over a small matter, a man assumes that she has misidentified it as a large matter – either her judgement is unsound, or she has 'got things out of proportion'. But a woman will be hurt more than a man by a personal criticism, because for her there is less of the clear division that men make between their working and their personal lives. Conversely, a woman values a professional compliment for its own sake, whereas with men praise is only valuable if it can be parlayed into promotion or a pay-rise.

This characteristic damages women in two ways; first, because the need for approval is not often satisfied in the workplace (blame is the basic corporate currency), and secondly because praise, though rare, is cheaper than equal pay.

For men, work is to a great extent a game – a very serious game, but then, to men games are a serious business. Men are in their element when it comes to the tactical manoeuvring of office politics, the snakes and ladders of corporate career structures. From their earliest years, they have delighted in play which is, according to one American sociologist 'more complex than girls' play, as indexed by . . . role differentiation, interdependence between players, size of play group, explicitness of goals, number of rules, and team formation.' The French psychologist Jean Piaget wrote that he did not find a single girls' game that had as elaborate an organisation of rules as the boys' game of marbles.

Men come to the world of work with an acceptance of a world of arbitrary rules, and an experience of working collectively with people they may not like, but who are useful to them. Women who, as girls, chose their friends with much greater, and more committed, care, try to like the people they work with, understanding their needs, breaking down the barriers of status. Women form groups. Men form teams.

One young woman struggling in a man's world of

work says: 'I think team sports teach you that there are a lot of jerks in powerful positions who you have to listen to and find some way of accomplishing your goals within theirs. You are an individual but have to work with the group.'

Ironically, relationships – in which women have the un-doubted supremacy over men – are easier for men to form at work; probably because they are not genuine relationships of feeling, but relationships of function. The backslapping and banter of the male world of work has little to do with deep personal sympathy.

Their very behaviour at work can be different for men and women. Because they see it as a game, men lubricate the machinery of the daily grind with jokes, teases and verbal rough-and-tumble. Male jocularity often has an edge of chal-lenge and aggression, which women either feel hurt by or simply don't find funny; and this leads to 'You know what her trouble is? No sense of humour.'

Men and women don't laugh at the same things, and they get upset by different things. Studies of worry and depression show that 'anxiety and neuroticism have different correlates in males and females, thus they have different meanings.' Women are generally found to be more anxious than men; the males only approach the female anxiety level in problems where their achievement is being put to the test – sitting an important examination, starting a new job, or giving an oral report.

At work, the man is almost literally 'one of the boys' again. He may not be challenging his peers to pull the funniest face or hold his breath the longest, but he is offering them the challenge of the biggest deal, the fastest promotion. That sort of competition holds no such compelling attraction for women; in fact, winning itself is less important. Young males are reluctant to participate in mixed-sex sport – be-cause the level of competitiveness falls when girls are included. For many men, every encounter in their profes-sional or personal life is a contest in which there must be a clear-cut winner and a loser. Maintaining the competitive edge is a basic masculine need. But women, given the choice,

172

'prefer sharing rather than seizing, smoothing rather than confrontation'. Hierarchies, structures and status mean less to them; but, like the rules and goals of the playground, they mean everything to men.

So, in important respects, men and women are not playing the same game at work. They have different attitudes to the rules, the teams, and the objective; which, in this respect at least, doesn't leave men and women very much else in common.

The tragedy of the differences between male and female at work is that they are denied, suppressed, or negatively exploited. Exploiting the differences in a positive way could yield astonishing results. Clinching a business deal, for instance, is usually a male preserve – and he has the benefit of competitive aggression. But if a women were part of the negotiating team, she would bring completely new insights to the task; with her emotional X-ray vision she is often able to pick up those discreet cues from the opposition's demeanour and tone of voice.

In industry, we have already suggested that labour negotiations and personnel management would seem to be areas in which women have a vast potential contribution to make; the men could huff and puff and sulk and threaten, while the women could get the problems resolved, if not solved.

A study of women-led businesses finds consistently good labour relations characterised by an absence of petty rules and regulations and hierarchical relationships – the very things that mean so much to men. The women bosses brought an 'intuitive' insight to bear upon the personal problems of the staff – an intuition which is simply a woman's superior interest in her fellow human beings – and developed a 'maternalistic' style of management which seems to be as successful as the now defunct, though not necessarily disastrous, paternalist style of days gone by.

Interestingly, a study of women who had set up their own businesses found that they had little time for conventional feminism.

Feminism? I don't like it. I think it's unnecessary. I was one of the first women to really start a big business on my own and I certainly did not have the feeling that I wanted to do it for women . . . I'm for all of us, not just for women.

The overwhelming complaint of successful women is that feminism identifies male goals and male methods as the ideal for women; that it denies the sexual difference, denies the very essence, and thus the very value, of the feminine. Some feel that so great is the difference between male and female attitudes to achievement that women are uncompetitive not because of their fear of failure but because of their fear of success, which would imply that they were somehow unfeminine.

Management itself would benefit from the male and female combination of stick and carrot motivation. At board level, membership should be reassessed to embrace people who are not simply very good financial directors (who may or may not be women) but who have proven success in other areas. They would be able to cast fresh, oblique light on old problems, and understand what makes people – and by extension companies – tick.

This sort of equality cannot be legislated for, partly because our legislators confuse equality with similarity; as yet, it is socially problematical to acknowledge what is scientifically true – that men and women are different. The hope lies in the simple self-interest of trades, professions, businesses and corporations. It would be a sad reflection on the intelligence of the world of work if, having understood the separate strengths and strategies that men and women can bring to bear, it ignored the potential of combining them.

Leadership, though it can be acquired, does not come naturally to the average woman, another study acknowledges. Yet she masters the art and adapts it in a particularly feminine way; mothering not in the sense of suffocating, but in encouraging, stimulating, supporting and eventually trusting and letting go.

> My whole philosophy (as a mother) was to find out the
> strength of the children and to go in that direction, and
> I apply the same philosophy to my employees. A person
> may be hired for one area and we see how he turns out
> and then move him on to something else. But once we
> trust him in the job he is left to do it on his own with
> the least interference.

Women industrialists, as well as Mrs Thatcher, are not in the least apologetic about running their enterprises, or the country, on the economics of housekeeping. Many prided themselves on running the business the same way that they ran the home – 'no waste and no extravagance'.

Most women have always known that they are not like men, that they see the world by the light of different values, different principles, different priorities. Men's minds are set, before birth, on a system of seeing the world through rules, codes, structures, things. It is men who feel driven to discover the secret clockwork of Creation itself, the laws of physics, motion, gravity, or to invent rules, procedures and constitutions to impose on the unruly society of mankind.

Women, while eminently the more law-abiding sex, are more interested in the personal, the individual; they recognise the social sense of the laws which benefit the human being – but when there is a conflict between the priorities of the law and the individual, women will champion the individual's case. It is women, more than men, who see nuclear weapons as an evil threatening life; men, more than women, who explain the theories of mutual deterrence and insist that laws protecting missiles must be obeyed.

There is a desperate, unwritten subtext to the nuclear debate; most men believe that, with nuclear weapons, they have the best chance in hundreds of years of not dying in the mud on the end of a sharp and rusty weapon. But with the coming of nuclear weapons, war has become much more personal to women; they, and their children, for the first time will very probably die in it as cheaply as men always have done.

In the past masculine values of power could not be changed

by women; for the very women who could attain the positions of power necessary to change them were motivated by, or imbued with, those masculine values. Today, more and more women are succeeding, especially in businesses they themselves have created – where they can make – or tear up, the rules. At the same time, intelligent businesses are learning the value of gentler management; that the businessman who neglects his wife and health for the sake of the company is not necessarily the company's best bet. Feminine virtues seem to be good for business.

But only the cleverest businessmen have realised this so far.

SUMMARY

WHEN A PROMINENT feminist friend of ours heard about this book, her eyes narrowed and she said, not without a hint of menace, 'It had better be good.'

She assumed, as many have done, that because this is a book about sexual differences, it must somehow be a book against women.

Untangling those assumptions (for we believe that they are in an unholy tangle), we find a political and social view – that men and women should be treated equally – somehow dependent upon a belief that men and women are the same. They are not. There is no longer any excuse, save mental indolence, to believe that

> many of the generally understood distinctions between
> the sexes in the more significant areas of role and
> temperament, not to mention status, have in fact
> essentially cultural rather than biological bases.

This isn't a prescriptive book; it merely explains how the brains of the sexes are different, and attempts to link those differences with the observably different behaviour of men and women – which men and women have been celebrating or bemoaning for centuries.

But the introduction of science into the sexual debate will inevitably mean more of the chaotic thinking that led American feminist Betty Friedan to write:

> Even if they are sorely handicapped by lack of
> testosterone, it is inescapably necessary for women at
> this stage in human evolution to move to equality in
> society.

Betty Friedan fails to see that a lack of testosterone means that many women may not want to move anywhere in particular, and so do not perceive themselves as handicapped. As Michael Levin, Professor of Philosophy of City College, New York, writes, athletes may be handicapped by a muddy track or weak hamstrings, but cannot be said to be handicapped by their own indifference to winning. Describing this feminist view that women really *ought* to want to emulate males, he writes,

> . . . such a view makes no literal sense, but a kind of
> emotional sense for those who see so much value in
> male pursuits that they cannot believe that women do
> not want what men do.

Even when difference is agreed, we also anticipate anger from those who believe that the difference between the sexes is the product of social conditioning.

Yet an hours-old girl baby behaves differently from an hours-old boy baby, and surely society doesn't act quite that fast. It is not society that makes women's eyes more sensitive to the longwave spectrum of light. At one week old, girls, but not boys, can distinguish between the sound of an infant's cry and general noise played at the same volume. Again, society was not coaching beside the crib.

Indeed, when you'd expect to see an adult influence at work, it seems to operate contrariwise. Baby boys receive significantly more affection and direct physical contact from their mothers, but nevertheless prefer objects to people, and show poorer speech development. In a telling example, we saw how some abnormal children are born looking like girls, and are brought up as girls – yet when puberty arrives they stand revealed as male, and behave as such; the instant that their male genitalia arrive, society's imprint disappears as if it had been written upon water. The imprint of the hormones in the womb is indelible.

What this means for women is that they will be more sensitive than men to sound, smell, taste and touch. Women pick up nuances of voice and music more readily, and girls acquire the skills of language, fluency and memory earlier than boys. Females are more sensitive to the social and personal context, are more adept at tuning to peripheral information contained in expression and gesture, and process sensory and verbal information faster. They are less rule-bound than men.

Men are better at the skills that require spatial ability. They are more aggressive, competitive, and self-assertive. They need the hierarchy and the rules, for without them they would be unable to tell if they were top or not – and that is of vital importance to most men.

These differences may account for the controversial assertion that there have been 'no women of genius, and very few of considerable talent in chess, mathematics, composing, and other pursuits for which a high-level abstracting aptitude is a necessary condition'. There will be those who look to the historical, sexist tyranny of society as an explanation; yet this sexually tyrannical society has 'allowed' the development of female genius in other fields, not associated with abstract reasoning, such as literature and the performing arts. While we are about it, we might also jettison the idea that women 'fail' in this field because of their lack of male drive. Why, then, do 'women equal or surpass men on all cognitive tests *not* related to mathematical reasoning or associated aptitudes'? The woman who cannot follow this logic is likely to be living proof of its validity.

The argument about the existence of brain sex differences has been won. It now begins to seem a little strange that the battle ever had to be fought at all, when men and women are so obviously different in physique and behaviour:

> It seems unrealistic to deny any longer the existence of
> male and female brain differences. Just as there are
> physical dissimilarities between males and females (size,

179

body shape, skeleton, teeth, age of puberty, etc.) there
are equally dramatic differences in brain functioning.

There is solid and consistent evidence from scientists all over
the world that a biochemical influence in the womb determines and directs the structure and function of our brains.
Through the influence of the hormones the brain cells 'acquire a "set" . . . highly resistant to change after birth'. Male
hormone organises the developing brain into a male pattern
which leads to male behaviour. Absence of male hormone
means that the brain persists in a female pattern, resulting in
a female pattern of behaviour. This organisation of the brain
into a male or female neural network is permanent; it can
only be modified by altering the hormonal milieu of the
womb.

As we have shown, girls who have been exposed to male
hormone in the womb become more assertive and confident,
preferring, as children, the company of boys and participa-
tion in active, outdoor activity. They are less interested than
their sisters in dolls, fantasy play, story-telling and talking
with other girls – and, later on, less interested in motherhood.
Boys exposed to female hormone in the womb have their
behaviour tilted towards a more female pattern. They are
less aggressive, assertive, and athletic.

There are also morphological differences between the
brains of men and women – that is, a difference in structure
or form. In men, the brain is more tightly and efficiently
organised for the processing of visual and spatial information, and for mathematical reasoning. Men, being stronger
in this area, call upon it more in their approach to the world
– analysing and theorising. In the same way, women's brains
are better designed for skills involving detail, sequential
tasks, and verbal fluency. Consequently the canvas of their
'world' is not like the men's bold abstracts; it's more like a
closely observed miniature.

Women have more connections between the two hemispheres of the brain. This helps their left- and right-hand
skills to be more in touch with each other. Sometimes this
very conversation between the two halves of the brain may

be confusing and may hinder efficiency – rather like trying to concentrate when someone is chattering away in the background – but the advantage is an enhanced ability to relate, perceive and communicate verbal and non-verbal information and emotion.

While the sex of the brain is determined at the time of neural organisation in the womb, the difference of brain sex doesn't show fully until the hormones of puberty come on stream. Then, the ebb and flow of the hormones activates and accentuates brain differences. In the extremes it will push men to violence, and women to irrational and disruptive swings of mood and behaviour. More commonly, it will give men more confidence, concentration, single-mindedness, and the channelled aggression of motivation and ambition, while in women it will stimulate the need and desire to form and maintain closer relationships with the people around them.

In men the level of male hormone at puberty also affects the efficiency of the brain. Levels which are too high or too low inhibit spatial and mathematical skills, in the same way that too rich, or too weak, a fuel mixture makes an engine run less efficiently. The mathematical genius is likely to have intermediate levels of male hormone.

In old age, as the hormonal springs begin to run dry, those differences in the brain that they accentuated begin to lose their sharp focus. Women tend to become more assertive and aggressive, because the female hormones lose their vigour, and their power to neutralise the masculine hormone present in all women: there is a biological basis for the stereotype of the whiskery and crotchety old woman. Men become less aggressive as their testosterone level drops, and, in turn, have less power to neutralise their own naturally occurring female hormones; as they contemplate the garden, they wonder why they wasted so much time struggling up the corporate career ladder.

Science, then, can offer an explanation for the way in which men and women come to be different. Some sexual politicians will deny the validity of the science; indeed, a few scientists will argue that sexual politics invalidates the science itself. One author maintains that we are sexually so strongly

181

conditioned and the sexual atmosphere is so highly charged, that, consciously or unconsciously, the researchers and their research are biased: all the thousands of clinical studies are meaningless; the morphological brain differences inconsequential; the countless academic articles so many wasted trees, pulped to perpetuate a scientific fallacy.

Others believe that even if the science is true, the truth has no right to be heard, because of the abuse to which it may be put. A Norwegian physiologist laments both attitudes:

> . . . it seems nevertheless frightening that well-educated people, some of whom have reached the highest levels within the scientific community, demonstrate ignorance of, or else simply seem to deny, elementary biological facts. Some . . . hold the view that even if behaviour differences between the sexes should be in part the result of biological differences between them, research discussions in this field should not take place because of the risk of supplying racists and undemocratic elements alibis for their views.

The writer of that paper believes science has a duty to resist this view; firstly, because it is unscientific, and secondly because it hampers our sense of justice, which can only be striven for through an understanding of our biologically determined potentials and limitations.

> Neglect of basic facts about human nature may be at least as dangerous as the risk of misinterpretation of these facts.

The argument, and it is one to which we subscribe, is that we are more likely to make the best out of the world that we have once we understand how it is made, rather than by trying to construct the world that we want from materials of which we are ignorant.

Ignorance, or denial, of difference has actually made the world a worse place for women. The American anthropologist Professor Lionel Tiger argues that the almost universally accepted notion that males and females are equal has led, in practical terms, to greater inequality. If you reject the evidence about sexual differences, you don't change the institutions or structures in a way that would accommodate those differences. So, 'at the moment, it is women who must accommodate themselves, and they are being asked to compete with men in male-orientated institutions. The net result of this is their continued deprivation and a recently increased resentment and anxiety.'

Tiger gives a telling example: the performance of young women writing examinations drops by as much as 14 per cent, depending on the timing of their menstrual cycle. Some first-class female brains are condemned by their biology, and the accident of the calendar, to a second-class result. This cannot in any sense be just; yet many women would rather accept this injustice than press for an examination system which would acknowledge, and take into account, this female biological disadvantage. If a similar proportion of men suffered a similar handicap, it is a fair bet that legislation would have been passed by now to mitigate its effects.

If sex differences, once acknowledged, are deemed to be wrong, hurtful, and unjust, there is a way to eliminate them. It is not, however, the way of education, propaganda or precept. (For close on two thousand years one strongly motivated, intellectually rigorous, and morally coherent philosophy has played a major part in Western civilisation; but there is still some way to go before Christianity persuades us universally to love one another, before envy and adultery are renounced, and the meek inherit the earth.)

No, if we want to eliminate sex differences we must use the means which created those differences in the first place; we must change the biological cocktail of Creation. We have, as they say, the technology. We will introduce selected sperm to suitable ova in clinically sterile surroundings; and having decided what our societal norm should be (men less aggressive, or women more so; women less responsive to the demands of parenthood, or men more so) we can sluice the developing foetal mind with the relevant synthetic chemical hormones. We can also decide the appropriate model for

183

society's sexuality – we may choose whether or not to allow homosexuality to exist, we can probably eliminate most extreme sexual perversions, and we can probably chemically tweak the male and female hypothalamus to produce a greater correspondence of libido. (As well as this re-engineering of the brain, we will also need regular topping up with additional hormones, or hormone neutralising agents.)

The absurdity of the effort illustrates the absurdity of the enterprise; yet well-intentioned politicians and educationalists are still determined, if by less drastic means, to engineer the demise of the sexual stereotype. In the progressive schoolroom, children read of princesses slaying dragons and rescuing princes, and picture books depict female fire-fighters and truck drivers. An anti-sexist teacher training pack suggests that the class be set projects like writing a non-sexist composition beginning with the words, 'Nadine put on the boxing gloves and stepped into the ring.' Girls should not be praised for excelling in neatness, nor boys receive more reprimands than girls for unruly behaviour – 'unless their behaviour clearly warrants this response'. 'Nonsexist teaching is a total process. It should involve all aspects of the classroom environment.'

There are two problems here. First of all, it inevitably involves telling lies in the name of education – worse still, lies that are palpably recognisable as such by the children. Secondly, this 'total process' would seem to leave very little time for learning anything else.

Perhaps the most fatuous example of sex-erasure is the word-processing programme which automatically inserts an 'or she' after the operator has typed a 'he'. This ensures that sexist writing will be automatically eliminated – the ultimate, mechanical tokenisation of the issue.

If it's social justice that we are worried about – and we should be – it makes infinitely more sense to reform our educational system in a way that acknowledges, and adapts to, our basic sex differences. If it means anything, equality of opportunity means the opportunity for equal, individual fulfilment. The alternative is a handicap system, with the brightest children being forced to receive less instruction, or, at exam time, being given pens designed to run out of ink every ten minutes.

There are practical ways in which we can, to some extent, redress the biological balance. If we genuinely want to encourage more women into engineering, and make maths more accessible to girls in school, we can surely find a way to teach it in a manner better adapted to the female brain. It might not work, but experiments could be made with a more verbal and less symbolic approach – maths without blackboards. Because of their comparative indifference to things, how they are assembled and what makes them work, and their greater bias towards the personal and collective, maybe girls, at a very early age, should be encouraged to investigate the structure and functioning of mechanical objects in groups, rather than individually.

After all, we have proof that children can overcome an initial handicap; boys suffer, at first, from an education unconsciously biased to the female, yet eventually learn to read and write and speak fluently, because their parents insist that they do so, and worry if these skills are not acquired by an early age. But 'no such insistence induces the female to learn about spatial-mechanical relationships; thus the male overcomes his initial handicap at school, but by the time certain spatial skills are required by the curriculum, the female may be too old to acquire them.'

It's a matter for the educationalists to ponder; but one thing is for certain – nothing is going to change if teachers persist in the illusion that girls are natural mathematicians, whose talents are suppressed by some sort of societal, mathematical machismo ethic, whose influence, by stupendous coincidence, happens to correspond with the ebb and flow of their hormones.

We can only begin to compensate for these differences by acknowledging them. If we acknowledge, for instance, that boys are by nature more boisterous, selfish, aggressive and dominant than girls, we might try to modify that nature by example, restraint, punishment or bribery. But we must first accept that boys *will* be boys, and, if we so desire, they will have to be changed from what they naturally are.

But, as we have said, this is not a prescriptive book, except in that it argues strongly that we accept who we are before arguing about what we should be.

> We ignore brain sex differences at the risk of confusing biology with sociology, and wishful thinking with scientific facts. The question is not 'are there brain differences?' but rather 'what is going to be our response to those differences?'

Or, in the American sociologist Dr Alice Rossi's words,

> An ideology that does not confront this basic issue is an exercise in wishful thinking, and a social science that does not confront it is sterile.

Ignoring the differences carries another risk – the risk of creating deep and unnecessary anger, and frustration. For what will happen if we are educated to believe that all men and women are equally capable of excellence in every sphere, and then find, as find we surely will, that this is not the case? Women, almost certainly, have not achieved all that they are capable of achieving; yet there may come a time when all social constraints have gone, all prejudices have been obliterated, and still women are not doing 'as well' as men. In the same way, the relative performance levels of men and women at tennis, or marathon running, have stabilised. As far as the gender gap is concerned, 'there has been no appreciable closing in any sport requiring strength, jumping or throwing, except when females have masculinised their bodies with steroids . . .'

So, with the best efforts of all concerned, men may still be society's technocrats, mechanics and inventors – 99 per cent of all patents applied for today are registered by men, and it is hard to see what would bring that figure down to 50 per cent. It may well be that, in the world of work, the present division of labour is found to represent a natural predisposition, rather than an artificial distortion of potential. It may be true that women would make better neurosurgeons than men, and it is certainly true that there have not been more female neurosurgeons in the past because of the male bias of the profession. But to reach the heights of a profession of this nature requires a single-minded desire to be top and for every woman who actually wants to be a top neurosurgeon there will forever be ten men who really want to be top neurosurgeons too. You can remove every obstacle in the path of success, but you cannot ensure that people will actually choose to follow that path; you can encourage aspiration, but you cannot inject ambition.

In any case, most people, men or women, fail to reach the top. Success usually demands a mixture of talent and aggression, a rare enough combination. Most men don't have it – very, very few are talented enough to be top scientist, captain of industry, prime minister or president. Most women don't have the elusive combination either; and they are additionally handicapped by the fact that those sex differences which may give them an abundance of talent do not, on average, also endow them with the aggression, ambition and obsessive drive necessary for its ultimate fulfilment. In the world as it is, the female politician is just as strongly motivated as her male equivalent, just as the six-foot-tall woman is as tall as the six-foot-tall man and, of course, just as rare.

It has been tellingly put that 'men and women invest their human capital differently'. For most women, material and career success are comparatively unimportant – there is more to life than climbing the corporate ladder. They haven't been conditioned by society to achieve this excellent, sensible and honest perception; indeed the strongest conditioning at the moment is the influence of successful women who maintain that their fellow women should feel badly about not doing better.

Some feminists argue that the differences between men and women can be minimised by a deliberate distortion of society. Men and women could compete on equal terms, and with equal success, in the marathon for example, if the finishing line for women were 11 per cent nearer the start. That is, after all, what affirmative action means, and it may be a perfectly reasonable strategy.

What we want to achieve is not compensation but an
improvement of the position of women until society
is fair to them and, as a matter of fact, probably the
best way to achieve this is to appoint to positions of
importance women who are rather less good at the
work than the men who are in competition with
them

The argument is that more women would do better once
they saw how well women could do – for without doubt, if
women could reach prominent positions without the necessity of striving for them, they would do the job perfectly
well. Artificially contrived role-models would widen the horizons of feminine aspiration.

This would, of course, be unjust to men, but then some
would say that men have been unjust to women for a very
long time and so at least there would be a just allocation of
injustice. An artificially contrived quota system would also
involve a degree of inefficiency; only about one fifth of
American girls in the elementary grades reach the average
level of male performance in tests of spatial ability – and,
according to the US Employment Service, all classes of engineering and most scientific and technical occupations require spatial ability in the top 10 per cent of the population.
So we would have to accept cars and space shuttles which
were even less well designed than at present. Would you let
your children fly on an affirmative action airline?

But before we go too far along this road – and Western
society has already gone some way, and is under pressure to
go further – maybe we should ask ourselves this question:
isn't it possible, or at least conceivable, that we already have
a society where everyone who *wants* to be a top engineer,
and everyone who has the talent to *be* a top engineer,
probably already *can* be a top engineer? May we not have
reached a plateau where women actually do have an education equal to that of men, and simply do not choose to
follow male pursuits? And that if anything militates against
this, it is more likely to be financial hardship rather than a
gender-based deprivation? That maybe the dragon to be slain

is not sexual prejudice, but good, old-fashioned social dis-advantage?

Before Saint Georgina sets out, it's worth asking if her mission is really necessary – if the dragon may not be a phantom. After all, this measurement of value – my job's more important than yours – is essentially a male sport, and not one which women, in the main, have ever taken very seriously. Female rats, after all, may perform less well in the maze because the rat race is not a particularly congenial activity in which to participate. Most women do a great amount of work at home, and most men do a different sort of work in the office or on the factory floor, and in truth one sort of work is not necessarily 'better' than the other. One happens to be paid, but that should not confer a special sort of honour on the work involved. Prostitutes are paid, but that does not make their work better than that of mothers.

There are practical reasons why the sexes cannot un-dertake the same work. There is no reason, however, why we could not value the different work of men and women equally. It has been argued that while men are paid for their ability to elaborate their mechanical expertise into complex edifices and machines, women should be valued for their skill in understanding and predicting human action, and their ability to sense motives and emotions. 'Communicative and spatial-mechanical skills, intelligently and logically employed, are equally necessary for the preservation of human civilisation.'

In the commercial world, then, we could try to find a way which values and exploits the skills of perception where women excel. Exactly how this unique contribution can be deployed and employed is a little more problematical. What's for sure at present is that in intelligent, non-sexist corpora-tions women tend to be promoted according to the degree to which they can play the male game, and suppress their uniquely female skills. There is a danger that a woman will gain admiration from her male colleagues and superiors because of the way, for example, she may put the company before her domestic responsibilities (how often, after all, do men seek advice about how to reconcile their marriage and their career?). But a woman's emotional strengths are an asset in themselves, which ought not to be sidelined for the supposed good of the corporation.

The thinking corporation should ask itself why it is wasting, and how it should capitalise upon, the unique skills of 50 per cent of its workforce. It is failing to exploit a woman's underlying superiority in her knowledge and understanding of how the world of people works.

In the unwaged economy of the home, the value of domestic effort has to be appreciated by men, but more importantly by women themselves. Here, one is not talking in the fatuous terms of putting a cash value on bed-making, shopping, or breast-feeding, but in relation to a self-value which can only be expressed in the ultimate currency of happiness and satisfaction. Levin writes (with a touch of hyperbole) that 'one can read the whole corpus of feminist writing without learning that most women find motherhood their greatest satisfaction'. Most women not only enjoy parenthood more than most men, but are also rather better at it. They are certainly better suited to it than men. Feeding, clothing, and educating the successor generation is as noble a task as earning the money to pay for its food, clothing, and education. It is also, ultimately, as rewarding, but most men have to wait until they are grandparents to appreciate the fact.

Some will find what we have written a justification for conservatism and the sexual status quo, and they will be wrong. We do not consecrate the natural, just because it is biologically true; men, for instance, have a natural disposition to homicide and promiscuity, which is not a recipe for the happy survival of society.

If this book is a prescription for anything – and it isn't intended to be – it's for a radical rethink of the relationship between the sexes, a relationship we can at last base on fact rather than theory. With the knowledge of who we are and why, we can clear the landscape of the clutter of prejudicial nonsense. There is no point, for instance, in laws and educational theories which both deny the differences between men and women, and then seek to eradicate them. We can clear the air, too, of the atmosphere of sexual ridicule and re-crimination. Women need not blame their supposed failure on men, and men need neither fear nor deride the efforts of women to beat them at their own game.

And when the air and the ground are cleared, maybe we can hope that men and women will be more honest about how they actually feel, and happier to be themselves. They may be relieved that they no longer have to strive towards the inevitable disappointment of something which in their hearts they know to be vain and illusory. Liberated by honesty rather than imprisoned by self-deception, they will have the confidence to strike their own balance between love and ambition, tenderness and striving. We can hope for an end to the slogans, for slogans do not change facts, and an end to the sterile pursuit of artificial equality; an abandonment of the arduous and unnatural process of denial and, instead, the enjoyment of our natural selves; the greening of a new relationship between men and women; a celebration of difference.

EPILOGUE TO THE AMERICAN EDITION

THIS EPILOGUE is a prologue, to all the work that is yet to come. Since the European publication of *Brain Sex*, new scientific research not only confirms what we have written about gender differences, but has widened our horizons and deepened our understanding. The knowledge is expanding so fast, at such an exponential rate, that we, as mere chroniclers of science, are hard put to keep up with it. We are at the end of the beginning, and at the beginning of the fascinating voyage of discovery into who we are and what makes us different.

In spite of the grim misgivings of our feminist friends, the sky didn't fall with the publication of *Brain Sex*, although there was the occasional purse-lipped review to the effect that the book should never have been written, and the inevitable over-simplification of the incorrigible British tabloid press (BRAINY BIRDS HAVE BLOKES' BRAINS, read one headline.) The very existence of the research still provokes anger and suspicion, according to Marie De LaCoste, now at Yale Medical school, who admits that one of her papers 'really hurt my career as opposed to enhancing it.' But like the mythical many-headed Hydra, just when those who are dogmatically opposed to gender difference research feel they've finally decapitated the enemy, a new head pops up in the form of fresh evidence of brain sex difference. The most welcome new evidence came in the area where knowledge was scantiest, and where the known differences were smallest; in the morphology, the physical structure of the male and female brain.

Some of these findings are as yet still too particular to analyse, like the confirmation of differences in the cell structure of the hypothalamus, that key control centre of mating and maternal behaviour, and where cyclical hormonal flow is regulated in men, and accelerated in women. Indeed, the research is so new that scientists are having to create names for the cell groups they are studying, like astronomers of old discovering and christening new galaxies. This exploration of mankind's inner space has already revealed two- to threefold sex-related size differences in cell structures. There is confirmation, too, that these physical differences are related to the exposure to varying degrees of hormone while the embryonic brain is developing in the womb. These areas have only just been named – the Interstitial Nuclei of the Anterior Hypothalamus, or INAH – so perhaps it is premature to speculate on their significance, but even cautious scientists believe they may have discovered those areas that Dörner hypothesised, the mating centres of the human brain. Independent studies have discovered significant differences in the nucleus of the nerve cells which control the muscles governing copulation. These are just two more pieces of the jigsaw of sexual knowledge; we cannot know the exact nature or size of the completed puzzle, but it is beginning to take shape.

Still in the area of physical difference, there are fresh findings in the area of the corpus callosum, that trunk of connective fibres which link one hemisphere of the brain to the other. Because brain functions are more spread about in women than in the tidier brains of men, the telephone exchange needed to link these scattered functions ought to be larger. Recently, an area called the splenum, in the back third of the corpus callosum, has been confirmed as being comparatively larger in women. Sandra Witleson has also published fascinating new research on another area next to the splenum, the isthmus. The isthmus contains the axons, or fibres which link verbal control areas in one hemisphere with visuo-spatial skill centres in the corresponding area of the other hemisphere.

Witleson thinks that this 'greater interhemispherical communication in women' can be related to women's observable superiority in communication with other people, while the relative poverty of men's central brain exchange has an effect on the male advantage in spatial skills; women, with this better link to the spatial side, can combine a visual imagination with their vocabulary, while men can focus better on practical images, because there's less 'interference' from the verbal side of their brains. The lesson seems to be: Let the men figure out how to solve the three-dimensional problem – how, for instance, to get from A to B or pack a trunk – but let the women explain it to everyone else. Most families at the outset of a vacation will be familiar with the phenomenon. It could also provide a clue as to why there have been more women poets and novelists than women painters and sculptresses.

The findings are reinforced by the discovery that the same comparatively larger area in the corpus callosum occurs in some men – specifically those who are left-handed. It is known that left-handed men have their brain functions less tidily and exclusively arranged than their right-handed male counterparts. Disposition of their brain functions is closer to the female than the tighter male pattern. But more later on the brains of left-handers. The observation in men and women confirms that a more widely-spread disposition of brain function, whether in the female or (left-handed) male brain, is accompanied by a correspondingly more developed corpus callosum. In women, left- or right-handedness makes no difference to the thickness of this bundle of nerves, since their brain functions are naturally more scattered than in the male, regardless of left- or right-handedness. A by-product of this research is the conclusion that there must be a brain sex difference in what determines hand preference in men and women. (For hand preference and sexual orientation studies, see later.)

'This anatomical difference is probably just the tip of the iceberg,' says Sandra Witleson, referring specifically to her findings in the isthmus, but other parts of the iceberg are emerging by the minute. By measuring brain activity scientists in Mexico have shown that while women use both hemispheres in solving geometric and mathematical problems, men, more successfully, used more of the specialised right-hand hemisphere – and greater success in higher mathematical problem solving was related to how tightly focussed the specialised activity was kept. The same study confirmed that women are superior at transferring 'information about the external world or of more abstract representations' between the two halves of the brain. Men were 'relatively disadvantaged.'

Similar exciting and intriguing findings arose from the study of blood-flow through the cortex. Cecile Naylor, a neurophysiologist with the Bowman Gray School of Medicine, Winston-Salem, North Carolina, admits that her discovery was accidental; she was simply studying the general brain geography of language when she found that men and women were using different parts of their brain while speaking. The traditional view (traditional, because for so long the male pattern has been accepted as the brain pattern for *Homo sapiens* in general) is that speech depends primarily on the connection between a space in the left temporal lobe called Wernicke's area, and a part in the left frontal lobe called Broca's area.

Wernicke's manages language-making and comprehension, while Broca's calls up the mechanisms of the tongue, throat and jaw to control the mechanical production of speech. Naylor found that pattern held good for men — but in women, evidence from the blood-flow monitor showed that other areas were being brought into play during female communication. Specifically, they were an area behind Wernicke's known to manage sight and sound input, and an area over in the right hemisphere involved with the experiencing and expression of emotion. 'Women are recruiting more areas of the brain that enable them to use more strategies than men,' says Naylor. Men, it seems, are the sex who say the first thing that comes into their heads, while women communicate by calling on a much wider repertoire.

Taken all together the evidence paints a comprehensive picture of a busier and wider interchange of information in the female brain. Shall we call it a freer and richer imagination? Witleson is cautious: 'What our results show is that there is a difference. It doesn't mean it's better to be male or female....' (The difference also has a dimension of age, at the beginning and the end of life. Males lose many of the axons, the connecting nerves between the hemispheres contained in the corpus callosum, while in the womb and in the first seven months of life, while testosterone levels are high; also, as they get older, the corpus callosum withers earlier in men than among women, decreasing the communication between the two halves of the brain.)

Like the female brain, the whole world of neurophysiology seems to be buzzing with the exchange of information and fresh discoveries. Biologists like Anne Fausto-Sterling of Brown University ('The evidence [of brain difference] is so fragmentary and so weak, it ought to stop there') are finding themselves increasingly isolated, stranded, and beached on the shores of dogma. The future, scientifically and politically, seems to belong more to the likes of Sandra Witleson, who says

> the sexes are different and it does no good to assume
> that they're not. We're not going to help equal
> opportunity when we assume both are equally good in
> all aspects, when it may well be that there are certain
> things each sex is somewhat better at.

The way men and women behave, and the difference in that behaviour, is not simply a matter of brain differences; it is a function of the interplay between the hormones and the brain, just as the intercession of the hormones first 'sexes' or 'wires' the brain. Since the publication of *Brain Sex* in Europe, further hormonal research throughout the world has confirmed what we already knew, and enriched our understanding.

Levels of testosterone have now been linked, more closely than ever, to career choice, attitude and achievement. Using a more accessible and accurate means of assessing testosterone levels from saliva rather than blood, Professor James Dabbs of Georgia State University compared male hormone levels among lawyers. He divided the profession into those who worked in court, and those who pursued a more sedentary, office-bound vocation. It will come as no surprise to those who have read the preceding pages that the trial lawyers had significantly higher levels. Women lawyers, when tested, had higher levels of male hormone than were found in housewives.

As in the case of higher mathematical ability, the highest levels of success correspond with testosterone at below the highest levels found. In a separate investigation into Vietnam veterans, Professor Dabbs found that those in the top 10 per cent of the testosterone range were twice as likely as their comrades to be engaged in antisocial behaviour such as drug abuse, trouble with the law, and fighting. The levels in those displaying such criminal behaviour was just slightly higher than those found in the most successful trial lawyers; the close affinity between the criminal and the sharpest legal mind has never been so intriguingly illustrated. Professor Dabbs' future plans include an assessment into the correlation between high testosterone levels and the success or failure of door-to-door salesmen.

We are not, of course, the prisoners of our hormones; society and self-discipline may channel them in different paths. A high testosterone level may lead one man to steal a car, another to smash it, and a third to buy the fastest one. Those with the highest testosterone levels are, however, two and a half times more likely to be in the disadvantaged levels of society, with less opportunity to buy the car in the first place. Cause and effect are hard to disentangle – very high hormone levels tend to disqualify men from high achievement because of the antisocial behaviour associated with it.

A new series of testosterone experiments has been conducted on both men and women by a team including Doreen Kimura, a pioneer in the field of brain sex difference. In tasks involving the perception of size and shape, as well as higher mathematical reasoning, the same relationship was observed – men with very high male hormone levels succeeded less well than those with lower levels, who in turn did better than those with subnormal degrees of testosterone. In women, the correlation was more straightforward – at all levels, the more testosterone, the better the result; because women obviously have less male hormone than men, they do not reach those levels where the sheer amount of male hormone seems, for men, to be counter-productive. In other tasks where women traditionally and naturally outperform men, like verbal and communication skills, testosterone levels made no difference, although there is a hint that high levels may have negative effects on some verbal tests. Where nature has equipped women with a natural superiority for their sex, it is hardly surprising that 'wrong sex'

197

hormones are irrelevant or deleterious. Kimura's study is significant in that it is the first study of the effects of male hormone on normal women, as opposed to women with a genetic irregularity. She admits that in biochemical terms the science is in its infancy, but 'we may speculate that testosterone enhances right-hemisphere functioning,' and that the effect of the hormones in early brain organisation has a crucial impact on right-brain skills.

On that same subject of prenatal brain organisation, two new studies from teams at the Kinsey Institute headed by June Reinisch consolidate and confirm the evidence we have already reviewed. There will be, however, exciting evidence to come in the longer term; already there are techniques to monitor, *in utero*, normal fetal exposure to testosterone. Linking that evidence to subsequent behaviour will provide a key to our understanding which has so far been available only from studies of abnormal exposure of the foetus to high levels of androgens, overdoses due to drugs or adrenal malfunctions.

Work on brain organisation in the female has been continuing at UCLA. Melissa Hines studied the effect on daughters whose mothers, during pregnancy, had taken DES (see The Case of Caroline, Chapter Two.) This hormone, although an estrogen, has a masculinising effect on developing animal brains. Hines found that the location of auditory centres of the brain in women exposed to DES followed the male pattern – tightly bunched functions in specific brain compartments – to a much greater extent than that of their unexposed sisters. Further tests on the effects of CAH (see the Case of Catherine, Chapter Six) have shown that girls thus exposed have a marked preference for playing with trucks, cars and other typically boyish toys. A puzzled Melissa Hines admits 'you don't think of there being a brain region governing toy preference.'

We have also been able to learn more about the effect on the brain of additional female hormones, thanks to study involving Hormone Replacement Therapy for postmenopausal women. In areas where women do better than men, such as rapid sequence of precise hand movements, additional female hormone improved performance still further. The same was found to be true when the women were tested on tongue-twisters. Estrogen was confirmed as having 'a strongly positive effect on functions which we know depend critically on the left hemisphere' – of which speech is one of the most obvious. High levels of female hormone detracted from women's performance at skills in which men enjoy a traditional superiority; other studies have added to our understanding of how the effect of the menstrual cycle affects, in Doreen Kimura's words, 'the apparent fluidity of certain abilities [in] the day-to-day functioning of women.'

In men and women, the latest literature seems agreed, the degree of male hormone affects the efficiency with which recognisedly male skills are performed, and the amount of female hormone influences the success of normal female aptitudes.

The explosion of research continues in that most politically explosive of areas – the effect of prenatal brain-sexing on homosexual development. Fascinating work has been done on the link between left-handedness and male homosexuality. We know that left-handedness can be connected with a brain which follows more the female than the male organisational pattern. We also know that a lack of male hormone at a crucial stage of male fetal development can lead to a feminine brain persisting in a male body. Do male homosexuals, then, have a more than average number of left handers among them? At the risk of creating the new prejudice of handism, Witleson predicted that this would be the case, and her survey confirmed the prediction. This does not, of course, mean all left handers are more likely to be homosexual, simply that 'homosexuality and its related left-hand preference are associated with decreased exposure to masculinising agents' in the womb. A confusing finding is that homosexual women are four times more likely to be left-handed than right-handed women. There is clearly a reason for this, although it may take some time to emerge.

Homosexual men, Witleson also found, performed below the average for heterosexuals, though still above the female average, in tasks involving the typically masculine spatial skills; but in tests of verbal fluency and articulacy they outperformed their 'straight' companions – though not reaching the levels achieved by women. Results of similar tests for lesbians were unfortunately not available at the time of going to press, but

Witleson told us that they broadly support what we would expect: a higher-than-average success in typically male skills, a lower-than-average achievement in those where females typically excel. Witleson is convinced that sexual orientation, as with so many other aspects of our behaviour, is crucially mediated by hormonal influences on the developing brain. We are or are not homosexual before we are born; society simply provides the environment where homosexuality is suppressed, encouraged, or tolerated. We can safely assume that same-sex institutions like prisons or boarding schools do not create homosexuality, but are simply providing the ideal conditions in which naturally occurring deviations have the best chance of flourishing. The old phrase 'hotbeds of vice' is close to the mark – they are the greenhouses offering optimal conditions for the natural seed to grow.

Meanwhile, Gunter Dörner's controversial work on the alchemy of sexual preference has yielded new clues. He believes that 'deviation' can be 'widely prevented' by the correction of abnormal hormone concentrations in prenatal or early postnatal life. Dörner, elaborating the theory we outlined in Chapter Eight, has produced a diagrammatic scheme of how abnormal hormones interact with neurotransmitters, the chemicals which direct the construction of the brain. This interaction determines the nature of his three key areas, the sex centres, mating centres, and so-called 'gender-role centres', all of which assume their structure – and sexual orientation – at subtly different times of brain development. Dörner is even prepared to attach a specific biochemical label to sexual deviations: 'Most subjects with female-to-male transsexuality and many subjects with female homosexuality display 21-hydroxylase deficiency.'

One area where, in the European edition of *Brain Sex*, we could merely hint at significant differences due to the organisation of the male and female brain, concerned mental illness. We made the general observation that abnormalities, be they criminal, sexual, or morally neutral like dyslexia and stuttering, are overwhelmingly a matter of the male. This, we suggested, was because the natural matrix of the brain was female; it needed the active intervention of androgens to rewire it into a male circuit, and such a conversion and restructuring inevitably provided scope for error. We also suggested that a male brain, being so discretely compartmentalised, or arranged in tidy little boxes, would be less capable of compensating for any such shortcoming. It's the eggs-in-one-basket analogy – damage to a control centre in man has drastic effects, whereas woman can summon up the resources of her more scattered cerebral sub-stations.

Now, thanks as always to the work of others, we can begin to fill out that admittedly somewhat sketchy hypothesis. An issue of *Schizophrenia Bulletin* devoted to Gender significantly broadens the horizons. Up to two-thirds of young adults with serious mental illnesses are male. The trend of male mental problems reveals itself early – boys react much more strongly than girls to stresses and conflicts in the family home. Young males are much more vulnerable to infantile autism. Later life reveals significantly large male majorities among a whole range of obsessives, suicides, fetishists, and schizophrenics.

In men schizophrenia develops earlier than in women, men respond less well than women to treatment, and have less chance of recovering and returning to a normal life in the community. Yet studies of schizophrenia have nevertheless largely ignored the evident male bias of the affliction. So great is the gender bias that some researchers now believe that the malignant form of schizophrenia is the result of neurological vulnerability in the male, while the incidence in females may have a more familial origin. Certainly at last the doctors are beginning to look to the different brain organisation in men and women as a possible key to their understanding of the illness: 'The organisational and activational effects of hor-mones on brain morphology...open up new areas of research in studies of schizophrenia.' A recent paper in *Comprehensive Psychiatry* agrees that disturbances in the normal process of brain growth cause structural abnormalities associated with schizophrenia, and 'one of the most crucial influences on this process may be the effect of sex hormones on brain growth.' This, scientists believe, may in turn explain the gender-related aspects of the illness. The paper admits that we still do not know whether or not gender differences in the brain are at the root of the gender differences in the clinical aspects of the disorder – but at least, and at last, the doctors are beginning to look, after decades of apparently deliberate dismissal of the very notion of 'gender differences in the brain'.

The interim conclusions are understandably tentative and cautious; yet few scientists, as little as ten years ago, would have ventured as bold a prediction as was offered in a recent academic paper: that the subtle sex differences in the organisation of the brain caused by the prenatal hormones are likely to 'define the scope and range of sex differences in the incidence, clinical presentation, and course of specific psychiatric diseases.'

Just as there is a marked gender difference in schizophrenia, it is possible that the overwhelming male bias in criminal behaviour may have a similar origin – in the wiring errors liable to occur when the natural female circuitry of the embryonic brain is reconnected into the male mode. Tests on a sample of aggressive psychopaths showed that 90 per cent suffered from an abnormal neuropsychological profile. Studies showed that offenders had a reduced verbal, as opposed to performance, IQ – correlating with damage to the left-hand side of the brain which houses the speech centres and which seems so vulnerable, in men, to physiological damage. There is an uncanny symmetry between schizophrenia and certain forms of extreme criminal behaviour (such as homicide, rape, and assault) both in their common male bias and in what part of the brain is damaged.

So if the brainsexing malfunctions of the hormones are proved to play a part in the underlying causes of schizophrenia, could they also be at the root of antisocial behaviour? If so, is it conceivable that we might, chemically, be able to abort the incidence not only of some psychiatric disorders, but of some aspects of criminality itself – just as we may be able to tinker with sexual orientation? Or, when sexuality and criminality merge, could we, for instance, anticipate and prevent the hormonal affects on the brain which have been detected among paedophiles? And should we? What eugenic implications may this new knowledge bring – what opportunities and what terrors?

As our understanding of the brain expands, a whole new agenda unfurls. We can only hope that our brains — male and female together — are capable of addressing it successfully.

REFERENCES

REFERENCES

GENERAL REFERENCES

BARASH, D., *Sociobiology: The Whispering Within*, Souvenir Press, London (1980).
BARDWICK, J. M., *The Psychology of Women*, Harper Row, New York (1971).
BEACH, F. A. (ed.), *Human Sexuality in Four Perspectives*, Johns Hopkins University Press, Baltimore (1976).
DE VRIES, G. J., DE BRUIN, J. P. C., UYLING, H. B. M. and CORNER, M. A. (eds.), 'Sex Differences in the Brain: The Relation between Structure and Function', *Progress In Brain Research*, 61, Elsevier, Amsterdam (1984).
DE WIED, D. and VAN KEEP, P. A. (eds.), *Hormones and the Brain*, MTP Press, Lancaster (1980).
DURDEN-SMITH, J. and DE SIMONE, D., *Sex and the Brain*, Pan Original, London (1983).
ELLIS, H., *Man and Woman*, 8th edition rev., William Heinemann (Medical Books), London (1934).
EYSENCK, H. J., *The Inequality of Man*, Temple Smith, London (1973).
FOSS, B. M. (ed.), *Sex Differences: Psychology Survey No. 1*, Allen and Unwin, London (1979).
FRIEDMAN, R. C. et. al. (eds.), *Sex Differences in Behaviour*, John Wiley & Sons, New York (1974).
GARAI, J. E. and SCHEINFELD, A., 'Sex differences in mental and behavioural traits', *Genetic Psychology Monographs*, 77 (1968), 169–299.
GOLDBERG, S., *The Inevitability of Patriarchy*, Temple Smith, London (1977).
GOY, R. W. and MCEWEN, B. S., *Sexual Differentiation of the Brain*, Massachusetts Institute of Technology Press, Cambridge, Mass. (1980).
HARRIS, L. J., 'Sex differences in spatial ability: possible environmental, genetic and neurological factors', *Asymmetrical Function of The Brain*, Kinsbourne, M. (ed.), Cambridge University Press (1978), 405–522.
HARRIS, L. J., 'Sex-Related Variations in Spatial Skills', *Spatial Representation and Behaviour Across the Life Span*, Liben, L. S. et al. (eds.), Academic Press, New York (1981), 83–112.
HUTCHISON, J. B. (ed.), *Biological Determinants of Sexual Behaviour*, John Wiley & Sons, New York (1978).
HOYENGA, K. B. and HOYENGA, K., *Sex Differences*, Little Brown and Company, Boston (1980).
HUTT, C., *Males and Females*, Penguin, London (1972).
KAGAN, J. and MOSS, H. A., *Birth to Maturity*, John Wiley & Sons, New York (1962).
KONNER, M., *The Tangled Wing*, Holt Rinehart and Winston, London (1982).
KOPP, C. B. and KIRKPATRICK, M. (eds.), *Becoming Female*, Plenum Press, New York (1979).
LEVIN, M., *Feminism and Freedom*, Transaction Books, New Brunswick, N.J. (1987).
LLOYD, B. and ARCHER, J. (eds.), *Exploring Sex Differences*, Academic Press, London (1976).
LLOYD, B. and ARCHER, J., *Sex and Gender*, Penguin Books, London (1982).
MACCOBY, E. (ed.), *The Development of Sex Differences*, Stanford University Press (1966).
MACCOBY, E. and JACKLYN, N., *The Psychology of Sex Differences*, Stanford University Press (1975).
MCGUINESS, D., *When Children Don't Learn*, Basic Books, New York (1985).
NICOLSON, J., *Men and Women*, Oxford University Press (1984).

OSBORNE, R. T., NOBLE, C. E. and WEYL, N., *Human Variation: The Biophysiology of Age, Race and Sex*, Academic Press, London (1978).

OUSTED, C. and TAYLOR, D. (eds.), *Gender Differences: Their Ontogeny and Significance*, Churchill Livingstone, London (1975).

PARSONS, J. E. (ed.), *The Psychobiology of Sex Differences and Sex Roles*, Hemisphere, London (1980).

PERLMUTTER, M. and HALL, E., *Adult Development and Aging*, John Wiley & Sons, New York (1985).

REID, I. and WORMALD, E. *Sex Differences in Britain*, Grant McIntyre, London (1982).

REINISCH, J. M. et. al. (eds.), *Masculinity and Femininity*, The Kinsey Institute Series, Oxford University Press (1987).

RESTAK, R., *The Brain. The Last Frontier*, Doubleday and Company, New York (1979).

ROSSI, A. S. (ed.), *Gender and the Life Course*, Aldine Publishing Company, New York (1985).

Sex, Hormones and Behaviour, CIBA Foundation Symposium 62 (New Series) Excerpta Medica, Amsterdam (1979).

VELLE, W., 'Sex, Hormones and Behaviour in Animals and Man', *Perspectives in Biology and Medicine*, 25, No. 2 (Winter 1982), 295–315.

WITTIG, M. A. and PETERSEN, A. C. (eds.), *Sex Related Differences in Cognitive Functioning*, Academic Press, London (1979).

CHAPTER ONE

BENBOW, C. P. and BENBOW, R. M., 'Biological correlates of high mathematical reasoning ability', *Progress in Brain Research*, 61, De Vries, G. J. et al. (eds.), Elsevier, Amsterdam (1984), 469–90.

BENBOW, C. P. and STANLEY, J. C., 'Sex differences in mathematical ability: fact or artifact', *Science*, 210 (1980), 1234–36.

BENBOW, C. P. and STANLEY, J. C., 'Sex differences in mathematical reasoning ability: more facts', *Science*, 222 (1983), 1029–31.

BURG, A., 'Visual acuity as measured by dynamic and static tests: a comparative evaluation', *J. Appl. Phychol.*, 50 (1966), 460–66.

COLTHEART, M. et al., 'Sex differences in imagery and reading', *Nature*, 253 (1975), 438–40.

BUFFERY, A. W. H. and GRAY, J. .A, 'Sex differences in the development of spatial and linguistic skills', *Gender Differences: Their Ontogeny and Significance*, Ousted, C. and Taylor, D. C. (eds.), Churchill Livingstone, London (1975), 123–57.

DE REINCOURT, A., *Women and Power in History*, Honeyglen Publishing, London (1983).

ELLIS, H., *Man and Woman*, William Heinemann, London (1934).

GAULIN, S. J. C. et al., 'Sex differences in spatial ability: An evolutionary hypothesis and test', *The American Naturalist*, 127, No. 1 (January 1986), 74–88.

GRAY, J. .A, 'Sex differences in emotional and cognitive behaviour in mammals including man: adaptive and neural bases', *Acta Psychologica*, 35 (1971), 89–111.

GOULD, S. J., 'Women's brains', *New Scientist*, 2 (November 1978), 364–66.

HARSHMAN, R. A. and PAIVIO, A., '"Paradoxical" sex differences in self-reported imagery', *Canadian Journal of Psychology*, 41 (3) (1987), 287–302.

HUTT, C., 'Biological bases of psychological sex differences', Paper given to The European Society for Paediatric Endocrinology, Rotterdam (June 1976).

HUTT, C., 'Neuroendocrinological, behavioural and intellectual differentiation in human development', *Gender Differences: Their Ontogeny and Significance*, Ousted, C. and Taylor, D. (eds.), Churchill Livingstone, London (1975), 73–121.

KIMURA, D., 'Are men's and women's brains really different?', *Canadian Psycol.*, 28 (2) (1987), 133–47.

KIPNIS, D. M., 'Intelligence, occupational status and achievement orientation', *Exploring Sex Differences*, Lloyd, B. and Archer, J. (eds.), Academic Press, London (1976), 95–122.

MCGEE, M. G., 'Human Spatial Abilities: Psychometric Studies and Environmental, Genetic, Hormonal, and Neurological Influences', *Psychological Bulletin*, 86, No. 5 (1979), 889–918.

MCGUINESS, D., 'Sex Differences in Organisation, Perception and Cognition', *Exploring Sex Differences*, Lloyd, B. and Archer, J. (eds.), Academic Press, London (1976), 123–55.

MCGUINESS, D., 'How schools discriminate against boys', *Human Nature*, (February 1979), 82–88.

MEADE, M., *Male and Female*, Pelican Books, London (1950).

MONEY, J. et al., 'An examination of some basic sexual concepts: the evidence of human hermaphroditism', John Hopkins Hospital, Baltimore, 97 (1955), 301–19.

REINISCH, J. M., 'Fetal hormones, the brain, and human sex differences: a heuristic, integrative review of the recent literature', *Archives of Sexual Behaviour*, 3, No. 1 (1974), 51–90.

SWAAB, D. F. and HOFMAN, M. .A., 'Sexual differentiation of the human brain', *Progress in Brain Research*, 61, De Vries, G. J. et al. (eds.), Elsevier, Amsterdam (1984), 361–74.

VANDENBERG, S. G., 'Sex differences in mental retardation and their implications for sex differences', *Masculinity and Femininity*, Reinisch, J. M. et al. (eds.), Oxford University Press (1987), 157–71.

WECHSLER, D., 'Sex differences in intelligence', *The Measurement and Appraisal of Adult Intelligence*, Williams and Wilking, Baltimore (1958).

WITLESON, S. F., 'Sex differences in the neurology of cognition: psychological, social, educational and clinical implications', *Le Fait Féminin*, Sullerot, E. (ed.), Fayard, France (1978), 287–303. [English translation obtained from Sandra Witleson.]

YARMEY, A. D., 'The effects of attractiveness, feature saliency and liking on memory for faces', *Love and Attraction*, Cook, M. and Wilson, G. (eds.), Pergamon Press, Oxford (1979), 51–53.

CHAPTER TWO

ARCHER, J., 'Biological explanations of psychological sex differences',. *Exploring Sex Differences*, Lloyd, B. and Archer, J. (eds.), Academic Press, London (1976), 241–65.

BEACH, F. A., 'Hormonal control of sex related behaviour', *Human Sexuality in Four Perspectives*, Beach, F. A. (ed.), Johns Hopkins University Press, Baltimore (1976), 245–67.

BEATTY, W. W., 'Gonadal hormones and sex differences in nonreproductive behaviours in rodents: organisational and activational influences', *Hormones and Behaviour*, 12 (1979), 112–63.

BEATTY, W. W., 'Hormonal organisation of sex differences in play fighting and spatial behaviour', *Progress in Brain Research*, 61, De Vries, G. J. et al. (eds.), Elsevier, Amsterdam (1984), 313–30.

BERG, I. et al., 'Change of assigned sex at puberty', *Lancet* (7 December 1963), 1216–18.

DIAMOND, M., 'Human sexual development: biological foundations for social development', *Human Sexuality in Four Perspectives*, Beach, F. A. (ed.), Johns Hopkins University Press, Baltimore (1977), 38–61.

DOMINIQUE TORAN-ALLERAND, C., 'On the genesis of sexual differentiation of the central nervous system: morphogenetic consequences of steroidal exposure and the possible role of alpha-fetoprotein', *Progress in Brain Research*, 61, De Vries, G. J. et al. (eds.), Elsevier, Amsterdam (1984), 63–98.

DÖRNER, G., 'Hormones and sexual differentiation of the brain', *Sex, Hormones and Behaviour*, CIBA Foundation Symposium 62, Excerpta Medica, Amsterdam (1979), 81–112.

DÖRNER, G., 'Sexual differentiation of the brain', *Vitamins and Hormones*, 38 (1980), 325–73.

DÖRNER, G., 'Sex hormones and neurotransmitters as mediators for sexual differentiation of the brain', *Endokrinologie*, 78 (December 1981), 129–38.

DÖRNER, G., 'Sex-specific gonadotrophin secretion, sexual orientation and gender role behaviour', *Endokrinologie*, 86 (August 1985), 1–6.

DURDEN-SMITH, J. and DE SIMONE, D., 'Birth of your sexual identity', *Science Digest*, (September 1983), 86–88.

EHRHARDT, A. A., 'Gender differences: a biosocial perspective', Nebraska Symposium on Motivation, 1984, *Psychology and Gender*, 32 (1985), 37–57.

EHRHARDT, A. A., 'A transactional perspective on the development of gender differences', *Masculinity and Femininity*, Reinisch, J. (ed.), Oxford University Press (1987), 281–88.

EHRHARDT, A. A. et al., 'Sexual orientation after prenatal exposure to exogenous estrogen', *Archives of Sexual Behaviour*, 14, No. 1 (1985), 57–77.

EHRHARDT, A. A. and BAKER, S., 'Fetal androgens, human central nervous system differentiation, and behaviour sex differences', *Sex Differences in Behaviour*, Friedman, R. C. et al. (eds.), John Wiley & Sons, New York (1974), 33–51.

EHRHARDT, A. A. and MEYER-BAHLBURG, H. F. L., 'Prenatal sex hormones and the developing brain', *Annual Review Med.*, 30 (1979), 417–30.

EHRHARDT, A. A. and MEYER-BAHLBURG, H. F. L., 'Effects of parental sex hormones on gender-related behaviour', *Science*, 211 (1981), 1312–14.

GORSKI, R. A., 'Critical role of the medial preoptic area in the sexual differentiation of the brain', *Progress in Brain Research*, 61, De Vries, G. J. et al. (eds.), Elsevier, Amsterdam (1984), 129–46.

GORSKI, R. A., 'Sex differences in the rodent brain: their nature and origin', *Masculinity and Femininity*, Reinisch, J. M. et al. (eds.), Oxford University Press (1987), 37–67.

GREEN, R., 'Sex-dimorphic behaviour development in the human: prenatal hormone administration and postnatal socialization', *Sex, Hormones and Behaviour*, CIBA Foundation Symposium 62, Excerpta Medica, Amsterdam (1979), 59–80.

GAULIN, S. J. C. et al.: see reference in Chapter One.

HAMILTON, W. H. and CHAPMAN, P. H., 'Biochemical determinants in gender identity', *Pädiatrie und Pädologie*, Suppl. 5 (1977), 69–81.

HARRISON, J., 'Warning: the male sex role may be dangerous to your health', *Journal of Social Issues*, 34, No. 1 (1978), 65–86.

HINES, M., 'Prenatal gonadal hormones and sex differences in human behaviour', *Psychological Bulletin*, 92, No. 1 (1982), 56–80.

HUTCHINSON, J. .B and STEIMER, T. H., 'Androgen metabolism in the brain: behavioural correlates', *Progress in Brain Research*, 61, De Vries, G. J. et al. (eds.), Elsevier, Amsterdam (1984), 23–51.

HUTT, C., 'Neurological, behavioural and intellectual aspects of sexual differentiation in human development', *Gender Differences: Their Ontogeny and Significance*, Outsted, C. and Taylor, D. (eds.), Churchill Livingstone, London (1975), 73–121.

IMPERATO-MCGINLEY, J. et al., 'Steroid 5 alpha-reductase deficiency in man: an inherited form of male pseudohermaphrodism', *Science*, 186 (1974), 1213–15.

IMPERATO-MCGINLEY, J. et al., 'Androgens and the evolution of male gender identity among male pseudohermaphrodites with 5 alpha-reductase deficiency', *New England Journal of Medicine*, 300, No. 22 (1979), 1233–37.

JOST, A., 'Basic sexual trends in the development of vertebrates', *Sex, Hormones and Behaviour*, CIBA Foundation Symposium 62, Excerpta Medica, Amsterdam (1979), 5–18.

KAPLAN, A. G., 'Human sex hormone abnormalities viewed from an androgenous perspective: a reconsideration of the work of John Money', *The Psychobiology of Sex Differences and Sex Roles*, Parsons, J. (ed.), Hemisphere (1980), 81–91.

LEIBERBURG, I. et al. 'Sex differences in serum testosterone and in exchangeable brain cell nuclear estradiol during the neonatal period in rats', *Brain Research*, 178 (1979), 207–12.

MACCOBY, E., 'The varied meanings of "Masculine" and "Feminine"', *Masculinity and Femininity*, Reinisch, J. M. et al. (eds.), Oxford University Press (1987), 225–39.

MACLUSKY, N. J. and NAFTOLIN, F., 'Sexual differentiation of the central nervous system', *Science*, 211 (1981), 1294–302.

MCEWEN, B. S., 'Neural gonadal steroid actions', *Science*, 211 (1981), 1303–11.

MCEWEN, B. S., 'Observations on brain sexual differentiation: a biochemist's view', *Masculinity and Femininity*, Reinisch, J. M. et al. (eds.), Oxford University Press (1987), 68–79.

MONEY, J. and SCHWARTZ, M., 'Biosocial determinants of gender identity differentiation and development', *Biological Determinants of Sexual Behaviour*, Hutchinson, J. B. (ed.), John Wiley & Sons, New York (1978), 767–84.

NAFTOLIN, F., 'Understanding the bases of sex differences', *Science*, 211 (1981), 1263–84.

PARSONS, J. E., 'Psychosexual neutrality: Is anatomy destiny?', *The Psychobiology of Sex Differences and Sex Roles*, Parsons, J. E. (ed.), Hemisphere, London (1980), 3–29.

PETERSON, A. C., 'Biopsychosocial processes in the development of sex related differences', *The Psychobiology of Sex Differences and Sex Roles*, Parsons, J. E. (ed.), Hemisphere, London (1980), 31–55.

PFAFF, D. W., *Estrogens and Brain Function: A Neural Analysis of Hormone Controlled Mammalian Reproductive Behaviour*, Springer-Verlag, New York (1980).

PHONENIX, C. H., 'Prenatal testosterone in the nonhuman primate and its consequences for behaviour', *Sex Differences in Behaviour*, Friedman, R. C. et al. (eds.), John Wiley & Sons, New York (1974), 19–32.

RAISMAN, G. and FIELD, P. M., 'Sexual dimorphism in the preoptic area of the rat', *Science*, 173 (1971), 731–33.

RAISMAN, G. and FIELD, P. M., 'Sexual dimorphism in the neuropil of the preoptic area of the rat and its dependence on neonatal androgen', *Brain Research*, 54 (1973), 1–29.

RATCLIFFE, S. G. et al., 'Klinefelter's Syndrome in adolescence', *Archives on Disease in Childhood*, 57 (1982), 6–12.

RESKE-NEILSEN, E. et al., 'A neuropathological and neurophysiological study of Turner's Syndrome', *Cortex*, 18 (1982), 181–90.

REINISCH, J. M. (1974): see reference in Chapter One.

REINISCH, J. M., 'Effects of prenatal hormone exposure on physical and psychological development in humans and animals: with a note on the state of the field', *Hormones and Behaviour*, Sachar, E. J. (ed.), Raven Press, New York (1976), 69–94.

REINISCH, J. M., 'Prenatal exposure of human foetuses to synthetic progestin and oestrogen affects personality', *Nature*, 266 (1977), 561–62.

REINISCH, J. M. et al., 'Prenatal influences on cognitive abilities: data from experimental animals and human genetic endocrine syndromes', *Sex Related Differences in Cognitive Functioning*, Wittig, M. A. and Petersen, A. C. (eds.), Academic Press, London (1979), 215–39.

REINISCH, J. M., 'Hormonal influences on sexual development and behaviour', *Sex and Gender: A Theological Scientific Inquiry*. Schwartz, M. F. et al. (eds.), The Pope John Center: St. Louis, Missouri (1983), 48–64.

REINISCH, J. M. and SAUNDERS, S. A., 'Prenatal gonadal steroid influences on gender-related behaviour', *Progress in Brain Research*, 61, De Vries, G. J. et al. (eds.), Elsevier, Amsterdam (1984), 407–15.

ROSSI, A. S., 'Gender and Parenthood', *Gender and Life Course*, Rossi, A. S. (ed.), Aldine, New York (1985), 161–91.

ROVET, J. and NETLEY, C., 'Processing deficits in Turner's Syndrome', *Developmental Psychol.*, 18, No. 1 (1982), 77–94.

SAUNDERS, S. A. and REINISCH, J. M., 'Behavioural effect on humans of progesterone related compounds during development in the adult', *Current Topics of Neuroendocrinology*, 15 (1985), 175–98.

SAVAGE, M. O. et al., 'Familial male pseudohermaphrodism due to deficiency of 5 alpha-reductase', *Clinical Endocrinology*, 12 (1980), 397–406.

SHAPIRO, B. H. et al., 'Neonatal progesterone and feminine sexual development', *Nature*, 264 (1976), 795–96.

SILER-KOHODR, T. M. and KHODR, G. S., 'Studies in human fetal endocrinology, *American Journal of Obstetrics and Gynecology*, 130 (1978), 795–800.

TAYLOR, D. C., 'Psychosexual Development', *Scientific Foundations of Paediatrics*, Davies, J. A. and Dobbing, J. (eds.), Heinemann (Medical Books), 2nd edition, London (1981), 290–301.

WAYNE BARDIN, C. and CATTERALL, J. F., 'Testosterone: a major determinant of extragenital sexual diamorphism', *Science*, 211 (1981), 1285–93.

WESTLEY, B. R. and SALAMAN, D. F., 'Role of oestrogen receptor in androgen-induced sexual differentiation of the brain', *Nature*, 262 (1976), 407–08.

WILSON, J. D. et al., 'The hormonal control of sexual development', *Science*, 211 (1981), 1278–84.

WITLESON, S. F., 'Sex differences in the neurology of cognition: social educational and clinical implications', *Le Fait Féminin*, Sullerot, E. (ed.), Fayard, France (1978), 287–303.

YALOM, I. D. et al., 'Prenatal exposure to female hormones', *Archives Gen. Psychiat.*, 28 (1973), 554–61.

CHAPTER THREE

BALKAN, P., 'The eyes have it', *Psychology Today* (April 1971), 64–67.

BUTLER, S., 'Sex differences in human cerebral function', *Progress In Brain Research*, 61, De Vries, G. J. et al. (eds.), Elsevier, Amsterdam (1984), 443–55.

CALVIN, W. and OJEMANN, G., *Inside the Brain*, New American Library, New York (1981).

DE LACOSTE-UTAMSING, C. and HOLLOWAY, R. L., 'Sexual dimorphism in the human corpus callosum', *Science*, 216 (1982), 1431–32.

DE LACOSTE-UTAMSING, C. and HOLLOWAY, R. L., 'Sex differences in the fetal human corpus callosum', *Human Neurobiology*, 5 (1986), 93–96.

DYER, R. G., 'Sexual differentiation of the forebrain-relationship to gonadotrophin secretion', *Progress in Brain Research*, 61, De Vries, G. J. et al. (eds.), Elsevier, Amsterdam (1984), 223–35.

FLOR HENRY, P., 'Gender, hemispheric specialization and psychopathology', *Social Science and Medicine*, 12b (1979), 155–62.

GAULIN, S. J. C.: see reference in Chapter One.

GORDON, H. W. and GALATZER, A., 'Cerebral organization in patients with gonadal dysgenesis', *Psychoneuroendocrinology*, 5 (1980), 235–44.

GUR, R. and GUR, R., 'Sex and handedness differences in cerebral blood flow, during rest and cognitive activity', *Science*, 217 (1982), 659–61.

HARSHMAN, R. A. et al., 'Individual differences in cognitive abilities and brain organisation: sex and handedness differences in ability', *Canadian Journal of Psychology*, 37, No. 1 (1983), 144–92.

HECGEN, H. et al., 'Cerebral organisation in left handers', *Brain and Language*, 12 (1981), 261–84.

HINES, M., 'Prenatal gonadal hormones and sex differences in human behaviour', *Psychological Bulletin*, 92, No. 1 (1982), 56–80.

INGLIS, J. and LAWSON, J. S., 'Sex differences in the effects of unilateral brain damage on intelligence', *Science*, 212 (1981), 693–95.

KIMURA, D. and HARSHMAN, R., 'Sex differences in brain organisation for verbal and non-verbal functions', *Progress in Brain Research*, 61, De Vreis, G. J. et al. (eds.), Elsevier, Amsterdam (1984), 423–40.

KIMURA, D., 'Male brain, female brain: the hidden difference', *Psychology Today* (November 1985), 51–58.

KIMURA, D., 'How different are the male and female brains?', *Orbit*, 17 (3) (October 1986), 13–14.

KIMURA, D., 'Are men's and women's brains really different?', *Canadian Psycol.*, 28 (2) (1987), 133–47.

LEVY, J., 'Lateral differences in the human brain in cognition and behaviour control', *Cerebral Correlates of Conscious Experience*, Buser, P. (ed.), North Holland Publishing Company, New York (1978), 285–98.

MATEER, C. A. et al., 'Sexual variation in cortical localisation of naming as determined by stimulation mapping', *The Behavioural and Brain Sciences*, 5 (1982), 310–11.

MCGLONE J. and DAVIDSON, W., 'The relation between cerebral speech laterality and spatial ability with special reference to sex and hand preference', *Neuropsychologia*, 11 (1973), 105–13.

MCGLONE, J., 'Sex differences in human brain symmetry: a critical survey', *The Behavioural and Brain Sciences*, 3 (1980), 215–63.

MCGLONE, J., 'The neuropsychology of sex differences in the human brain organisation', *Advances in Clinical Neuropyschology*, 3, Goldstein, G. and Tarter, R. E. (eds.), Plenum Publishing Corp. (1986), 1–30.

NYBORG, H., 'Spatial ability in men and women: review and new theory', *Adv. Behav. Res. Ther.*, 5 (1983), 89–140.

NYBORG, H., 'Performance and intelligence in hormonally different groups', *Progress in Brain Research*, 61, De Vries, G. J. et al. (eds.), Elsevier, Amsterdam (1984), 491–508.

REINISCH, J. M.: see reference in Chapter Two.

SPERRY, R., 'Some effects of disconnecting cerebral hemispheres', *Science*, 217 (1982), 1223–26.

SPRINGER, S. P. and DEUTSCH, G., *Left Brain, Right Brain*, W. H. Freedman and Co., New York (1985).

TUCKER, D. M., 'Sex differences in hemispheric specialization for synthetic visuospatial functions', *Neuropsychologia*, 14 (1976), 447–54.

WADA, J. et al., 'Cerebral hemispheric asymmetry in humans', *Arch. Neurol.*, 32 (April 1975), 239–45.

WITLESON, S. F., 'Left hemisphere specialization for language in the newborn brain', 96 (1973), 641–46.

WITLESON, S. F., 'Hemispheric specialization for linguistic and non-linguistic tactual perception using a dichotomous stimulation technique', *Cortex*, 10 (1974), 3–7.

WITLESON, S. F., 'Sex and the single hemisphere: specialization of the right hemisphere for spatial processing', *Science*, 193 (1976), 425–27.

WITLESON, S. F. (1978): see reference in Chapter Two.

WITLESON, S. F., 'The brain connection: the corpus collosum is larger in left handers', *Science*, 229 (1985), 665–68.

WITLESON, S. F., 'An exchange on gender', *New York Review* (24 October 1985), 53–55.

ZAIDEL, E., 'Concepts of cerebral dominance in the split brain', *Cerebral Correlates of Conscious Experience*, Buser, P. A. and Rougeul-Buser, A. (eds.), North-Holland Publishing Company, Amsterdam (1978), 261–83.

CHAPTER FOUR

BHAVNANI, R. and HUTT, C., 'Divergent thinking in boys and girls', *J. Child Psycho. Psychiat.*, 13 (1972), 121–27.

BUFFERY, A. W. H. and GRAY, J. A.: see reference in Chapter One.

COLTHEART, M. et al.: see reference in Chapter One.

DIAMOND, M.: see reference in Chapter Two.

EISENBERG, N. et al., 'Children's reasoning regarding sex-typed toy choices', *Child Dev.*, 53 (1982), 81–86.

GOLDBERG, S. and LEWIS, M., 'Play behaviour in the year old infant: early sex differences', *Child Dev.*, 40 (1969), 21–31.

HUTT, C.: see reference in Chapter One.

JURASKA, J. M., 'Sex differences in dendritic response to differential experience in the rat visual cortex', *Brain Res.*, 295 (1984), 27–34.

JURASKA, J. M., 'Sex differences in developmental plasticity of the visual cortex and hippocampal dentate gyrus', *Progress in Brain Research*, 61, de Vries, G. J. et al. (eds.), Elsevier, Amsterdam (1984), 205–14.

KAGAN, J., 'Sex differences in the human infant', *Sex and Behaviour: Status and Prospectus*, McGill, T. E. et al. (eds.), Plenum Press, New York (1978), 305–16.

KORNER, A. F., 'Methodological considerations in studying sex differences in the behavioural functioning of newborns', *Sex Differences in Behaviour*, Friedman, R. C. et al. (eds.), John Wiley & Sons, New York (1974), 197–208.

LEVER, J., 'Sex differences in the games children play', *Social Problems*, 23 (1976), 478–87.
LEVER, J., 'Sex differences in the complexity of children's play and games', *American Sociological Review*, 43 (1978), 471–83.
MCGEE, M. G.: see reference in Chapter One.
MCGUINESS, D. (1976): see reference in Chapter One.
MCGUINESS, D. (1979): see reference in Chapter One.
PARIZKOVA, J. et al., 'Sex differences in somatic and functional characteristics of preschool children, *Human Biol.*, 49, No. 3 (1977), 437–51.
REINISCH, J. M.: see reference in Chapter One.
ROSENBLUM, L. A., 'Sex differences in mother-infant attachment in monkeys', *Sex Differences in Behaviour*, Friedman, R. C. et al. (eds.), John Wiley & Sons, New York (1974), 123–41.
SMITH, ANTHONY, *The Mind*, Hodder and Stoughton, London (1984).
STEIN, S., *Girls and Boys: The Limits of Non-Sexist Rearing*, Chatto and Windus, London (1984).
STERN, D. N. and BENDER, E. P., 'An ethological study of children approaching a strange adult: sex differences', *Sex Differences in Behaviour*, Friedman, R. C. et al. (eds.), John Wiley & Sons, New York (1974), 233–58.
SUTTON-SMITH, B., 'The play of girls', *Becoming Female: Perspective on Development*, Kopp, C. B. (ed.), Plenum Press, New York (1980), 229–57.
TIGER, L. and SHEPHER, J., *Women in the Kibbutz*, Penguin Books, London (1977).
WITELSON, S. (1976 and 1978): see references in Chapter One.
WHITING, J. W. M., *Children of Six Cultures: A Psychocultural Analysis*, Harvard University Press, Camb., Mass. (1975).

CHAPTER FIVE

BUSS, A. H., 'Aggression pays', *The Control of Aggression and Violence: Cognitive and Physiological Factors*, Singer, J. (ed.), Academic Press, New York (1971), 7–18.
DALTON, K., 'Premenstrual tension: an overview', *Behaviour and the Menstrual Cycle*, Friedman, R. C. (ed.), Dekker, New York (1982), 217–42.
DALTON, K., *Once a Month*, Fontana Original, 4th Edition, Glasgow (1987).
DAVIS, P. C. and MCEWEN, B. S., 'Neuroendocrine regulation of sexual behaviour', *Behaviour and the Menstrual Cycle*, Friedman, R. C. (ed.), Dekker, New York (1982), 43–59.
DE JONGE, F. H. and VAN DE POLL, N. E., 'Relationship between sexual behaviour in male and female rats: effects of gonadal hormones', *Progress in Brain Research*, 61, De Vries, G. J. et al. (eds.), Elsevier, Amsterdam (1984), 283–302.
FERIN, M., 'The neuroendocrinological control of the menstrual cycle', *Behaviour and the Menstrual Cycle*, Friedman, R. C. (ed.), Dekker, New York (1982), 23–32.
FRIEDMAN, R. C. (ed.), *Behaviour and the Menstrual Cycle*, Dekker, New York (1982).
GLICK, I. D. and BENNETT, S. E., 'Oral contraceptives and the menstrual cycle', *Behaviour and the Menstrual Cycle*, Friedman, R. C. (ed.), Dekker, New York (1982), 345–65.
GOVE, W. R., 'The effect of age and gender on deviant behaviour: a biopsychological perspective', *Gender and the Life Course*, Rossi, A. S. (ed.), Aldine, New York (1985), 115–44.
GRAHAM, D. A. J. and BEECHER, E. A., (eds.), *The Menstrual Cycle: A Synthesis of Interdisciplinary Research*, 1, Springer, New York (1980).
GRANT, E. C. G. and PRYSE-DAVIES, J., 'Effect of oral contraceptives on depressive mood changes', *Brit. Med. Journal*, 3 (September 1968), 777–80.
HERZBERG, B. and COPPEN, A., 'Change in psychological symptoms in women taking oral contraceptives', *Brit. J. Psychiat.*, 116 (1970), 161–64.
HUNTINGFORD, F. H. and TURNER, A. K., *Animal Conflict*, Chapman and Hall, London (1987).
KAGAN, J.: see reference in Chapter Four.
KOPERA, H., 'Female hormones and brain function', *Hormones and the Brain*, de Wied, D. and Van Keep, P. A. (eds.), MTP Press, Lancaster (1980), 189–203.

KRUCK, M. R. et al., 'Comparison of aggressive behaviour induced by electrical stimulation in the hypothalamus of male and female rats', *Progress in Brain Research*, 61, De Vries, G. J. et al. (eds.), Elsevier, Amsterdam (1984), 303–13.

LANGEVIN, R. (ed.), *Erotic Preference, Gender Identity and Aggression In Men: New Research Studies*, Lawrence Erlbaum Associates Publisher, Hillsdale, New Jersey (1985).

LEVINE, S., *Hormones and Behaviour*, Academic Press, London (1972).

LINKIE, D. M., 'The physiology of the menstrual cycle', *Behaviour and the Menstrual Cycle*, Friedman, R. C. (ed.), Dekker, New York (1982), 1–10.

LORENZ, K., *On Aggression*, Methuen, London (1966).

MARSH, P. and CAMPBELL, A. (eds.), *Aggression and Violence*, Basil Blackwell, Oxford (1982).

MCGUINESS, D. (ed.), *Dominance Aggression and War*, Paragon House, New York (1987).

MELEGES, F. T. and HAMBURG, D. A., 'Psychological effects of hormonal changes in women', *Human Sexuality in Four Perspectives*, Beach, F. A. (ed.) Johns Hopkins University Press, Baltimore (1976), 269–95.

MESSANT, P. K., 'Female hormones and behaviour', *Exploring Sex Differences*, Lloyd, B. and Archer, J. (eds.), Academic Press, London (1976), 183–211.

MEYER-BAHLBURG, H. F. L. and EHRHART, A. A., 'Prenatal sex hormones and human aggression: a review and new data on progesterone effects', *Aggressive Behaviour*, 8 (1982), 39–62.

MEYER-BAHLBURG, H. F. L., 'Aggression, androgens and the XYY Syndrome', *Sex Differences in Behaviour*, Friedman, R. C. et al. (eds.), John Wiley & Sons, New York (1974), 433–53.

MOYER, K. E., 'The physiology of aggression and the implications for aggression control', *The Control of Aggression and Violence*, Singer, J. L. (ed.), Academic Press, New York (1971), 61–92.

MOYER, K. E., 'Sex differences in aggression', *Sex Differences in Behaviour*, Friedman, R. C. et al. (eds.), John Wiley & Sons, New York (1974), 335–72.

MOYER, K. E., 'The biological basis for dominance and aggression', *Dominance Aggression and War*, McGuiness, D. (ed.), Paragon House, New York (1987), 1–34.

MOYER, K. E., *Violence and Aggression: A Physiological Perspective*, Paragon House, New York (1987).

NIESCHLAG, E., 'The endocrine function of the human testes in regard to sexuality', *Sex, Hormones and Behaviour*, CIBA Foundation Symposium 62, Excerpta Medica, New York (1979), 183–208.

NOTMAN, M., 'Adult life cycles: changing roles and changing hormones', *The Psychobiology of Sex Differences and Sex Roles*, Parsons, J. E. (ed.), Hemisphere, London (1980), 209–23.

PERSKY, H. et al., 'Relation of psychologic measures of aggression and hostility to testosterone production in man', *Psychosomatic Med.*, 33, No. 3 (1971), 265–77.

RAUSCH, J. L., 'Premenstrual tension: etiology', *Behaviour and the Menstrual Cycle*, Friedman, R. C. (ed.), Dekker, New York (1982).

REINISCH, J. M., 'Prenatal exposure to synthetic progestins increase potential for aggression in humans', *Science*, 211 (1981), 1171–73.

REINISCH, J. M. and SAUNDERS, S. A., 'A test of sex differences in aggressive response to hypothetical conflict situation', *Journal of Personality and Social Psychol.*, 50, No. 5., (1986), 1045–49.

RESKE-NEILSEN, E.: see reference in Chapter Two.

ROSE, R. M., 'Androgens and behaviour', *Hormones and the Brain*, De Wied, D. and Van Keep, P. A. (eds.), MTP Press, Lancaster (1980), 175–85.

ROSSI, A. S. and ROSSI, P. E., 'Body time and social time: mood patterns by menstrual cycle phase and day of the week', *The Psychobiology of Sex Differences and Sex Roles*, Parsons, J. E. (ed.), Hemisphere, London (1980), 269–301.

ROVERT, J. and NETLEY, C.: see reference in Chapter Two.

RUBIN, R T. et al., 'Postnatal gonadal steroid effects on human behaviour', *Science*, 211 (1981), 1318–24.

RUBIN, R. T., 'Testosterone and aggression in men', *Handbook of Psychiatry and Endocrinology*, Beumont, P. C. and Burrows, G. (eds.), Elsevier, Amsterdam (1982), 355–66.

SAVIN-WILLIAMS, R., 'Dominance systems among primate adolescents', *Dominance Aggression and War*, McGuiness, D. (ed.), Paragon House, New York (1987), 131–73.

SINGER, J. L., 'The psychological study of aggression', *The Control of Aggression and Violence*, Singer, J. L. (ed.), Academic Press, New York (1971), 1–5.

STONE, M. H., 'Premenstrual tension in borderline and related disorders', *Behaviour and the Menstrual Cycle*, Friedman, R. C. (ed.), Dekker, New York (1982), 317–43.

Young People in the 80's: A Survey, Department of Education and Science, London HMSO (1983).

CHAPTER SIX

BAKER, S. and ERHARDT, A. A., 'Prenatal androgen, intelligence and cognitive sex differences', *Sex Differences in Behaviour*, Friedman, R. C. et al. (eds.), John Wiley & Sons, New York (1974), 53–76.

BALDING, J, *Young People in 1986*, University of Exeter, Exeter (1987).

BENBOW, C. P. and BENBOW, R. M.: see reference in Chapter One.

BENBOW, C. P. and STANLEY, J. C.: see references in Chapter One.

BROVERMAN, D. M. et al., 'The automisation of cognitive style and physical development', *Child Development*, 35 (1964), 1343–59.

BROVERMAN, D. M. et al., 'Roles of activation and inhibition in sex differences in cognitive abilities', *Psychological Review*, 75, No. 1 (1968), 23–50.

BROVERMAN, D. M. et al., 'Gonadal hormones and cognitive functioning', *The Psychobiology of Sex Differences and Sex Roles*, Parsons, J. E. (ed.), Hemisphere, London (1980), 57–80.

BROVERMAN, D. M. et al., 'Changes in cognitive task performance across the menstrual cycle', *J. Comp. Physiol. Psychol.*, 95 (1981), 646–54.

DALTON, K., 'Ante-natal progesterone and intelligence', *Brit. J. Psychiat.*, 114 (1968), 1377–82.

DALTON, K., 'Prenatal progesterone and educational attainments', *Brit. J. Psychiat.*, 129 (1976), 438–42.

DAWSON, J. L. M. 'Effects of sex hormones on the cognitive style in rats and man', *Behaviour Genetics*, 2, No. 1 (1972), 21–42.

EHRHARDT, A. A. and MEYER-BAHLBURG, H. F. L., 'Prenatal sex hormones and the developing brain: effects on psychosexual differentiation', *Ann. Rev. Med.*, 30 (1979), 417–30.

EHRHARDT, A. A. and MEYER-BAHLBURG, H. F. L., 'Effects of prenatal sex hormones on gender-related behaviour', *Science*, 211 (1981), 1312–14.

EHRHARDT, A. A. and MEYER-BAHLBURG, H. F. L., 'Idiopathic precocious puberty in girls: long term effects on adolescent behaviour', *Acta Endocrinologica Suppl.*, 279 (1986), 247–53.

HAMPSON, E. and KIMURA, D., 'Reciprocal effects of hormonal fluctuations on human motor and percepto-spatial skills', Research Bulletin 656, Department of Psychology, University of Western Ontario, London, Canada (June 1987).

HAMPSON, E. and KIMURA, D., 'Reciprocal effects of hormonal fluctuations on human motor and perceptual-spatial skills', *Behavioural Neuroscience*, 102, No. 3 (1988), 456–59.

HIER, D. and CROWLEY, W., 'Spatial ability in androgen deficient men', *New England Journal of Medicine*, 306 (1982), 1202–05.

KELLY, A., *Girls and Science: International Study of Sex Differences in School Achievement*, Almqivst and Wiksell, Stockholm (1978).

KLAIBER, E. L. et al., 'Effects of infused testosterone on mental performances and serum LH', *Journal of Clinical Endocrinology and Metabolism*, 32 (March 1971), 341–49.

KLAIBER, E. L. et al., 'Estrogens and central nervous system function: electroencephalography, cognition and depression', *Behaviour and the Menstrual Cycle*, Friedman, R. C. (ed.), Dekker, New York (1982), 267–89.

KOPERA, H.: see reference in Chapter Five.

MCGEE, M. G.: see reference in Chapter One.

MCGUINESS, D.: see reference in Chapter One.

MONEY, J., 'Prenatal hormones and intelligence: a possible relationship', *Impact of Science on Society*, XXI, No. 4 (1971), 285–90.

NYBORG, H., 'Spatial ability in men and women: review and new theory', *Adv. Behav. Res. Ther.*, 5 (1983), 89–140.

NYBORG, H., 'Performance and intelligence in hormonally different groups', *Progress in Brain Research*, 61, De Vries, G. J. et al. (eds.), Elsevier, Amsterdam (1984), 491–508.

RATCLIFFE, S. G., 'Klinefelter's Syndrome in adolescence', *Archives of Disease in Childhood*, 57 (1982), 6–12.

RESKE-NEILSEN et al., 'A neuropathological and neurophysiological study of Turner's Syndrome', *Cortex*, 18 (1982), 181–90.

REINISCH, J. M.: see references in Chapter Two.

RESNICK, S. M. et al. (eds.), 'Early hormonal influences on cognitive functioning in cogenital adrenal hyperplasia', *Developmental Psychol.*, 22, No. 2 (1986), 191–98.

ROSE, R. M.: see reference in Chapter Five.

ROSENTHAL, K., 'Hormonal influences on cognitive ability patterns', Research Bulletin 653 (March 1987), Department of Psychology, University of Ontario, London, Canada.

ROVET, J. and NETLEY, C., 'Processing deficits in Turner's Syndrome', *Developmental Psychol.*, 18, No. 1 (1982), 77–94.

SAUNDERS, S. A. and REINISCH, J. M.: see reference in Chapter Two.

SHUTE, V. J. et al., 'The relationship between androgen levels and human spatial abilities', *Bulletin of the Psychonomic Society*, 21, No. 2 (1983), 465–68.

YALOM, I. D.: see reference in Chapter Two.

Young People in the 80's: see reference in Chapter Five.

CHAPTERS SEVEN, NINE AND TEN

BAKKEN, D., 'Regulation of intimacy in social encounters: the effect of sex interactants and information about attitude similarity', *Love and Attraction*, Cook, M. and Wilson, G. (eds.), Pergamon Press, Oxford (1979), 83–89.

BARDIS, P. D., 'The kinetic-potential theory of love', *Love and Attraction*, Cook, M. and Wilson, G. (eds.), Pergamon Press, Oxford (1979), 229–35.

BECK, S. B., 'Women's somatic preferences', *Love and Attraction*, Cook, M. and Wilson, G. (eds.), Pergamon Press, Oxford (1979), 15–19.

BEACH, F. A., 'Animal models for human sexuality', *Sex, Hormones and Behaviour*, CIBA Foundation Symposium 62, Excerpta Medica (1979), 113–43.

BEACH, S. R. H. and TESSER, A., 'Love in Marriage', *The Psychology of Love*, Sternberg, R. J. and Barnes, M. L. (eds.), Yale University Press, New Haven (1988), 330–55.

BELENKY, M. F. et al., *Woman's Ways of Knowing*, Basic Books, New York (1986).

BENTLER, P. M. and NEWCOMB, M. D., 'Longitudinal study of marital success and failure', *Love and Attraction*, Cook, M. and Wilson, G. (eds.), Pergamon Press, Oxford (1979), 189–94.

BERSCHEID, E., 'Some comments on love's anatomy', *The Psychology of Love*, Sternberg, R. J. and Barnes, M. L. (eds.), Yale University Press, New Haven (1988), 359–74.

BUCK, R. W. et al., *Human Motivation and Emotion*, Wiley, New York (1976).

BUSS, D. M., 'Love acts: the evolutionary biology of love', *The Psychology of Love*, Sternberg, R. J. and Barnes, M. L. (eds.), Yale University Press, New Haven (1988), 69–118.

BYRNE, D. and MURNEN, S. K., 'Maintaining loving relationships', *The Psychology of Love*, Sternberg, R. J. and Barnes, M. L. (eds.), Yale University Press, New Haven (1988), 293–310.

CANCIAN, F. M., 'Gender politics: love and power in the private and public spheres', *Gender and the Life Course*, Rossi, A. S. (ed.), Aldine, New York (1985), 253–64.

COOK, M. and WILSON, G. (eds.), *Love and Attraction*, Pergamon Press, Oxford (1979).

D'ANDRADE, R. G., 'Sex differences and cultural institutions', *The Development of Sex Differences*, Maccoby, E. E. (ed.), Stanford University Press (1966), 174–204.

DEAUX, K., *The Behaviour of Women and Men*, Brooks/Cole Publishing Co., New York (1976).

DEAUX, K., 'Psychological constructions of masculinity and femininity', *Masculinity and Femininity*, Reinisch, J. M. et al. (eds.), Oxford University Press (1987), 289–303.

DIAMOND, M.: see reference in Chapter One.

DÖRNER, G. (1980): see reference in Chapter Two.

DRAUGHTON, M., 'Mate selection and the lady role', *Love and Attraction*, Cook, M. and Wilson, G. (eds.), Pergamon Press, Oxford (1979), 163–65.

ELIAS, J. and ELIAS, V., 'Dimensions of masculinity and female reactions to male nudity', *Love and Attraction*, Cook, M. and Wilson, G. (eds.), Pergamon Press, Oxford (1979), 475–80.

ERHARDT, A. A.: see references in Chapter Two.

EYSENCK, H. J., *The Inequality of Man*, Temple Smith, London (1973).

EYSENCK, H. J., 'Sex, society and the individual', *Love and Attraction*, Cook, M. and Wilson, G. (eds.), Pergamon Press, Oxford (1979), 337–45.

FISHER, H. E., *The Sex Contract*, William Morrow, New York (1982).

FORD, C. S. and BEACH, F. A., *Patterns of Sexual Behaviour*, Harper Row, New York (1951).

GALENSON, E. and ROIPE, H., 'The emergence of genital awareness in the second year of life', *Sex Differences in Behaviour*, Friedman, R. C. et al. (eds.), John Wiley & Sons, New York (1974), 223–31.

GILLAN, P. and FRITH, C., 'Male-female differences in response to erotica', *Love and Attraction*, Cook, M. and Wilson, G. (eds.), Pergamon Press, Oxford (1979), 461–63.

GILLIGAN, C., *In a Different Voice*, Harvard University Press, Cambridge, Mass. (1982).

GOVE, W.: see reference in Chapter Five.

GREEN, M., *Marriage*, Fontana Paperbacks, London (1984).

HENLEY, N. M., 'Power, sex and nonverbal communication', Prentice Hall, New Jersey (1977).

HITE, S., *The Hite Report: Women and Love*, Alfred A. Knopf, New York (1987).

HOBART, C. W., 'Changes in Courtship and Cohabitation Patterns in Canada, 1968–1977', *Love and Attraction*, Cook, M. and Wilson, G. (eds.), Pergamon Press, Oxford (1979), 359–71.

HUNTINGFORD, F. H. and TURNER, A. K.: see reference in Chapter Five.

INEICHEN, B., 'The social geography of marriage', *Love and Attraction*, Cook, M. and Wilson, G. D. (eds.), Pergamon Press, Oxford (1979), 115–49.

KINSEY, A. et al., *Sexual Behaviour in the Human Male*, W. B. Saunders, Philadelphia (1948).

LANCASTER, J. B., 'Evolutionary perspectives on sex differences in the higher primates', *Gender and the Life Course*, Rossi, A. S. (ed.), Aldine, New York (1985), 3–27.

LANCASTER, J. B. and LANCASTER, C. S., 'Parental investment: the hominid adaption', *How Humans Adapt: A Biocultural Odessey*, Ortner, D. J. (ed.), Smithsonian Institution Press, Washington D.C. (1983), 33–65.

LANCASTER, J. B. and LANCASTER, C. S., 'The watershed: change in parental-investment and family-formation strategies in the course of human evolution', *Parenting Across the Life Span*, Lancaster, J. B. et al. (eds.), Aldine de Gruyter, New York (1987), 187–203.

LA ROSSA, R. and LA ROSSA, M. M., *Transition to Parenthood*, Sage, Beverly Hills, California (1981).

LANGFELT, T., 'Processes in sexual development', *Love and Attraction*, Cook, M. and Wilson, G. (eds.), Pergamon Press, Oxford (1979), 493–97.

218

LEDWITZ-RIGBY, F., 'Biochemical and neurophysiological influences on human sexual behaviour', *The Psychobiology of Sex Differences and Sex Roles*, Parsons, J. E. (ed.) Hemisphere, London (1980), 95–104.

LEE, A. J., 'The styles of loving', *Psychology Today* (October 1974), 44–51.

LEGRAS, J. J., 'Hormones and sexual impotence', *Hormones and the Brain*, De Wied, D. and Van Keep, P. A. (eds.), MTP Press, Lancaster (1980), 205–17.

MESSANT, P.: see reference in Chapter Five.

MOSS, R. L. and DUDLEY, C. A., 'Hypothalmic peptides and sexual behaviour', *Behaviour and the Menstrual Cycle*, Friedman, R. C. (ed.), Dekker, New York (1982), 65–76.

MURSTEIN, B. I., *Love, Sex and Marriage Through the Ages*, Springer, New York (1974).

MURSTEIN, B. I., 'A taxonomy of love', *The Psychology of Love*, Sternberg, R. J. and Barnes, M. L. (eds.), Yale University Press, New Haven (1988), 13–37.

NIAS, D. K. B., 'Marital choice: matching or complementation?', *Love and Attraction*, Cook, M. and Wilson, G. D. (eds.), Pergamon Press, Oxford (1979), 151–55.

NIESCHLAG, E.: see reference in Chapter Five.

RIENISCH, J. M.: see reference in Chapter Two.

ROSENTHAL, R., 'Body talk and tone of voice: the language without words', *Psychology Today*, (September 1974), 64–68.

ROSSI, A. S., 'A biosocial perspective on parenting', *Daedelus*, 106 (1977), 1–32.

ROSSI, A. S.: see reference in Chapter Two.

ROSSI, A. S. and ROSSI, P. E.: see reference in Chapter Five.

SCARF, M., *Intimate Partners: Patterns in Love and Marriage*, Random House (New York), 1987.

SHELLY, D. S. A. and MCKEW, A., 'Pupillary dilation as a sexual signal and its links with adolescence', *Love and Attraction*, Cook, M. and Wilson, G. (eds.), Pergamon Press, Oxford (1979), 71–74.

STEIN, G.: see reference in Chapter Four.

STERNBERG, J. K. and BARNES, M. L., *The Psychology of Love*, Yale University Press, New Haven (1988).

SYMONS, D., *The Evolution of Human Sexuality*, Oxford University Press (1979).

TIGER, L. and SHEPHER, J.: see reference in Chapter Four.

TIGER, L., 'Alienated from the meanings of reproduction', *Masculinity and Femininity*, Reinisch, J. M. et al. (eds.), Oxford University Press (1987).

VEITCH, R. and GRIFFITT, W., 'Erotic arousal in males and females as perceived by their respective same and opposite sex peers', *Love and Attraction*, Cook, M. and Wilson, G. (eds.) Pergamon Press, Oxford (1979), 465–73.

WHALEN, R. E., 'Brain mechanisms controlling sexual behaviour', *Human Sexuality in Four Perspectives*, Beach, F. A. (ed.), Johns Hopkins University Press (1976), 213–42.

WILSON, G. D. and NIAS, D. K. B., *Loves Mysteries: The Psychology of Sexual Attraction*, Open Books, London (1976).

WILSON, G. D., 'The sociobiology of sex differences', *Bulletin of the British Psychological Society*, 32 (1979), 350–53.

YARMEY, A. D.: see reference in Chapter One.

CHAPTER EIGHT

BANCROFT, J., 'The relationship between gender identity and sexual behaviour: some clinical aspects', *Gender Differences: Their Ontogeny and Significance*, Ousted, C. and Taylor, D. (eds.), Churchill Livingstone, London (1972), 57–73.

BANCROFT, J., 'The relationship between hormones and sexual behaviour in humans', *Biological Determinants of Sexual Behaviour*, Hutchison, J. B. (ed.), John Wiley & Sons, New York (1978), 493–519.

BELL, A. P. et al., *Sexual Preference: Its Development in Men and Woman*, Indiana University Press, Bloomington, Indiana (1981).

BELL, G., *The Masterpiece of Nature: Evolution and the Genetics of Sexuality*, Croom Helm, London (1982).

BERAL, V. and COLWELL, L., 'Randomised trial of high doses of stilboestrol and ethisterone therapy in pregnancy: long term follow up of children', *Journal of Epidemiology and Community Health*, 35 (1981), 155–60.

BUCK, R. W.: see reference in Chapter Seven.

COMFORT, A., 'Deviation and variation', *Variant Sexuality: Research and Theory*, Wilson, G. (ed.), Croom Helm, London (1987), 1–20.

CROWN, S., 'Male homosexuality: perversion, deviation or variant?', *Sex, Hormones and Behaviour*, CIBA Foundation Symposium 62, Excerpta Medica, Amsterdam (1979), 145–64.

DIAMOND, M.: see reference in Chapter Two.

DÖRNER, G., 'Prenatal stress and possible aetiogenetic factors of homosexuality in human males', *Endokrinologie*, 75 (1980), 365–68.

DÖRNER, G.: also see references in Chapter Two.

EHRHARDT, A. A.: see references in Chapter Two.

FLOR-HENRY, P., 'Cerebral aspects of sexual deviation', *Variant Sexuality: Research and Theory*, Wilson, G. D. (ed.), Croom Helm, London (1987), 49–83.

GREEN, R., 'The behaviourally feminine male child: pretransexual? pretransvestic? prehomosexual?', *Sex Differences in Behaviour*, Friedman, R. C. et al. (eds.), John Wiley & Sons, New York (1974), 301–25.

GREEN, R., 'Gender identity in childhood and later sexual orientation: follow up of 78 males', *Am. J. Psychiat.*, 142 (1985), 339–41.

GREEN, R. et al., 'Lesbian mothers and their children: a comparison with solo parent heterosexual mothers and their children', *Archives of Sexual Behaviour*, 15, No. 2 (1986), 167–84.

GREEN, R.: also see reference in Chapter Two.

KOHLBERG, L. and ULLIAN, D. Z., 'Stages in the development of psychosexual concepts and attitudes', *Sex Differences in Behaviour*, Friedman, R. C. et al. (eds.), John Wiley & Sons, New York (1974), 209–22.

KORNFELD, H., 'T-lymphoctye sub-populations in homosexual men', *New England Journal of Medicine*, 307, No. 12 (1980), 729–31.

LANGEVIN, R. (ed.), *Erotic Preference, Gender Identity, and Aggression in Men: New Research Studies*, Lawrence Erlbaum Associates, New Jersey (1985).

MACCULLOCK, M. J. and WADDINGTON, J. L., 'Neuroendocrine mechanisms and aetiology of male and female homosexuality', *British Journal of Psychiatry*, 139 (1981), 341–45.

MEYER-BAHLBURG, H. F. L. et al., 'Cryptorchidism, development of gender identity and sex behaviour', *Sex Differences in Behaviour*, Friedman, R. C. et al. (eds.), John Wiley & Sons, New York (1974), 281–99.

MEYER-BAHLBURG, H. F. L., 'Homosexual orientation in women and men: a hormonal basis?', *The Psychobiology of Sex Differences and Sex Roles*, Parsons, J. (ed.), Hemisphere, London (1980), 103–30.

MEYER-BAHLBURG, H. F. L., 'Hormones and homosexuality', *Advances in Psychoneuroendocrinology*, 3, No. 1 (1980), 349–64.

MEYER-BAHLBURG, H. F. L., 'Hormones and psychosexual differentiation: implications for the management of intersexuality, homosexuality and transsexuality', *Clinics in Endocrinology and Metabolism*, 11, No. 3 (1982), 673–93.

MEYER-BAHLBURG, H. F. L., 'Psychoendocrine research on sexual orientation: current studies, future options', *Progress in Brain Research*, 61, De Vries, G. J. et al. (eds.), Elsevier, Amsterdam (1984), 375–98.

MEYERSON, B. J., 'Hormone-dependant socio-sexual behaviours and neurotransmitters', *Progress in Brain Research*, 61, De Vries, G. J. et al. (eds.) Elsevier, Amsterdam (1984), 271–81.

MONEY, J., 'Human Hermaphroditism', *Sexuality in Four Perspectives*, Beach, F. A. (ed.), Johns Hopkins University Press, Baltimore (1976), 62–83.

MORRIS, J., *Conundrum*, Penguin Books, London (1987).

MILARDO, R. M. and MURSTEIN, B. I., 'The implications of exchange orientation on dyadic function of heterosexual cohabitors', *Love and Attraction*, Cook, M. and Wilson, G. (eds.), Pergamon Press, Oxford (1979), 279–85.

NEISCHLAG, E.: see reference in Chapter Five.

REINISCH, J. M. and SAUNDERS, S. A., 'Early barbiturate exposure: the brain, sexually dimorphic behaviour and learning', *Neuroscience and Biobehavioural Reviews*, 6 (1982), 311–19.

SIMPSON, M. J. A., 'Tactile experience and sexual behaviour: aspects of development with special reference to primates', *Biological Determinants of Sexual Behaviour*, Hutchison, J. B. (ed.), John Wiley & Sons, New York (1978), 783–807.

SYMONS, D.: see reference in Chapter Seven.

WARD, I. L., 'Sexual behaviour differentiation: prenatal hormonal and environmental control', *Sex Differences in Behaviour*, Friedman, R. C. et al. (eds.), John Wiley & Sons, New York (1974), 3–17.

WAYNE, C. B. and JAMES, F. C., 'Testosterone: a major determinant of extragenital sexual differentiation', *Science*, 211 (1981), 1258–93.

WILSON, G. D. and NIAS, D. K. B.: see reference in Chapter Seven.

WILSON, G. D., 'An ethological approach to sexual deviation', *Variant Sexuality: Research and Theories*, Wilson, G. D. (ed.), Croom Helm, London (1987), 84–115.

WILSON, G. D. and FULFORD, K. W. M., 'Sexual behaviour, personality and hormonal characteristics of heterosexual, homosexual and bisexual men', *Love and Attraction*, Cook, M. and Wilson, G. D. (eds.), Pergamon Press, Oxford (1979), 387–93.

YALOM, I. D. et al.: see reference in Chapter Two.

CHAPTERS ELEVEN AND TWELVE

BARON, N. J. and BIELBY, W. T., 'Organisational barriers to gender equality: sex segregation of jobs and opportunities', *Gender and the Life Course*, Rossi, A. S. (ed.), Aldine, New York (1985), 233–51.

BELEKY, M. F. et al., *Women's ways of knowing*, Basic Books, New York (1986).

BENBOW, C. P. and BENBOW, R. M.: see reference in Chapter One.

BENBOW, C. P. and STANLEY, J. C.: see references in Chapter One.

BRADWAY, K. and THOMPSON, C., 'Intelligence and adulthood: a twenty-five year follow-up', *Journal of Educational Psychology*, 53, No. 1 (1962), 1–14.

BRASLOW, J. B. and HEINS, M. H., 'Women in medical education', *New England Journal of Medicine*, 304 (19) (1981), 1129–35.

BRODY, E. L., 'Gender differences on standardized examinations used for selection applicants to graduate and professional schools', paper presented at annual meeting of American Educational Research Assoc., Washington, D.C., 24 April 1987.

BURNSTEIN, B. et al., 'Sex differences in cognitive functioning: evidence, determinants, implications', *Human Development*, 23 (1980), 289–313.

CALLAHAN-LEVY et al., 'Sex differences in the allocation of pay', *Journal of Personality and Social Psychology*, 37 (1979), 433–46.

CANCIAN, F. M.: see reference in Chapter Seven.

CONRAD, H. S. et al., 'Sex differences in mental growth and decline', *Journal of Educational Psychology*, XXIV, 3 (1933), 161–69.

D'ANDRADE, R. G., 'Sex differences and cultural institutions', *The Development of Sex Differences*, Maccoby, E. E. (ed.), Stanford University Press (1966), 174–204.

DAUBER, S. L., 'Sex differences on the SAT-M, SAT-V, TSWE, and ACT among college-bound high school students', paper presented at annual meeting of American Educational Research Assoc., Washington, D.C., 24 April 1987.

ECCLES, J. S., 'Gender roles and the achievement patterns: an expectancy value perspective', *Masculinity and Femininity*, Reinisch, J. M. et al. (eds.), Oxford University Press (1987), 240–80.

EKEHAMMER, B. and SIDANIUS, J., 'Sex differences in sociopolitical attitudes: a replication and extension', *British Journal of Psychology*, 21 (1982), 249–57.

Equal Opportunities Commission: Annual Report 1986, HMSO London (1987).

Equal Opportunities Commission: Women and Men in Britain, A Statistical Profile, HMSO London (1987).

ERHARDT, A. A., 'A transactional perspective on the development of gender differences', *Masculinity and Femininity*, Reinisch, J. M. et al. (eds.), Oxford University Press (1987), 281–311.

Everywoman, 'The gender gap', No. 7 (September 1985).

FINN, J. D. et al., 'Sex differences in educational attainment: a cross-national perspective', *Harvard Educational Review*, 49, No. 4 (1979), 477–503.

GILLIGAN, C., *In a Different Voice*, Harvard University Press, Cambridge, Mass. (1982).

GILLIGAN, C., 'Why should a woman be more like a man?' *Psychology Today*, (June 1982), 68–77.

GOFFEE, R. and SCASE, R., *Women in Charge*, Allen and Unwin, London (1985).

GOULD, R. E., 'Measuring masculinity by the size of the paycheck', *Men and Masculinity*, Pleck, J. H. and Sawyer, J., Prentice Hall, London (1974), 96–100.

HENNIG, M. and JARDIM, A., *The Managerial Woman*, Pan, London (1979).

HERTZ, L., *The Business Amazons*, Methuen Paperback, London (1986).

HEWLETT, S. A., *A Lesser Life*, Michael Joseph, London (1987).

'Hospital and dental staff in England and Wales', *Health Trends*, 18 (1986), 50.

HORNER, M. S., 'Toward an understanding of achievement-related conflicts in women', *Journal of Social Issues*, 28, No. 2 (1972), 157–75.

KIPINIS, D., 'Intelligence, occupational status and achievement orientation', *Exploring Sex Differences*, Lloyd, B. and Archer, J. (eds.), Academic Press, London (1976), 93–122.

KOSTICK, M. M., 'A study of transfer: sex differences in the reasoning process', *Journal of Educational Psychology*, 45 (December 1954), 449–58.

LEVER, J.: see references in Chapter Four.

LUPKOWSKI, A. E., 'Sex differences on the differential aptitude tests', paper presented at annual meeting of American Educational Research Assoc., Washington D.C., 24 April 1987.

MACCOBY, E., 'Sex differences in intellectual functioning', *The Development of Sex Differences*, Maccoby, E. (ed.), Stanford University Press (1966), 23–55.

MAHONE, C. H. Fear of Failure and Unrealistic Vocational Aspirations. Journal of Abnormal and Social Psychology, 60, No. 2 (1960), 253–66.

MCCLELLAND, D. C., *Power: The Inner Experience*, Irvington Publishers, New York (1979).

MCGEE, P. E., *Humor: Its Origin and Development*, W. H. Freeman, San Francisco (1979).

MEADE, M.: see reference in Chapter One.

Medical Women's Federation, London. Unpublished statistics on women in medicine supplied by them.

National Management Survey, British Institute of Management, London (1988).

NEWMAN, L., 'Pride and prejudice: female encounters in general practice', *Medical Woman*, 6, No. 2 (Summer 1987), 3–7.

NOTMAN, M.: see reference in Chapter Five.

PIAGET, J., *The Moral Judgement of Children*, Free Press, New York (1965).

RAPAPORT, R. and RAPAPORT, R., *Dual Career Families Re-Examined*, Oxford University Press (1976).

SAVIN-WILLIAMS, R.: see reference in Chapter Five.

SILVERMAN, J., 'Attentional styles and a study of sex differences', *Attention: Contemporary Studies and Analysis*, Mostofsky, D. (ed.), Appleton-Century-Croft, New York (1970), 61–98.

STANLEY, J. C., 'Gender difference on the College Board Achievement Tests and the Advance Placement Examinations', paper presented at the annual meeting of American Educational Research Assoc., Washington, D.C., 24 April 1987.

STANLEY, J., 'Study of mathematically precocious youth', paper presented at the annual meeting of American Educational Research Assoc., Washington, D.C., 24 April 1987.

STEPHEN, P. J., 'Career patterns of women medical graduates 1974–84', *Medical Education*, 21 (1987), 225–59.

STEIN, A. H. and BAILEY, M. M., 'The socialization of achievement orientation in females', *Psychological Bulletin*, 80, No. 5 (November 1973), 345–66.

STRECHERT, K., *The Credibility Gap*, Thorsons Publishing Group, Wellingborough, Northamptonshire (1987).

TIGER, L., *Men in Groups*, Random House, New York (1969).

TIGER, L., 'The possible biological origins of sexual discrimination', *The Impact of Science on Society*, XX, No. 1 (1970).

TIGER, L. and FOX, R., *The Imperial Animal*, Secker and Warburg, London (1972).

TIGER, L. and SHEPHER, J.: see reference in Chapter Four.

TIGER, L. (1987): see reference in Chapter Seven.

TURNER, R. H., 'Some aspects of women's ambition', *American Journal of Sociology*, LXX, No. 3 (November 1964), 271–85.

WITLESON, S., 'Exchange on Gender', *The New York Review*, 24 October 1985, 53–55.

VETTER, B., 'Working women scientists and engineers', *Science*, 207 (1980), 28–34.

SUMMARY REFERENCES

FAUSTO-STERLING, A., *Myths of Gender*, Basic Books, New York (1985).

FRIEDAN, B., *New Statesman* (23 September 1977).

GOLDBERG, S., see General References.

LEVIN, M., see General References.

MCGUINNESS, D., see reference in Chapter One.

MILLET, K., *Sexual Politics*, Virago, London (1977).

RESTAK, R., see General References.

RICHARDS, J., *The Sceptical Feminist*, Routledge and Kegan Paul, Boston (1980).

ROSSI, A., see references in Chapter Seven, Nine, Eleven.

TIGER, L. See reference in Chapter Eleven.

VELLE, W., see General References.

WITLESON, S., see reference 'Exchange on Gender', Chapter Three.

EPILOGUE

Brain Differences:

ALLEN, L.S. et al., 'Two sexually dimorphic cell groups in the human brain', *The Journal of Neuroscience*, 9(2), (February 1989), 497-506.

CORSI-CABRERA, M. et al., 'Correlation between EEG and cognitive abilities: sex differences', *Intern. J. Neuroscience*, 45 (1989), 133-141.

HINES, M., 'Why can't a man be more like a woman?', *Omni* (October 1990), 42-68; and personal communication (1991).

NAYLOR, C., 'Why can't a man be more like a woman?', *Omni* (October 1990), 42-68; and personal communication (1991).

POTTER, S.M. and GRAVES, R.E., 'Is interhemispheric transfer related to handedness and gender?', *Neuropsychologia*, 26(2) (1988), 319-325.

WITLESON, S.F., 'Hand and sex differences in the isthmus and genu of the human corpus callosum', *Brain*, 112 (1989), 799-835; and personal communication (1991).

WITLESON, S.F., 'Structural correlates of cognition in the human brain', *Neurobiology of Higher Cognitive Function*, Scheibel, A.B. and Welchsler, A.F. (eds.), Guilford Press, New York (1990), 167-183.

Hormonal Affects:

DOBBS, J., Personal communication (1991) regarding testosterone levels and behaviour in the legal profession and amoung Vietnam Veterans.

GOUCHIE, C. and KIMURA, D., 'The relation between testosterone levels and cognitive ability patterns', *Research Bulletin 690*, Department of Psychology, University of Ontario, London, Canada (May 1990).

KIMURA, D., 'Monthly fluctuations in sex hormones affect women's cognitive skills', *Psychology Today* (November 1989), 63-66.

KIMURA, D. and HAMPSON, E., 'Neural and hormonal mechanisms mediating sex differences in cognition', *Research Bulletin 689*, Department of Psychology, University of Ontario, London, Canada (April 1990).

HAMPSON, E. and KIMURA, D., 'Reciprocal effects of hormonal fluctuations on human motor and perceptual spatial skills', *Behavioural Neuroscience*, 102, No. 3 (1988), 456-459.

REINISCH, J.M. and SANDERS, S.A. 'Sex differences and human personality development', *Handbook of Behavioural Neurobiology*, 10, *Sexual Differentiation: A Lifespan Approach*, H. Molts et al (eds.), New York, Plenum Publishing Corporation (in press: 1991).

REINSCH, J.M. et al., 'Hormonal contributions to sexually dimorphic behavioural development in humans', *Psychoneuroendocrinology* (in press: 1991).

Homosexuality:

DORNER, G., 'Hormone-dependent brain development and neuroendocrine prophylaxis', *Exp. Clin. Endocrinol.*, 94, No. 1/2 (1989), 4-22.

MCCORMICK, C.M., WITLESON, S.F. and KINGSTONE, E., 'Left-handedness in homosexual men and women: neuroendocrine implications', *Psychoneuroendocrinology*, 15 (1990), 69-76.

Mental Illness (BrainSex differences):

DELISI, L.E. et al., 'Gender differences in the brain: are they relevant to the pathogenesis of schizophrenia?', *Comprehensive Psychiatry*, 30, No. 3 (1989), 197-207.

Schizophrenia Bulletin, National Institute of Mental Health. Issue Theme: *Gender and Schizophrenia*, 16, No. 2, 1990.

SIKICH, L. and TODD, R.D., 'Are the neurodevelopmental effects of gonadal hormones related to sex differences in psychiatric illness?', *Psychiatric Developments*, 4 (1988), 277-309.

Crime Sex Differences:

FLOR-HENRY, P., 'Influence of gender in schizophrenia as related to other psychopathalogical syndromes', *Schizophrenia Bulletin*, 16, No. 2. (1990), 211-228.

NOTES ON THE CHAPTERS

Specific references that are quoted in the text can be found by using the References for each Chapter. Where a fact(s) is quoted in the text the opening words of the sentence containing the information are quoted, followed by the reference(s) on which that information is based.

CHAPTER ONE

p. 9.   'When a Canadian psychologist . . .' Kimura, D.

p. 11.   'The Germans were . . .' Swaab, D. F. and Hofman, M. A.

          'The French scientist . . .' Gould, S. J.

p. 12.   'At least one researcher . . .' in conversation, Harris, L. J.

          'Another told us . . .' in conversation, Broverman, D.

          'The first systematic . . .' Garai, J. E. and Scheinfeld, A. (See General References).

          'Ten years later in the US . . .' Garai, J. E. and Scheinfeld, A.

          'Havelock Ellis . . .' Ellis, H., 339 (See General References).

p. 13. 'Wechsler, among others . . .' Garai, J. E. and Scheinfeld, A.; McGuinness, D., 18, p. 72; Nicolson, J.; Lloyd, B. and Archer, J. (See General References).
'Our findings confirm . . .' Wechsler, D.
p. 14. 'What an early British . . .' Hutt, C. (1975).
'The main group championing . . .' Money, J.
p. 15. 'The area where the biggest . . .' Gaulin, S. J. C. et al.; Garai, J. E. and Scheinfeld, A.; Harris, L. J. (1978) (See General References); McGee, M. G.
'One scientist who has reviewed . . .' Harris, L. J.
'A typical test . . .' Harris, L. J.
p. 16. 'From school age onwards . . .' Benbow, C. P. and Benbow, R. M.; Benbow, C. P. and Stanley, J. C., (1980) and (1983).
'Boys also have the superior . . .' Burg, A.; Garai, J. E. and Scheinfeld, A.
p. 17. 'The better spatial ability . . .' Harris, L. J. (1978) and (1981); McGee, M. G.; Maccoby, E. and Jacklin, N., 85–98. (See General References.)
'It has been shown . . .' McGuinness, D. (1976) (See General References) and Rienisch, J. M.
'Girls say their . . .' Garai, J. E. and Scheinfeld, A.; Harris, L. J. (1978) and (1981); McGuinness, D.; Maccoby, E. and Jacklin, N., 75–85. (See General References.)
'Boys outnumber . . .' Durden-Smith, J. and Simone, D. (See General References); McGuinness, D. (1985), 21 and 115–19.
'Girls and women hear . . .' Garai, J. E. and Scheinfeld; McGuinness, D. (1985) (1976) and (1979).
p. 18. 'Men and women even see . . .' McGuinness, D. (1976) and (1979).
'They are more sensitive to the red . . .' as above.
'They have a better visual . . .' Bardwick, J. M., (See General References) 102; Buffery, A. H. W. and Gray, J. A.; McGuinness, D. (1976) and (1979), 162.
'Men see better . . .' McGuinness, D. (1976) and (1979).
'They have a wider . . .' as above.
'They have more rods . . .' as above.
'Women react faster . . .' Hutt, C., 92; Reinisch, J. M.; Restak, R. (See General References), 81.
'In a sample of young adults . . .' Garai, J. E. and Scheinfeld, A.
'In childhood and maturity . . .' McGuinness, D. (1976) and (1979).
'There is strong evidence . . .' Garai, J. E. and Scheinfeld, A.
'Women's noses . . .' Rienisch, J. M.; Hutt, C. 91.
p. 19. 'Women are better at . . .' Bardwick, J. P., 102; Hoyenga, K. B. and Hoyenga, K., 303–08.
'Older females . . .' McGuinness, D. (1976); Yarmey, A. D.
'Sex differences have been noted . . .' Hutt, C., 97.
'It seems unrealistic to deny . . .' Restak, R., 204.

CHAPTER TWO
p. 26. 'It took microscopic examination . . .' Goy, R. W. and McEwen, B. S. (See General References), 102–15; McEwen, B. S. (1981) and (1987); Raisman, G. and Field, P. M. (1971) and (1973).
p. 27. 'Their curiosity aroused . . .' Dörner, G. articles; Goy, R. W. and McEwen, B. S. (See General References), 102–15; Gorski, R. A., articles; McEwen, B. S. articles; Raisman, G. and Field, P. M., articles.
'Further research revealed . . .' Hines, M.; Gaulin, S. J. C., et al.
'There is a graphic . . .' Goy, R. W. and McEwen, B. S., 115–19.
p. 28. '"The brain" according to . . .' Witleson, S.
'Scientists can now . . .' Goy, R. W. and McEwen, B. S., 44–54; Phoenix, C. H.
p. 29. '"The brains of male and female . . .' Gorski, R. A. (1984).
'Male rats are better . . .' Goy, R. W. and McEwen, B. S., 31–32; Hoyenga, K. B. and Hoyenga, K. (See General References), 79–80.
The Case of Jane is based on Ehrhardt, A. A., articles; Ehrhardt, A. A. and Baker, S.; Ehrhardt, A. A. and Meyer-Bahlburg, H. F. L. articles; Hutt, C.; Kaplan, A. G.; Reinisch, J. M., articles; Reinisch, J. M. and Saunders, S. A.

p. 31. **The Case of Caroline** is based on Hutt, C.; Reske-Neilsen; Reinisch, J. M., articles; Rovet, J. and Netley, C.

p. 32. 'The findings of this study . . .' Reinisch, J. M. articles; Reinisch, J. M. and Saunders, S. A.; Shapiro, B. H., et al.; Siler-Kohodr, T. M.; Saunders, S. A. and Reinisch, J. M.; Yalom, I. D., et al.

    The Case of Jim is based on Reinisch, J. M. articles; Reinisch, J. M. and Saunders, S. A.; Saunders, S. A. and Reinisch, J. M., Yalom, I. D., et al.

p. 33. 'The psychologist Dr June . . .' Reinisch, J. M. articles; Reinisch, J. M. and Saunders, S. A.; Saunders, S. A. and Reinisch, J. M.

p. 35. **The case of Juan, née Juanita** is based on Berg, I., et al., Imperato-McGinley, J., et al. articles.

p. 36. 'As one of them sums . . .' Rossi, A. S.

CHAPTER THREE

p. 42. 'The first indications . . .' Durden-Smith, J. (See General References), 54; McGlone, J., articles.

    'Numerous studies . . .' Butler, S.; Flor Henry, P.; Harshman, R. A., et al.; Hines, M.; Inglis, J. and Lawson, J. S.; Kimura, D. and Harshman, R.; Kimura, D. articles; McGlone, J. articles; Tucker, D. M.; Witleson, S. articles.

p. 43. 'Tests have measured . . .' Tucker, D. M.

    'Men faced with a test . . .' Harris, L. J. (1978); McGlone, J. (1980).

    'Another piece of the puzzle . . .' Gordon, H. W.; Hines, M.

    'Men who are known . . .' Gaulin, S. J. C.; Hines, M.; Rienisch, J. M. articles.

    'New research has added . . .' Kimura, D. and Harshman, R. A.; Kimura, D. (1985) and in conversation.

p. 44. 'since confirmed by other . . .' Mateer, C. A. and in conversation.

p. 45. 'A leading Canadian . . .' Witleson, S. (1978) and (1985) and in conversation.

    'The differences in brain . . .' Harris, L. J. (1978) and (1981); Hines, M. and in conversation; Nyborg, N. articles; Restak, R. (See General References), 192–204 and in conversation; Witleson, S. (1978) and (1985) and in conversation.

    'There is a further difference . . .' Butler, S.; Durden-Smith, 53; Harris, L. J. (1978) and (1981); Hines, M.; Levy, J. and in conversation; McGlone, J. articles.

    'The superiority of women . . .' Kimura, D. and Harshman, R. A.; Kimura, D. (1985) and in conversation.

p. 46. 'Sandra Witelson . . .' Witleson, S. (1978).

p. 47. 'In women the corpus . . .' De Lacoste-Utamsing, C., et al. articles; in conversation with Kimura, D. and Hines, M.

    'And the latest research . . .' in conversation with Hines, M.

p. 48. 'Some scientists suggest . . .' Butler, S.; McGuinness, D., 45–46; Restak, R., 192–204; Witleson, S. (1978) and (1985) and in conversation.

    'Sandra Witleson calls . . .' Witleson, S. (1978).

CHAPTER FOUR

p. 53. 'He or she comes into . . .' Diamond, M.

    'Rats develop bigger . . .' Juraska, J. M. articles; Restak, R. (See General References), 104–06.

p. 54. 'Kittens reared in . . .' Restak, R., 98.

    'In humans, too . . .' Restak, R., 86–101; Smith, A., 35–55.

    The Case of Genie, McGuinness, D. (See General References), 88–87.

p. 55. 'At a few hours old . . .' McGuinness, D. articles; Rienisch, J. M.

    'When it comes to sound . . .' McGuinness, D. articles and in General References, 76–83.

    'Baby girls are more . . .' Hutt, C.; McGuinness, D. (1976).

p. 56. 'One study involves . . .' McGuinness, D., 90.

    'From the cradle . . .' Hutt, C.; McGuinness, D. articles; Reinisch, J. M.; Restak, R., 199.

    'Boys are more active . . .' Korner, A. F.; Hutt, C.; McGuinness, D. articles.

    'At four months old . . .' McGuinness, D. articles; Restak, R., 199.

'A one-week-old baby . . .' Korner, A. F.' Kagan, J., McGuinness, D. articles.
p. 57. 'That bias in girls . . .' Hutt, C. McGuinness, D. articles; Restak, R., 199; Rienisch, J. M.
'In a study of 2–4 year . . .' Buffrey, A. W. H. and Gray, J. A.; Harris, L. J. articles (See General References); Rienisch, J. M.
p. 58. 'At the age of three . . .' Harris, L. J. (1978).
'Scientists have devised . . .' Goldberg, S. and Lewis, M.; Hutt, C.
'"The boy more naturally . . .' Harris, L. J. (1979).
p. 59. 'According to one English . . .' Hutt, C.
'There they will play . . .' Garai, J. E. and Scheinfeld, A. (See General References); Harris, L. J. articles; Hutt, C.
'In the playschool class room . . .' Garai, J. E. and Scheinfeld, A.; Harris, L. J. articles; Hutt, C.; McGuinness, D. articles.
'A newcomer . . .' Hutt, C. (See General References), 96; McGuinness, D. (1976).
'By the age of four . . .' Garai, J. E. and Scheinfeld, A.; Reinisch, J. M.; Stein, S., 20, 100.
'Boys tend not to bother . . .' Kagan, J.; Sutton-Smith, B.
'Boys will make up stories . . .' Garai, J. E. and Scheinfeld, A.; Sutton-Smith, B.
p. 60. 'Boys' games involve . . .' Diamond, M.; Harris, L. J. articles; Hutt, C.; Kagan, J.; Sutton-Smith, B.
The Case of Mandy is based on the same research as **The Case of Jane** (See Chapter Two).
p. 61. 'In one study of nursery . . .' McGuinness, D. (1979).
'Even in the Israeli . . .' Tiger, L. and Shepher, J.
'But a few lonely . . .' McGuinness, D. P., 55–106.
p. 62. '"Sex difference research . . .' as above, 75.
'Boys are actually better . . .' McGee, M. G.; McGuinness, D., 84–90.
'It is not the relative . . .' McGuinness, D. (1979); Restak, R., 199; Witleson, S. (1976).
'"It is clear that the . . .' McGuinness, D., 70.
'Boys do better than . . .' Coltheart, M., et al.
p. 63. 'The female infant's . . .' Harris, L. J. (1978); McGuinness, D., 89.
'At all ages between six . . .' Buffery, A. H. W. and Gray, J. A.; Garai, J. E. and Scheinfeld, A.; McGuinness, D. articles.
'A study of nine and ten . . .' Harris, L. J. (1978).
p. 64. 'As early as the age of six . . .' Witleson, S. (1976).
p. 65. '"In the early school years . . .' McGuinness, D. (1979).
'Over 95 per cent . . .' Restak, R., 205.
'"Hiding the knowledge . . .' McGuinness, D., 32.

CHAPTER FIVE
p. 70. '"It is essential . . .' Meleges, F. T. and Hamburg, D. A.
p. 71. 'It is now accepted . . .' Bardwick, J. (See General References), 301; Kopera, H.; Hoyenga K. B. and Hoyenga, K. P. (See General References), 122–52; Meleges, F. T. and Hamburg, D. A.; Messant, P. K.; Notman, M.; Rossi, A. S. and Rossi, P. E.
p. 72. 'Evolution has equipped . . .' Meleges, F. T. and Hamburg, D. A.; Messant, P. K.; Rossi, A. S. and Rossi, P. E.
'Progesterone, on the . . .' Kopera, H.
p. 73. 'In evolutionary terms . . .' Meleges, F. T. and Hamburg, D. A.
p. 74. 'One study has found . . .' Stone, M. H.
'Most female prisoners . . .' Dalton, K. articles; Messant, P. K.; Moyer, K. E. (1974) and *Violence* (1987), 78–9.
'"The psychological . . .' Meleges, F. T. and Hamburg, D. A.
p. 75. **The Case of Moira**, in conversation, Katherine Dalton.
p. 76. '"From mouse to man . . .' Moyer, K. E. book (1987), 1.
'"Human aggression is . . .' Buss, A. H.
'First, they induced . . .' Moyer, K. E. book (1987), 2; (1974).

'If the male is castrated . . .' as above.

'It's not just a matter . . .' Hoyenga, K. B. and Hoyenga, K., 94–110; Reinisch, J. M. and Saunders, S. J.; Rubin, R. T. articles.

p. 77. The Case of Erika is based on the same research as The Case of Caroline (See Chapter Two).

p. 78. The Case of Colin is based on the same research as The Case of Jim (See Chapter Two).

'June Reinisch . . .' Reinisch, J. M.

'It is not just aggression . . .' Hoyenga, K. B. and Hoyenga, K., 122–38; Reinisch, J. M. and Saunders, S. A.

p. 79. 'The most placid . . .' Hoyenga, K. B. and Hoyenga, K., 31–32; Reske-Neilsen, E.; Rovet, J. and Netley, C.

p. 80. 'Most criminals . . .' Moyer, K. E. article (1987); book (1987), 23–25.

'One study reveals . . .' Persky, H., et al.

p. 81. ' "All their old antisocial tendencies . . .' Moyer, K. E. (1987), 45.

'The capacity for aggression . . .' Hoyenga, K. B. and Hoyenga, K., 289.

'In another test . . .' same as above.

'Boys, as they grow up . . .' Kagan, J.; Moyer, K. E. (1987), 4.

'When watching television . . .' Garai, J. E. and Scheinfeld, A.

p. 82. 'According to a study . . .' Young People in the 80's.

'A study of responses to . . .' Reinisch, J. M. and Saunders, S. A.

'It has been found that . . .' Maccoby, E. and Jacklin, N. (See General References), 239.

'At the extreme . . .' Moyer, K. E. book (1987), 4.

'In one study, a sample . . .' Reinisch, J. M. and Saunders, S. A.

p. 83. 'As Walter Gove . . .' Gove, W. R.

'When it comes to dominance . . .' Velle, W. (See General References).

'Young male humans . . .' Huntingford, F. H. and Turner, A. K., 330.

p. 84. 'At the University of Chicago . . .' Savan-Williams, R.

'Another study . . .' Hoyenga, K. B. and Hoyenga, K. P., 275–76.

p. 85. 'The pursuit of power . . .' Goldberg, S. (See General References).

'To rise in . . .' same as above.

CHAPTER SIX

p. 88. 'A leading Danish . . .' Nyborg, H. (1983).

p. 89. 'Male IQ scores . . .' Hoyenga, K. B. and Hoyenga, K. P. (See General References), 237–39; Nyborg, H. articles.

'A talent search . . .' Benbow, C. P. and Stanley, J. C. articles.

'The male hormone . . .' Erhardt, A. A. articles; Hampson, E. and Kimura, D.; Heir, D. and Crowley, W.; Hoyenga, K. B. and Hoyenga, K., 140–45; Rovet, J. and Netley, C.

p. 90. 'Most boys seem to . . .' McGuinness, D. (1979).

p. 91. 'Men find it easier . . .' Harris, L. J. articles (See General References); McGee, M. G.; McGuinness, D.

'Research into human . . .' Erhardt, A. A. articles; Hampson, E. and Kimura, D. articles; Hoyenga, K. B. and Hoyenga, K., 237–39; Hutt, C. (See General References), 118; Nyborg, H. articles.

'Teenage girls whose . . .' Dalton, K., articles.

The Case of Catherine is based on the same research as The Case of Jane (See Chapter Two).

p. 92. 'Previous studies of . . .' Baker, S. and Erhardt, A. A.

'A new study in 1986 . . .' Shute, V. J., et al.

p. 93. The Case of Ginette is based on the same research as The Case of Caroline (See Chapter Two).

'The variation is related . . .' Hampson, E. and Kimura, D. articles; Rosenthal, K.

p. 94. 'Boys with XXY . . .' Hoyenga, K. B. and Hoyenga, K. P., 246; Nyborg, H. articles; Ratcliffe, S. G.

'And boys whose . . .' Yalom, I. D., et al.

'The very highest level . . .' Heir, D. and Crowley, W.; Hoyenga, K. B. and Hoyenga, K., 245–46; Nyborg, H. articles.

p. 95. 'Experiments have been . . .' Hoyenga, K. B. and Hoyenga, K., 141–42; Boroverman, D., et al. articles, Klaiber, E. L., et al. (1971).

'"Strong automatisers . . .' Broverman, D. (1980).

p. 96. 'Women's capacity for . . .' Hampson, E. and Kimura, D. articles; Klaiber, E. L., et al. (1982); Nyborg, H. articles.

'Other tests . . .' Rosenthal, K.

p. 97. 'Studies of school-age . . .' Hoyenga, K. B. and Hoyenga, K., 272–74.

'For instance, when girls . . .' same as above.

CHAPTER SEVEN

p. 99. 'The rule has . . .' Wilson, G. D. and Nias, D. K. B., 30.

p. 102. '"We know more about the maze . . .' Eysenck, H. J. (1979).

'We are nature's sexiest . . .' Murstein, B I., p. 418–26, Symons, D., 97–110.

'In many surveys . . .' Hoyenga, K. B. and Hoyenga, K. (See General References), 330–32; Murstein, B. I., 422–23; Wilson, G. D. and Nias, D. K. B., 131.

p. 103. 'Professor Hans . . .' Eysenck, H. J. (1979).

'Testosterone, the aggression . . .' Hoyenga, K. B. and Hoyenga, K., 133–37; Nieschlag, E.; Wilson, G. D. and Nias, D. K. B., 79; Symons, D., 105.

p. 104. 'In a woman's menstrual cycle, . . .' Buck, R. W., et al., 211; Messant, P.; Rossi, A. E. and Rossi, P. E.; Wilson, G. D. and Nias, D. K. B., 81.

'In men, testosterone . . .' Nieschlag, E.

'Sexual awareness . . .' Bardwick, J. M., 51–59; Buck, R. W., et al., 209; Galenson, E. and Roipe, H.; Wilson, G. D. and Nias, D. K. B., 131.

'Some girls, however, do dream . . .' Hoyenga, K. B. and Hoyenga, K., 330; Symons, D., 290.

'High concentrations of . . .' D'Andrade, R. G.; Murstein, B. I.; 422–23; Wilson, G. D. and Nias, D. K. B., 79, 131.

'A male-voice choir . . .' Nieschlag, E.

p. 105. 'But a word of caution . . .' Huntingford, F. H. and Turner, A. K., 340.

'"There seems to be no . . .' Kinsey, A., et al.

'In an American questionnaire . . .' Murstein, B. I., 425.

'Men, deprived of sex, . . .' Murstein, B. I., 422.

p. 106. 'In men, the key . . .' Diamond, M.; Gillan, P. and Frith, C.; Hoyenga, K. B. and Hoyenga, K., 327–30; Murstein, B. I., 423.

'Women are not . . .' Elias, J. and Elias, V.; Hoyenga, K. B. and Hoyenga, K., 327–30; Murstein, B. I., 426; Symons, D., 170–84; Vietch, R. and Griffitt, W.

'Two magazines . . .' Symons, D., 174–75.

'The same findings . . .' Symons, D., 178–79.

p. 108. 'Preferences tend to be . . .' Wilson, G. D. and Nias, D. K. B., 30.

'"In most societies . . .' Ford, C. S. and Beach, F. A.

'When the testosterone . . .' Dörner, G. (1980), Murstein, B. I., 418.

p. 109. 'With these inbuilt . . .' Beck, S. B.

'Sexual gratification . . .' Murstein, B. I., 387–97; Cancian, F. M.

'This is also, for women, . . .' Murstein, B. I., 425.

'One interesting study . . .' Murstein, B. I., 431–32.

p. 110. '"Women do tend . . .' Hoyenga, K. B. and Hoyenga, K., 303; Wilson, G. D. and Nias, D. K. B., 62–76.

p. 111. 'They certainly need love . . .' Cancian, F. M.

'It is hard to talk to . . .' same as above.

'Another man, told . . .' same as above.

CHAPTER EIGHT

p. 113. 'One of the most dramatic . . .' Comfort, A.; Langevin, R.; Wilson, G. D. articles;
Wilson, G. D. and Nias, D. K. B., 92–95, 104–07.

'Indeed, sexual deviancy . . .' Langevin, R.

p. 114. 'The East German . . .' Dörner, G. articles.

p. 116. 'A British psychologist . . .' Wilson, G. D., 100.

p. 117. 'Another American . . .' Diamond, M.

p. 118. 'To back up the general . . .' Hoyenga, K. B. and Hoyenga, K., 32–36; Nieschlag,
E.; Dörner, G. (1980).

'Then, there are those . . .' Beral, V. and Colwell, L.

'another study of six . . .' Yalom, I. B. et al.

'Some girls, as we have described . . .' Buck, R. W., 213; Erhardt, A. A. articles;
Dörner, G. (1980); Rienisch, J. M. articles; Symons, D. 289–90.

p. 119. 'In a fascinating . . .' Dörner, G. (1981).

'Although an American . . .' in conversation Meyer-Bahlburg, H. F. L.

'A sophisticated British . . .' MacCullock, M. J. and Waddington, L. J.

p. 120. 'Testosterone levels in . . .' Symons, D., 292–305; Wilson, G. D. (1987).

'A minority of . . .' Comfort, A.; Wilson, G. D. and Nias, D. K. B., 95–96.

'Female homosexuals . . .' Symons, D., 298–305; Wilson, G. D. (1987).

p. 121. 'Homosexual or heterosexual, . . .' Symons, D., 301.

'Transexuality is one . . .' Morris, J.

'The classic male . . .' Hoyenga, K. B. and Hoyenga, K. (See General References),
32–36.

'An American . . .' Diamond, M.

'The subject seems . . .' Hoyenga, K. B. and Hoyenga, K., 177.

'But most studies of . . .' Diamond, M., Wilson, G. D. and Nias, D. K. B., 99;
Wilson, G. D. articles.

'The book . . .' Bell, A. P., et al.

p. 123. 'The first clues . . .' Ward, I. L.

'Dörner was intrigued . . .' Dörner, G. (1980).

'Among the observed results . . .' Rienisch, J. M. and Saunder, S. A.

CHAPTER NINE

p. 126. '"An appreciation of . . .' Symons, D., 274.

p. 127. '"We don't seem to . . .' Green, M., 159.

'A woman brings to the . . .' Cancian, F. M.; Wilson, G. D. and Nias, N. K. S., 62–76.

'Men are usually . . .' Hite, S.

p. 129 'Dr Alice Rossi . . .' Rossi, A. S. (1985).

p. 130. 'In a survey of six . . .' Hoyenga, K. B. and Hoyenga, K. (See General References), 203.

'In an other survey . . .' Hoyenga, K. B. and Hoyenga, K., 315.

'Studies of married . . .' same as above, 337.

'Intriguingly, women . . .' same as above, 338.

'This is around the time . . .' same as above, 65; Perlmutter, M. and Hall, E. (See
General References); Rossi, A. S. (1985).

'Women show a greater . . .' Cancian, F. M.; Henley, N. M., 8–13; Hoyenga, K. B.
and Hoyenga, K., 335; Gove, W.; Rosenthal, R.

'"Women's sense of . . .' Gilligan, C.

p. 131. '"genetically equipped . . .' Rossi, A. S. (1977).

p. 132. 'Male promiscuity . . .' Barash, D., 47–50; Hoyenga, K. B. and Hoyenga, K., 63–65;
Symons, D., 201–2.

p. 133. 'This has been happily . . .' Symons, D., 210–11.

'All the research shows . . .' Symons, D., 206–53; Wilson, G. D. and Nias, N. K. S.,
125–39.

p. 134. 'So different are . . .' Fisher, H. E. and in conversation.

'However it is still . . .' Wilson, G. D. and Nias, N. K. S., 131.

'The happily married . . .' D'Andrade, R. G.; Hoyenga, K. B. and Hoyenga, K.,
203; Symons, D., 232–37.

p. 135. 'Understanding, even within . . .' Murstein, B. I., 427, Symons, D., 232–37.
'In spite of all this . . .' Symons, D., 232–37.
'Sex apart . . .' Cancian, M. F.
'Ninety-eight . . .' Hite, S.
p. 136. 'But most wives . . .' same as above.
p. 137. 'They experience other . . .' Hoyenga, K. B. and Hoyenga, K., 307.
'Women rarely understand . . .' Henley, N. M.; Hoyenga, K. B. and Hoyenga, K.;
Huntingford, F. H. and Turner, A. K.
'At Boston University . . .' Henley, N. M.
p. 139. 'We have already mentioned . . .' Henley, N. M.; Hoyenga, K. B. and Hoyenga, K.,
308; McGuinness, D. (See General References), 145; Wilson, G. D. and Nias,
N. K. S., 51; Yarmley, A. D.

CHAPTER TEN
p. 141. 'Social scientists . . .' Rossi, A. S. (1985).
'Female attachment . . .' Barash, D., (See General References), 88–115; Goy, R. and
McEwen (See General References), 60; Hoyenga, K. B. and Hoyenga, K. (See
General References), 159–61); Velle, W. (See General References).
'This bias towards . . .' Goy, R. and McEwen, 60; Hoyenga, K. B. and Hoyenga,
77–79; Messant, P.
p. 142. 'Baby monkeys . . .' Buck, R. W., 233; Wilson, D. G. and Nais, D. K. B., 149.
'The youngsters "reared" . . .' Wilson, D. G. and Nais, D. K. B. 149.
p. 143. 'But according to . . .' Hoyenga, K. B. and Hoyenga, K., 159–61.
'Parenthood means . . .' same as above, 39.
'All the literature . . .' Barash, D. P.; Rossi, A. S. articles.
'Studies on both sides . . .' Green, M., 126; Hoyenga, K. B. and Hoyenga, K., 338–39.
p. 144. 'The female hormones . . .' Green, M., 129; Hoyenga, K. B. and Hoyenga, K., 305,
159–61); Lancaster, J. B. articles papers; Symons, D., 108.
'The evidence for this . . .' Erhardt, A. A. articles; Rienisch, J. M. articles.
'Meanwhile the Turner's . . .' Hoyenga, K. B. and Hoyenga, K., 305, 33–34.
'The roles of hormones . . .' Hoyenga, K. B. and Hoyenga, K., 53; Rossi, A. S. (1985).
p. 145. 'Men may fret . . .' Barash, D., 88–115; Goy, R. and McEwen, B. S., 60; Hoyenga,
K. B. and Hoyenga, K., 159–61; Rossi, A. S. articles; Symons, D., 108; Velle, W.
'Even in the most . . .' Stein, G.
'American sociologist . . .' Rossi, A. S. (1985).
p. 146. 'Compare that description . . .' Stein, G.
p. 147. '"By always having . . .' Rossi, A. S. (1985).
p. 148. 'Three or four generations . . .' Tiger, L. and Shepher, J.
'Other studies of . . .' Rossi, A. S. (1985).
'"Modern" mothering . . .' same as above.
p. 149. 'Studies of primative . . .' same as above.
p. 150. 'Even in Scandanavian countries . . .' Hoyenga, K. B. and Hoyenga, K., 202.
'In the self-consciously . . .' Tiger, L. and Shepher, J.
'"I feel it is a personal . . .' Hite, S.
p. 151. 'In the kibuttz . . .' Tiger, L. and Shepher, J.

CHAPTER ELEVEN
p. 154. 'This decade, in Britain . . .' Equal Opportunities (1987).
'It takes more than . . .' Tiger, L. and Shepher, J.
'Even so, data on . . .' same as above.
'"Our data about education . . .' same as above.
p. 155. 'The pattern is repeated . . .' Eccles, J. S.
'In fact some of that . . .' Kipinis, D.
'Sylvia Hewlett . . .' Hewlett, S. A., 268.
'In Britain, women's . . .' Equal Opportunities (1987).
'Power in the professions . . .' same as above.
'There are only nine . . .' National Management Survey.

'There has been a big increase . . .' *Equal Opportunities* (1987).
p. 156. 'Even in a trade or . . .' Strechert, K., 11–13.
'A recent British . . .' *Health Trends*.
p. 157. 'A key study . . .' Hoyenga, K. B. and Hoyenga, K. (See General References), 274–75.
'An early British . . .' Hutt, C. (See General References), 122.
'In another study . . .' Eccles, J. S.
'The male need . . .' Hoyenga, K. B. and Hoyenga, K., 275.
p. 158. 'Again, the elaborate . . .' Hoyenga, K. B. and Hoyenga, K., 205.
'A more recent study . . .' Tiger, L. (1987).
'In economic terms . . .' D'Andrade, R. G.
p. 159. 'A study of work . . .' Baron, N. J. and Bielby, W. T.
'In the words of an American . . .' Bardwick, J. P. (See General References), 158.
'There was a startling . . .' Levin, M. (See General References), 142–43.
p. 160. 'Another study of women . . .' Hutt, C., 138.
'A study of college . . .' Hoyenga, K. B. and Hoyenga, K., 275.
'American studies . . .' Kipinis, D.
p. 161. 'Talking of money . . .' Gould, R. E.
'One psychiatrist claims . . .' same as above
'For men, success . . .' same as above; Strechert, K., 160.
'A 1979 study . . .' Callahan-Levy, et al.
'Putting these two aspects . . .' Levin, M., (See General References), 145.
p. 162. '"To have power . . .' Witleson, S.
'In great measure . . .' Bardwick, J., 150; Cancian, F. M.; Notman, M.
'The job of bank teller . . .' Kipinis, D.
'Margaret Meade . . .' Meade, M.
p. 163. 'Just as lower pay . . .' Kipinis, D.
p. 164. 'A study of twenty-five . . .' Hennig, M. and Jardim, A.
'Corrine Hutt noted . . .' Hutt, C., 277.
'Many clinical studies . . .', see Chapter Two.
'Towards the end . . .' Hoyenga, K. B. and Hoyenga, K., 315.
'As we have seen . . .' Gilligan, C.; Hutt, C., 119–21.

CHAPTER TWELVE
p. 165. 'If there is any question . . .' Hewlett, S. A.
p. 166. 'Self-esteem is equally . . .' Hoyenga, K. B. and Hoyenga, K. (See General References), 274–79.
'In one important study . . .' same as above, 276–78.
p. 167. 'In every case . . .' same as above.
'"You have to act . . .' Goffee, R. and Scase, R.
'"We don't believe . . .' same as above.
p. 168. '"I certainly don't think . . .' same as above.
'The difference between . . .' Gilligan, C., 21–26.
p. 170. 'The difference in the . . .' McClelland, D. C., 89.
'A wide range . . .' Silverman, J.
p. 171. 'For men, work is . . .' Lever, J. articles; Strechert, K., 74–80; Turner, R. H.
'The French . . .' Piaget, J.
p. 172. 'Men and women don't . . .' McGee, P. E.
'Studies of worry . . .' Ekehammer, B; Honyenga, K. B. and Hoyenga, K., 337.
'Maintaining the competitive . . .' Strechert, K., 132.
p. 173. 'A study of women . . .' Goffee, R. and Scase, R.
'Interestingly, a study . . .' same as above.
p. 174. 'Leadership, though . . .' Hertz, L.
p. 175. 'My whole philosophy . . .' Goffee, R. and Scase, R.
p. 177. '"Many of the generally . . .' Millet, K., 28.
p. 178. '"Even if they . . .' Friedan, B.
'"Such a view . . .' Levin, M. (See General References), 38.
p. 179. '"It seems unrealistic . . .' Restak, R. (See General References), 204.
p. 181. 'One author maintains . . .' Fausto-Sterling, A.

p. 182. '"It seems nevertheless . . .' Velle, W. (See General References).
'The American anthropologist . . .' Tiger, L. (1970).
p. 183. 'So, "at the moment . . .' same as above.
p. 184. 'In the progressive . . .' Levin, M., 16368.
p. 185. 'But " no such . . .' McGuiness, D. (1976).
p. 186. '"We ignore brain sex . . .' Restak, R., 206.
'"An ideology that . . .' Rossi, R. A. (1985).
p. 187. 'It has been tellingly . . .' Goldberg, S. (See General References).
p. 188. '"What we want to achieve . . .' Richards, J., 111.
'Only about one fifth . . .' Levin, M., 99.
p. 189. '"Communicative and spatial . . .' McGuinness, D. (1976).
p. 190. 'Levin writes . . .' Levin, M., 267.

EPILOGUE

p. 192 'The very existence...' DeLascoste, M., *Omni* (1990).
p. 193 'Some of these...' Allen, S.L. (1989).
p. 193 'Still in the...' Witleson, S. (1989) (1990) (1991).
p. 194 'These findings are...' Potter, S. (1988); Witleson, S. (198).
p. 195 'Similar exciting and...' Naylor, C. (1990).
p. 196 'The sexes are...' Witleson, S. (1990, 1991).
p. 196 'Levels of testosterone...' Dabbs, J. (1991).
p. 197 'A new series...' Gouchie, C. (1990).
p. 198 'On that same...' Reinisch, J.M. (1991).
p. 198 'Work on the...' Hines, M. (1991).
p. 198 'We have also...' Kimura, D. (1990).
p. 199 'Fascinating work...' McCormick, C.M. (1990).
p. 201 'Now, thanks...' *Schizophrenia Bulletin* (1990).
p. 201 'A recent paper...' DeLisi, L.E. (1989).
p. 202 'The interim...' Sikich, L. (1988).
p. 202 'Just as there...' Flor-Henry, P. (1990).

Index

Index

problem-solving, 168–70
professions, 153–64
progesterone, 69, 71–73, 141
  level after birth, 142–43
promiscuity, 132
  wives' knowledge of, 139–40
Proxmire, Senator, 101
puberty, 88, 89, 96, 178–79
  hormonal influence at, 38, 68–
  69, 75–76, 80–81, 93, 95

rats
  brain development/structure of,
  25–29, 53–54
  experiments on, 115, 142, 189
  and stress, 122–23
reading, 17, 61–62, 63
  disorders/remedial, 62, 65
Reinisch, June, 33, 78
Restak, Richard, 20
rhesus monkeys, 77
  and dominance, 83
  experiments with, 28
'role-sharing' families, 145
Rossi, Alice, 129, 145, 146, 148, 186

schoolmastering, 162
science/scientists, 12, 89–90
seafaring, 137
seeing and relating, 58–59, 63
self-esteem, 166
senses/sensory stimuli, 15–19
sex, 109
  affectionate and social side of,
  109
  attitudes to, 105–12
  behaviour, 102–12
  casual, 109
  centres *see* sexual identity:
  formation of
  deprivation of, 105
  determination, and genetics, 21–
  22
  deviant, 113–24
  enthusiasm for, 102
  hormone *see* testosterone

male/female arousal, 106–107
sexual revolution/liberation 107–
  108, 134–35
  see also homosexuality; marriage;
  orgasm; sex differences
sex differences, 177–91
  at early stages, 54–55
  attentional styles, 170
  breaking relationships, 110
  and equality, 129, 177–78
  in marriage, 126–40
  and parenthood, 143
  and self-perception, 130
  selfish/selfless differentiation,
  85–86
  and sexual diversity, 133–35
  sexual status quo, 126, 128, 131,
  187–88
  sociological explanations, 14
  and stereotyping, 10, 96, 130–32,
  147–57, 184
  variations in, 15
  'wrong-sex' skills, 15
  see also childhood differences;
  hearing; old age; parenthood;
  physical attraction; reading;
  seeing; sexual identity; singing; smelling; spatial ability;
  speaking; tactile sensitivity;
  talking; tasting; verbal ability
Sex Differences (Hoyenga), 164
sex offenders, 79, 81
sexual identity,
  formation of, 24–26, 114–19
*Sexual Preference – its development
  in Men and Women*, 121
singing (in tune), 17
single-mindedness, 95–96, 108,
  159, 181
smelling, 100
social and cultural conditioning, 5,
  15, 29, 82–83, 97
songbirds, 27
space (as status) requirements, 137–
  38